blue
rider
press

RG3

RG3

THE PROMISE

DAVE SHEININ

BLUE RIDER PRESS
a member of
Penguin Group USA (Inc.)
New York

blue
rider
press

Published by the Penguin Group
Penguin Group (USA) Inc., 375 Hudson Street,
New York, New York 10014, USA

USA · Canada · UK · Ireland · Australia
New Zealand · India · South Africa · China

Penguin Books Ltd, Registered Offices:
80 Strand, London WC2R 0RL, England
For more information about the Penguin Group visit penguin.com

Library of Congress Cataloging-in-Publication Data

Sheinin, David.
RG3 : the promise / Dave Sheinin.
p.   cm.
Includes index.
ISBN 978-0-399-16545-0
1. Griffin, Robert, III. 1990—Juvenile literature.   2. Football players—United
States—Biography—Juvenile literature.   3. Quarterbacks (Football)—United
States—Biography—Juvenile literature.   I. Title.
GV939.G775S54   2013   2013017865
796.332092—dc23
[B]

Printed in the United States of America
1   3   5   7   9   10   8   6   4   2

BOOK DESIGN BY SUSAN WALSH

To my mother, Kathy Lowry,

for teaching me to love words

And to my wife, Amy Sheinin,

for teaching me to love life

CONTENTS

RG3

THE PROMISE

It was the last moment when everything was still uncomplicated, when the story of Robert Griffin III was still a legend—growing richer and deeper by the week, by the day, and here, as he hobbled valiantly on a wounded leg toward the line of scrimmage, by the second. This, late in the fourth quarter of his first NFL playoff game, was the last moment when the trajectory was still unquestionably pointed skyward, when nobody yet worried about the future or held him up as a cautionary tale, when all that mattered was this moment and this drive, when all anybody asked this twenty-two-year-old rookie quarterback to do was to move the ball 88 yards in 6 minutes 25 seconds, all that remained on the game-clock, for the tying score.

It was the last moment you still had faith that the man known as RG3, bum knee and all, could do it, all of it: put the ball in the end zone, win the game, redeem the Washington Redskins franchise, become the face of the NFL, maybe even change the world someday. Your faith may not have been what it was an hour earlier, when his limp was less noticeable, or a month earlier, when there was no limp at all. But the kid had this way of making people believe in him.

The ball was at the 12-yard line, on the right hash mark, atop the chopped-up turf at FedEx Field in Landover, Maryland. It was just after seven o'clock in the evening on January 6, 2013, with Griffin's Redskins trailing the visiting Seattle Seahawks by a touchdown in their NFC wild-card playoff game. It was second-and-22.

In those last few moments before the ball was snapped, as Griffin crouched four yards behind the center, held his hands in front of him, and barked out the signals, the mind could fathom no outcome that wasn't at the very least a satisfying one—full of hope for the future and the singular type of awe that comes from witnessing the rise of a transcendent young athlete before our eyes. The Redskins would either come back to beat the Seahawks here and advance to the next stage of the playoffs, or they wouldn't. But even if they lost and saw their season come to an end, on this particular day—as the Redskins played their first home playoff game in thirteen years—the future seemed bigger than any one victory or loss. The Redskins had already done more this season than anyone could have reasonably expected. Largely because of Griffin's immense talents and the sheer force of his personality, they were relevant again, regardless of what happened here, and the coming years were all but certain to be full of epic victories, highlight-reel plays starring number 10, and, one suspected, February parades down Pennsylvania Avenue.

Win or lose here, Griffin had already done the heavy lifting in restoring the Redskins to prominence and establishing himself as the top rookie and arguably the most exciting player in the league. Less than a month later, he would be named the NFL's Offensive

Rookie of the Year. With an off-the-field magnetism that matched his on-field brilliance—his replica jersey that season sold more units than any other player's since they started keeping track of the numbers—he was the future face of the NFL, adored by fans nationwide as well as by Madison Avenue.

Griffin's sprained knee had been getting worse throughout the game, his limp more pronounced, and here in the fourth quarter the crowd was getting nervous. Shouldn't the Redskins get him out of there? He had been wearing a brace over the knee since injuring it a month earlier, and the team had said he couldn't injure himself further by playing. The leading sports orthopedist in the nation was right there on the Redskins' sideline, keeping watch on him. But this didn't look good. Every step seemed a struggle.

The snap was low and to Griffin's left. Perfect. When Griffin was a boy, his father used to put him through improvisation drills just like this: Now the ball is snapped over your head. Now it's way off to the side. The play-call is worthless now. Toss it out the window. You're going to have to make it up from here—and with the ball on the ground, the defense smells blood. They're closing in. Quick, what are you going to do? You have to be prepared for that, son. It's going to happen. And sure enough, a couple of times during Griffin's stellar career at Baylor University, when the ball was snapped over his head, or when he simply dropped it, he calmly scooped it up, circled past the defenders, and delivered it to the end zone.

But here, with the ball suddenly at his feet, Griffin half-lunged and half-bent down for the ball, planting on his right foot, and something in his knee gave way.

. . .

They locked their pinkies together, little Robby Griffin and his mother, Jacqueline, and he promised—again, but this time a Pinkie Promise, which meant you absolutely could not break it—that he wouldn't get hurt. That in fact no one was even fast enough to catch him, let alone hurt him.

There was every reason to believe the boy. There wasn't another twelve-year-old in all of Copperas Cove, Texas, who could run like him, and everyone knew it. He was already gaining a measure of renown as the best young athlete in that part of central Texas—the best basketball player, the fastest hurdler. In those days, the boy worshipped Michael Jordan and wanted nothing more than to grow up to be the next MJ. But football was king in Texas, of course, and as his seventh-grade year approached at S. C. Lee Junior High School, the boy wanted to play the sport that everyone talked about.

Nobody knew him as "the Third" back then, as a twelve-year-old, even though he was the third in a line of Robert Griffins. He was either Rob or Robby or Little Rob, so as to distinguish the youngster from his father, who was simply Robert, or if you preferred, Big Robert or Big Rob or Mr. Griffin or Coach Griffin—but never Robert Junior, and never, ever, ever just plain Junior. Big Robert, a huge football fan, was fine with the idea of his son playing the sport, but it was Jacqueline who needed convincing. In the end, Big Rob and Robby talked her into it, but only if her son Pinkie Promised her.

"If you get tackled, then you'll quit football?" she asked the boy, locking her pinkie around his.

"Yes, Mom," he replied. "But they'll have to catch me to tackle me—and they won't catch me."

And so began, for young Robert Griffin III and his family, a lifetime of grappling with the dangers of football—of rationalization and internal deal-making, of precautions taken and precautions ignored, of hits avoided and hits absorbed, of maternal worry and paternal pride in the boy's growing toughness.

But actually, the reckoning had begun even earlier than that. When he was seven years old and living with relatives in New Orleans while his parents, both sergeants in the Army, were deployed in Korea, little Robby was on his way to get signed up for peewee football, in the passenger seat of a car being driven by his uncle Shane Griffin, when Uncle Shane suddenly turned the car around. What had made him change his mind? Deep down, he knew the boy wasn't cut out to play football with the rougher, harder "project kids" of the Iberville Projects where they lived. Robby was an outsider, a kid raised mostly on Army bases, and he was a little soft. If he played, there was a good chance he was going to get himself hurt, and Uncle Shane couldn't let that happen on his watch.

"So," Shane Griffin recalled, "we went and got some snowballs instead." (Snowballs, for the uninitiated, are frozen, fruity treats known in other parts of the country as snow cones or shaved ice.)

Fifteen years, two concussions, and one knee surgery later, as Robert Griffin III stood behind the center in the fourth quarter of his first NFL playoff game, with the Redskins' season ticking away, he could have used a little luck, a little divine intervention, a little stronger knee brace, a little healthier playing field.

But maybe what he really needed was an Uncle Shane.

. . .

Vou notice things when you cover one person for the better part of a year, as I did in 2012 covering Robert Griffin III for the *Washington Post*. You watch through binoculars, and you jot things down in a notebook or type them into a computer file—seemingly unrelated, trivial things, stuff that's probably not even worth a line in a three-thousand-word story but that strikes you at the time as curious or telling or emblematic of something—and when you look back on all these trivial things, you find that perhaps, taken together, they do mean something. There's a piece of a narrative there.

You notice Griffin, during one of the Redskins' first pre-training camp workouts in May—the ones called "organized team activities," or OTAs—spitting on the artificial turf of the team's indoor practice facility as he jogs past. Then you notice him stopping in his tracks, doubling back, and sheepishly smushing the dollop of spit into the turf with his foot. It's as if he's hearing his mother's voice in his head saying, *You wouldn't do that in somebody's house, would you?*

You notice the Gatorade cups strewn all over the Redskins' sideline as players, in the heat of battle on a regular-season Sunday afternoon, grab a cup off a table filled with cups, throw back its contents, and toss the cup on the ground—too busy, or too psyched-up, or too important to put the empty cup in the trash can that sits behind the bench. And then you see Griffin drinking from his cup, and you see him walking around the bench and dropping the cup in the trash can. The great ones are often meticulous like that, whether about their schedules, their lockers, or their appearance. But Griffin doesn't just seem meticulous. He seems overwhelmingly polite.

You notice how he pauses in the middle of his news conferences, in the shade of a tree outside the Redskins' headquarters in Ashburn, Virginia—almost directly below the flight path for runway 19L of Dulles International Airport—whenever an approaching jet passes overhead so that the audio isn't ruined for the TV and radio stations. You note that nobody else around the Redskins does that.

You notice the way he stands in the huddle, leaning forward on one leg, with his other leg behind him, so that his face is near the center of the huddle but he is still at eye level with his teammates—rather than crouching down, as some do, so that you have to look up at everyone, or leaning in sideways, halfheartedly, as if you've got better things to do. The way Griffin does it, he can look into everyone's eyes.

And you notice, on September 16, 2012—in the waning minutes of the Redskins' gut-wrenching 31–28 loss to the St. Louis Rams in Week 2—Griffin approaching a teammate sitting alone on the bench in misery. The player is Josh Morgan, a veteran wide receiver, and moments earlier he had single-handedly blown the Redskins' final chance at a comeback by throwing the ball at an opponent out of frustration and drawing a fifteen-yard unsportsmanlike conduct penalty, pushing them out of field goal range—a lapse in judgment that would later make him the target of death threats and racist taunts. As those final seconds ticked down, no other Redskins player would go anywhere near Morgan on the bench until Griffin, who that day made his second regular-season NFL start and was about to absorb his first NFL loss, walked over, rubbed Morgan's head, leaned in, and said something to him.

"Keep your head up and keep going," Griffin told him.

Morgan looked up, nodded, and went back to his thoughts—but right there something had changed.

"Yeah, it did mean a lot to me," Morgan recalled later. "He didn't have to do that."

Clearly, Griffin was different. The question was, different how?

In his famous biography of Bill Bradley, *A Sense of Where You Are,* author John McPhee wrote of his subject, "Basketball was more a part of him than he a part of basketball. The most interesting thing about Bill Bradley was not just that he was a great basketball player, but that he succeeded so amply in other things that he was doing at the same time, reached a more promising level of attainment, and, in the end, put basketball aside because he had something better to do."

It was easy to view Griffin in similar terms. Don't misunderstand—Bradley was a unique figure in sports history: a Rhodes Scholar and Princeton man who enjoyed a Hall of Fame basketball career, then went on to become a three-term United States senator. But just as with Bradley and basketball, Griffin seemed like someone for whom football wasn't the destination, but merely the vehicle to get him to something bigger and more important. Whether he eventually went into politics or some other field, Griffin, like Bradley, seemed destined to rise above his sport.

There was only one difference: Bradley's sport didn't have the potential to maim him for life.

When Jackie Griffin told me the Pinkie Promise story, we were
sitting on the metal bleachers of the football field at S. C. Lee
Junior High in Copperas Cove, where her son had first played
organized football. It was April 16, 2012, a beautiful, cloudless Texas spring day, just ten days before her son would be chosen by the Redskins with the No. 2 overall selection of the NFL
draft.

Petite and stylish, with a toothy smile that left no doubt as to
where her son had gotten his, she could have passed for Robert
Griffin III's sister, though she was already a grandmother (the
Griffins' oldest daughter, Jihan, had a four-year-old daughter,
Jania). While her son gave an interview on the black asphalt track
below, Jacqueline sat on the bleachers next to Robert's fiancée,
Rebecca Liddicoat, and watched him. She had never missed one of
her son's games, at any level, and was already figuring on moving
to whatever NFL city Robert wound up in, in order to keep that
streak alive.

In those days, the NFL seemed to be at something of a cross-
roads. Less than a month earlier, the league had suspended three
New Orleans Saints coaches, plus the team's general manager, for
their roles in what had come to be known as "Bountygate"—the
alleged payment system whereby defensive players were rewarded
with cash bonuses for hits that injured opposing players. A few
weeks later, suspensions would also be announced for four players
allegedly involved in the bounties. This came, of course, on top
of the ongoing concussion scandal that was proceeding along

incrementally—another lawsuit filed here, another ex-player revealed to have brain damage there.

This was the NFL into which Robert and Jacqueline Griffin were about to entrust the youngest of their three children, and I wondered if Mrs. Griffin had any reservations about seeing her son play such a violent sport at the highest, fastest, biggest level, given all that had emerged in recent months. That's when she told the story of the Pinkie Promise. It was a cute story, and she chuckled and smiled throughout, but it was clear that, below the surface, some reckoning had been necessary—some soul-searching, some bargaining, some compartmentalizing—in order to live with the danger. For Jacqueline Griffin, that reckoning involved constant prayer.

"Everybody knows I pray the whole game," she said with a laugh. "It's like, 'Oh, she's not ignoring you—she's praying.'"

Robert and Jackie Griffin were the perfect parents for raising a future superstar. Not perfect parents, mind you, because there is no such thing, but perfect in their concept of parenthood, and their dedication to it. There was a military precision to their approach, as might befit two retired Army sergeants. They had discussed and planned their strategy for parenthood from the very beginning, and they were on the same page in terms of the sacrifices they would make, the lifestyle they would choose, the discipline they would deliver. There was also a clear delineation of duties between them when it came to raising their three children—daughters Jihan and De'Jon and son Robert—as much due to the natural differences in their temperaments as to any clear lines they had drawn.

"They're like the yin and the yang," Robert Griffin III told me in April.

The father was the hard one, the tough one, the kind of man who never cried in front of his children—the kind of man who had risen from private E1 to staff sergeant E6 in less than two years after joining the Army, the kind of father who, when little Robert, then seven years old, told him he wanted to be the best basketball player ever, said okay, then took the boy to a basketball court and made him shoot 120 layups, left-handed, to see if the boy really had the kind of commitment it takes to be the best.

The mother, meanwhile, was the one to whom the boy ran home afterward, in tears. She comforted the boy and told him that his father knew what he was doing, even if neither she nor the boy could quite understand it at that moment.

Once, in June, when I was interviewing Robert Griffin Jr. in the living room of his Copperas Cove home, in the middle of an answer about parenting he pointed across the room at the door that led to the section of the house where the three kids' bedrooms were.

"I hardly ever went over there," he admitted. "That's where their bedrooms are. Even now, I never go over there."

By the end of Robert Griffin III's rookie season, ten-time all-pro linebacker Junior Seau was dead from suicide at age forty-three, his brain showing signs of football-inflicted brain damage; the number of concussion-related lawsuits against the NFL had grown to more than two hundred, representing more than four thousand former players or their estates; President Barack Obama, in an interview with the *New Republic,* had said he would "have to think long and hard" about letting a son play football; and Griffin himself was holed up in the Florida Panhandle, rehabbing from his second reconstructive knee surgery in three and a half years.

The final toll on Griffin's body during his rookie season included one confirmed concussion, one additional blow to the head that necessitated concussion testing (which he passed), one unspecified rib injury that required X-rays (negative), and finally, one torn lateral collateral ligament, one re-torn anterior cruciate ligament, and one partially torn medial meniscus, all in his right knee.

And that was only what had been revealed publicly—to say nothing of the invisible toll. By the time Griffin's season ended with the shredded knee, he seemed wholly diminished—not only physically but emotionally and mentally as well, a sense that was only confirmed when he went underground for months following the surgery, his only communication with the outside world coming through a trickle of platitude-heavy tweets that read as if ripped from a motivational text ("God would not test you if you were not ready," he wrote on January 19). Was he disillusioned by what he encountered during his rookie season—not only the injuries but also perhaps the inflexibility of the Redskins' play-calling and the minefield of questions about race from the media? The answers apparently would have to wait until the new season, if they would be offered at all.

There were any number of stand-out moments from what was arguably the most dazzling rookie season in recent NFL history: The seventy-six-yard touchdown run against Minnesota, the longest by a quarterback in sixteen years. The eighty-eight-yard touchdown pass to Pierre Garcon against New Orleans in Griffin's NFL debut. The scramble-juke-and-pass conversion of a fourth-and-10 against the New York Giants. The sixty-eight-yard touchdown heave to Aldrick Robinson against the Dallas Cowboys in a nationally televised Thanksgiving Day game.

He was that rare, heavily hyped, supposedly once-in-a-generation phenom who actually surpassed the immense expectations. Think about that list: who else in the last quarter-century might be on it? Perhaps Tiger Woods. Perhaps LeBron James. But it's a very short list. Not only did Griffin set all-time NFL records for passer rating (102.4), interception percentage (1.3), and rushing yards (815) by a rookie quarterback—while leading the entire NFL in both yards per pass attempt and yards per rush attempt—he also guided the Redskins to a 10-6 record and the franchise's first NFC East title since 1999.

But he was never the same after the original injury, suffered on a scramble out of the pocket on December 9 against Baltimore— when his knee absorbed the full force of a hit by a 340-pound defensive tackle named Haloti Ngata. He would miss one game (against his will) with what was originally diagnosed as a grade-1 ligament sprain and would play in three more, including the play-off game against the Seahawks. But his explosiveness was largely gone, and his passes lost their zip as his back, push-off leg weakened—a process that seemed to accelerate during the course of that playoff game.

The season produced indelible images: Griffin seated on the turf of the Superdome during his debut, with his arms raised in the air, fingers pointed skyward, after the touchdown pass to Garcon. Griffin engulfed by enraptured female fans in the front row of FedEx Field after an impromptu leap into the stands following the touchdown sprint against the Vikings. And always, Griffin smiling that perfect smile. Ultimately, however, the lingering image of

Griffin from the 2012 season—because it was the final image, and because of the visceral reaction it produced—will always be of him crumpling to the turf at FedEx Field on January 6, having been unwilling to take himself out of the game until it was too late, and unspared by anyone else willing to take the decision out of his hands. In the end, he embodied, to a fault, the football code that says you never willingly come out of a game.

"It doesn't matter how many times they hit me, I'm going to continue to get back up," Griffin had said months earlier, in a telling moment after a brutally physical game against the Cincinnati Bengals in which he was battered mercilessly. "Even if they have to cart me off the field, I'm going to get off that cart and walk away."

Indeed, when the doctors and trainers finally came onto the field on January 6 to get Griffin out of the game, after the low snap and the lunge and the knee giving out, he rose to his feet with some help, then brushed away offers for a shoulder or an arm to lean on as he made his way off the field. He walked off on his own, giving a grim little half-wave, half-salute to the crowd as he neared the sideline.

He had become not only a part of football's twisted, violent, play-at-all-costs culture—football being the only arena, other than the battlefield, where it is considered normal to play through the type of knee injury Griffin was dealing with—but its ultimate expression. Just twenty-two years old (the first quarterback born in the 1990s to play in the NFL), the brightest rookie star in America's most popular sport, the darling of Madison Avenue, Griffin had more to lose than anyone by putting his health on the line to stay in that game. And still he stayed. Where did that get him? In a hospital bed in Florida, with a future that now seemed a little less certain, if not a little less bright.

He had opened his rookie season as a symbol of everything that is beautiful and alluring about the NFL—his dazzling performance at New Orleans on September 9 was arguably the greatest debut by a rookie quarterback in league history, and it practically demanded that no game with Robert Griffin III in it should ever be missed again—and he ended it four months later as a symbol of everything that is rotten about the NFL.

As for the Pinkie Promise with his mother, it had been broken long before. But on the shredded turf of FedEx Field that day, it felt as if he had effectively spit on it and smushed it into the ground.

ONE

THE PERFECT QUARTERBACK

If you were to assemble the perfect NFL quarterback from the attributes of various existing specimens, you might take Michael Vick's speed, Drew Brees's accuracy, Jay Cutler's arm strength, Peyton Manning's intelligence and field vision, Tom Brady's pocket awareness and clutchness, and Aaron Rodgers's evasiveness. You might want to go even further in constructing the man who will be the face of your franchise for the next decade or so and also give him some helpful, intangible skills: Ben Roethlisberger's leadership ability, Philip Rivers's hard-nosed toughness, and the solid character and camera-ready magnetism of . . . well, let's go ahead and say it: Tim Tebow.

No such creature exists, of course, just as there similarly exists no hideous, opposite creature—you know, with Vick's prison record, Brees's receding hairline, Cutler's petulance, Manning's Manning Face, Brady's whininess, and so on and so forth. But as the NFL draft approached in the first part of 2012, certain observers around the league, including some residing high up in the Washington Redskins' organization, were beginning to think that the closest thing to it anyone had seen in a long, long time was hurtling toward the NFL in the form of Baylor University quarterback Robert Griffin III.

Griffin's highlight reel alone was enough to warrant checking off several of those "perfect" attributes—full of flick-of-the-wrist deep balls, thread-the-needle throws in heavy traffic, and breathtaking sprints, scrambles, and jukes around and through defenses. Just that winter, in December 2011, he had been awarded the Heisman Trophy—punctuating the night by delivering a memorable, quotable speech and charming the assembled media with his silly socks (specifically, Superman, complete with little red capes on each) and his big, toothy smile.

"Robert Griffin III will be the next quarterback to revolutionize the game," former NFL player and scout Bucky Brooks wrote on the NFL.com website in late 2011. ". . . Griffin possesses the speed and explosiveness of Michael Vick and the arm strength and pocket presence of Drew Brees. He combines those remarkable athletic traits with a keen football sense that translates into spectacular play on the field."

You want fast? He was an elite hurdler, having set a pair of state records as a Texas high schooler, winning a Big 12 championship as a Baylor freshman, and qualifying for the 2008 U.S. Olympic Trials (where he advanced to the semifinals but failed to qualify for the Beijing Games) before putting aside his track career (only temporarily, he has insisted) in the interest of football. Two months before the 2012 draft, at the NFL scouting combine—where prospective draft picks are measured and sized up and looked over like sides of beef—he ran a 4.41 time in the 40-yard dash, the third-fastest ever recorded by a quarterback, behind only Vick (4.33) and Reggie McNeal (4.40).

You want accurate? He completed 67.1 percent of his passes as a collegian—getting better with each season, from 59.9 percent as a freshman to 72.4 percent as a junior (his final season before turning pro).

You want intelligent? He finished high school a semester early (graduating seventh in his class), completed his bachelor's degree in political science at Baylor in three years, and was a thesis shy of completing a master's in communications by the spring of 2012. Had he stayed at Baylor for his senior season of eligibility, he was planning to enroll in law school—another childhood dream he had given up (again, he has insisted, only temporarily) for football.

You want character? He was the son of two retired Army sergeants, had never so much as tried alcohol or drugs, and as a high schooler was often seen in his hometown of Copperas Cove pulling a tire up a hill for a couple of hours—after football practice was over.

You want magnetism? Sponsors—big-time ones, like Subway, Gatorade, and Adidas—were lining up at his agents' doors to sign him up, well in advance of the actual draft. It scarcely mattered what NFL team he ultimately played for. His market was clearly bigger than whatever local area claimed him as its own. This guy was going national.

You want size? Well, okay—that's one attribute we conveniently neglected to ascribe to our mythical "perfect" quarterback.

Ideally, you would want him to have Cam Newton's size and strength—a chiseled, six-foot-five, 248-pound monster capable of breaking tackles, seeing over defensive linemen, and absorbing a season's worth of pounding. Griffin, on the other hand, at six-two, 225 pounds, was not small by any means—Brees, at six feet, 205 pounds, is among the quarterbacks who have proven that size is not everything—but not as big as you might hope for someone who was certain to be a running threat in the NFL.

As it happened, there was another quarterback pointed toward the April 2012 draft who had arguably as much claim to the title of the "Perfect Quarterback" as did Griffin—or, judging from their expected draft order, even more of a claim.

Andrew Luck and Robert Griffin III had been crossing paths and career trajectories since the days before Griffin regularly had a "III" attached to his name—since 2007, in fact, when Griffin, then a rising high school senior, took an official recruiting visit to Stanford University in Palo Alto, California, where then head coach Jim Harbaugh was putting the hard sell on him to join another highly touted recruit, Luck, as co-quarterbacks of the Cardinal.

Though Griffin ultimately declined the scholarship offer— "That system never works," he would say later of the dual-quarterback plan—he and Luck would continue to be measured against each other as collegians, straight through the 2011 season, when Griffin, almost an afterthought to voters when the season began, outplayed Luck, especially on their respective games on the biggest stages, and took home a Heisman Trophy that most experts at season's start had figured was Luck's to lose.

Bigger (six-four, 234 pounds) and a more polished drop-back passer than Griffin (and thus, at least according to conventional wisdom, better suited to the NFL style of play), Luck also displayed surprising speed for a bigger quarterback, clocking a 4.67 in the 40-yard dash at the combine—slower than Griffin by more than a few steps, but significantly faster than other successful drop-back passers of recent vintage, including Brady (5.28), Rivers (5.08), Joe Flacco (4.86), and Brees (4.83).

As the NFL draft approached, it was widely expected that the Indianapolis Colts, who were on the verge of letting the future Hall of Famer Manning depart via free agency, would take Luck with the No. 1 overall pick.

The No. 2 pick, meanwhile, was held by the St. Louis Rams, who already had a promising young quarterback in Sam Bradford and who were letting it be known to the thirty teams behind them in the draft order that the pick was available to any team willing to mortgage a sizable chunk of its future to move up.

It is an exceedingly difficult thing to pull off: taking a flagship NFL franchise, a semi-dynasty with thirteen playoff appearances and three Super Bowl titles in a twenty-two-season span from 1971 to 1992, and with a fan base so rabid and loyal that the waiting list for season tickets was said to be hundreds of thousands of names long, and turning it into a laughingstock—the punch line of late-night television jokes, a sad, irrelevant has-been of a franchise. At a certain point, success in professional sports, even the parity-crazed NFL, can become so self-sustaining, with fan support swelling and free agents crawling all over each other to come play for you, that it is nearly impossible to go from dynastic greatness to abject misery for more than a year or two at a time.

But by God, that's what the Washington Redskins had managed to do under owner Daniel Snyder, the billionaire communications mogul who purchased the team in 1999 and set about systematically ridding the franchise of all its glory, its standing as an NFL flagship, and, ultimately, its charm. Under Snyder, the Redskins lost big, and his response was always to double-down on another shiny, expensive (and aging) bauble (or two or three), which was how recent Redskins history had come to be littered with the bloated corpses of ill-fated acquisitions such as Deion Sanders, Jeff George, Bruce Smith, Mark Brunell, Adam Archuleta, Albert Haynesworth, and Donovan McNabb. Snyder's record with head coaches was not much better—he had cycled through seven of them in thirteen years.

Snyder's Redskins made the playoffs in his first season as owner, 1999, but would do so only two more times in the next twelve years. And things were only getting worse. As the 2012 draft approached, the Redskins were coming off their fourth consecutive last-place finish in the NFC East division, and most if not all of the fans' vitriol—at least from those who still cared—was directed squarely at Snyder.

Snyder's most recent plot to dig himself out of his mess, in January 2010, was to throw $35 million at Mike Shanahan, the two-time Super Bowl–winning former coach of the Denver Broncos, to entice him into coaching the Redskins. To seal the deal, Snyder also had named Shanahan vice president of football operations, giving him the final say on personnel matters—a power afforded to few other head coaches in the NFL. Not to say that Shanahan didn't believe Snyder's promise to stay out of personnel matters, but just to be sure, he insisted that such a clause be written into his Redskins contract.

The Redskins went 6–10 and 5–11 in Shanahan's first two seasons at the helm—a horrific stretch that was perhaps most memorable for the very ugly, very public endings to the brief Redskins careers of Haynesworth and McNabb, both of whom had clashed with Shanahan. Haynesworth, the oversize, overpaid, and under-motivated defensive tackle whom they jettisoned in July 2011, may go down as the single worst free agent signing in the history of the NFL, a $100 million bust from which the Redskins still have not completely recovered. Meantime, McNabb's rancorous departure that same month, after one full season during which he was twice benched unceremoniously, had kept alive the franchise's losing streak with quarterbacks—which dated back, some would say, to the days of Joe Theismann—and left the Redskins' quarterbacking duties in the hands of veterans Rex Grossman and John Beck, who proceeded to combine for a whopping twenty-four interceptions during the horrific 2011 season.

If ever there was a franchise in need of a bold move in an altogether new direction, it was the Redskins—even if few trusted them to do it right.

The Redskins' first target that winter was Manning, the then thirty-five-year-old future Hall of Famer who had missed the entire 2011 season with the Indianapolis Colts while recovering from surgery to fuse together two vertebrae in his neck. As difficult as it was for the Colts to part with the quarterback who had spent thirteen seasons in their uniform, winning a Super Bowl in 2006, they were coming off a 2-14 train wreck of a season with Manning sidelined, and they saw themselves in need of a rebuilding project. As they saw it, Luck was the answer.

But the Redskins' chances of landing Manning were slim to begin with—some doubted whether the superstar quarterback wanted to play in the same division as his brother, Eli, which would mean two head-to-head games per year—and got even thinner after the NFL docked the Redskins $36 million in salary-cap space over a two-year period as a penalty for allegedly attempting to gain an unfair competitive advantage during the uncapped 2010 season. Shanahan and his son Kyle, the Redskins' offensive coordinator, met secretly with Manning at the elder Shanahan's Colorado home, but the Redskins never appeared to be serious contenders for Manning's services, and he eventually signed with the Broncos.

At the same time, however, the Redskins had begun to explore the possibility of making a trade with the Rams for the No. 2 overall draft pick—and the chance to get Griffin. At the NFL combine in February, Shanahan had whispered in Griffin's ear that the Redskins would try to trade up and get him. The move, if they could pull it off, would only be four spots in the order, from the Redskins' assigned No. 6 position, but they knew the cost would be steep. The market for such trades essentially had been set in 2004 when the New York Giants had given up two first-round picks, plus a third-rounder and a fifth-rounder, to the San Diego Chargers in order to get Eli Manning with the first overall pick. If anything, the NFL was even more of a quarterback-driven league now—coming off a 2011 season in which three quarterbacks had passed for more than 5,000 yards and three others had surpassed 4,500—than it had been eight years earlier. In other words, the price had gone up.

There is perhaps no more valuable or rare commodity in American professional sports than what has come to be known as the "franchise quarterback"—the type of talented, commanding signal-caller who might run your offense for a decade or more. How many honest-to-God, unquestioned, slam-dunk franchise quarterbacks even existed in the NFL in the spring of 2012? Let's see: certainly Brady, Brees, Rodgers, Roethlisberger, and the Manning brothers—the six quarterbacks responsible for the previous nine Super Bowl titles. But who else? Maybe Rivers? Maybe Newton? Maybe Cutler? Matt Ryan? Matthew Stafford? Tony Romo? Joe Flacco? Even if you generously counted all of them, that meant fewer than half of the league's thirty-two teams were at that moment in possession of a franchise quarterback. And the ones who didn't have one were constantly in search of one.

Once upon a time it may have been possible to win a Super Bowl with an average quarterback (see: Dilfer, Trent, 2000), but several pass-friendly rules changes in recent years and the growing sophistication of offenses throughout the league had made it more imperative than ever to acquire a franchise quarterback.

And now here was a draft with—potentially, anyway—two of them.

Quietly, Mike Shanahan had spent much of the first part of 2012 holed up in front of a television screen, watching every play of every season of the collegiate careers of Griffin and Luck. Why Luck too? Because the Redskins, if they traded up to the No. 2 overall spot, couldn't be sure the Colts wouldn't change their minds at some point and take Griffin at No. 1. It wasn't likely, but as Shanahan would say later, "You don't make that move unless you think the world of both guys."

Apparently, he did. On March 9, word began to leak that the Redskins had pulled off the deal, outmaneuvering and outbidding the Cleveland Browns to nab that No. 2 overall pick from the Rams. The cost was indeed steep: in addition to giving up their first-round pick in 2012 (sixth overall), the Redskins had to part with their first-round picks in both 2013 and 2014, plus their second-round pick in 2012.

"When you bought your home, you probably wanted to pay a little less too," Redskins general manager Bruce Allen told reporters after the details of the trade made their way to the public. "[But] you like your home once you've lived in it."

The Redskins had their man, but with the price they paid in draft picks—plus the $36 million salary-cap hit hanging over them—they could pretty much forget any notion of rebuilding around him. Robert Griffin III was going to have to do this dirty job, turning around the Redskins, more or less on his own.

So who was this man—this telegenic, multifaceted, crazy-sock-wearing, Heisman Trophy–sporting, sort-of-dorky, sort-of-cool, gunslinging, swashbuckling Texan with the meticulous braids and the Dylanesque pencil-thin mustache? In the days following the trade, you could practically hear the Internet groaning and straining around the Washington area as a gazillion Redskins fans took to YouTube and Google in search of answers. Meantime, the *Washington Post* put me on a plane to Texas in search of the same.

In the days and weeks that followed the trade, it started to become clear that Griffin was not only some mad scientist's rendering of the Perfect Quarterback—or as close to it as is humanly possible—but quite possibly also the perfect superstar for our times, potentially an icon for the ages. This was a guy who, if all went according to plan, was going to win not only a lot of games, a lot of titles, and a lot of awards but a lot of hearts as well—someone who was going to sell not only a lot of tickets but a lot of sneakers, foot-long sandwiches, and bottles of neon-colored sports drink.

His press conferences were epic, ad-libbed, virtuoso performances, utterly devoid of the sort of eye-roll-inducing, well-coached, clichéd quotes spouted by 99 percent of athletes, but also never coming close to veering off the rails. He was, in a word, charming.

"Who are you?" a reporter asked bluntly at Griffin's news conference following the NFL scouting combine in February, some two weeks before the trade. The intent was clearly to throw him off guard, make him think on his feet: *Here, kid—let's see what you're made of.*

"Heh heh," Griffin laughed. "What? That sounds like a paper from my English class." After a pause to let the laughter die down in the room, he continued, "I'm just the person that I am."

Later, someone asked about the possibility of a team trading up in the draft to pick him.

"As a player, you want a team that really wants you," he said. "Head coach, GM, owner—everybody that really wants you in that place and [where] the players believe in you. That's what I'm looking forward to. I'm looking forward to making somebody fall in love with me."

There was a duality about Griffin that was downright disarming—springing, one could speculate, from "the yin and the yang" of his parents. He was raised under strict military discipline, yet cherished and flaunted his individualism (sock choice at the combine: Teenage Mutant Ninja Turtles). He expertly straddled the line between humility and confidence, neither trait appearing forced in any way. He seemed extroverted and outgoing, yet described himself as a loner by nature—someone whose idea of a great night was listening to music and watching movies on his couch. He sported no tattoos or piercings, but wore his hair in the sort of long braids that might take some getting used to in middle America. He was African American and deeply Christian, yet kept his thoughts about race and religion to himself. He played the meanest, most violent team sport in the world—and by all accounts played it with alarming aggressiveness and toughness—yet also wrote poetry and once composed a love song that he sang to his girlfriend during an elaborate marriage proposal in 2010. (She said yes, of course.)

"He has two sides," the girlfriend-turned-fiancée, Rebecca Liddicoat, said. "What everyone sees is the serious, football side. But really, he's kind of goofy."

Seriously, though—poetry?

"Yeah, I'm a hopeless romantic," Griffin explained. "So anything I write about is love or the sky. I have a weird fascination with the sky. It's pretty cool. Whenever you're flying and you just look at the clouds—that's pretty sweet. Those are the types of things I write about. I don't write about heartbreak and things of that nature."

Above all, Griffin possessed a self-awareness that was rare for an elite athlete, let alone an NFL rookie fresh out of college. He seemed fully cognizant of his rare gifts and the power for good that was bestowed upon him by them. He possessed the innate sense to know exactly when to flash the big smile, when to crack a joke, when to be serious, when to be humble—and not because he was coached in the art of press conferences. He was just a natural.

He also seemed to be of no specific place: born in Okinawa, Japan, shuttled from one military base to another as a young boy, raised primarily in Texas, with roots that trace back on both sides of his family to New Orleans—but with no identifying features such as an accent or a style of dress that would peg him to one locale. He was of the world—the kind of guy who had possessed a passport since he was two months old, the kind of guy who could name-drop President Obama and not sound boastful.

"Maybe me and the president can actually live up to the deal we made," Griffin said when it started to appear likely he was heading to Washington. Back in January 2012, he had attended the National Prayer Breakfast at the White House and met Obama. "I challenged him to a basketball game, but he said he wouldn't play against me—he'd play with me. So, two-on-two—whoever wants it, let's go."

It wasn't immediately clear that Griffin loved football, but he loved the competition, and he loved the platform the sport had given him. He acknowledged that basketball was his first love, and that his best sport was probably track and field—but the former had been ruled out because he felt he wasn't tall enough to make it big, and the latter didn't offer the same type of stage. He didn't seem to court fame as much as he courted *greatness,* and if that brought fame along with it, well, that was cool too.

He also seemed wholly unfazed by the notion of pressure, even the sort of stomach-churning pressure that one would expect to come from being pegged as the new savior of a floundering, once-proud franchise such as the Redskins. Anytime he was asked about pressure, he spouted a phrase that had become a motto of sorts to him and his Baylor teammates during the 2011 season (and that he would eventually seek to trademark): "No pressure, no diamonds."

But when pressed about it, he was expansive and thoughtful with his answer.

"I think the mistake a lot of guys make is looking at the big picture," he said in April. "If you look at the big picture—yeah, you're going to be paid millions. You're going to have millions of fans out there cheering for you, and then if you throw one interception you're going to have millions of fans saying you should be benched. So I think a lot of guys look at the big picture and say, 'I've got all these people leaning on me.' But if you go to work every day and get better, [if] you watch film and work on your footwork, [if] you understand the playbook—then you can worry about the big things later at the end of season, when you go 10-6 and win the Super Bowl. Then you can say, 'I had all these people leaning on me.'

"You can't let your emotions or how you feel about yourself sway with the tide that's going to be [there] when you have millions of people watching. Some people are going to love you, some aren't. You just have to do what you have to do to make sure the guys in the locker room support you and the coaches support you. That's what I say about the pressure: Don't look at the big picture. Worry about the little things, and the big things will fall into place."

He had said he wanted someone to fall in love with him, and—well, it was abundantly clear that wasn't going to be a problem. If Griffin was indeed on his way to Washington, and if he was as good as advertised, this was going to be a love affair—giddy, sloppy, head-over-heels love—the likes of which the city had never seen.

It is often said in Washington that the second-most-important person in town, behind only the occupant at 1600 Pennsylvania Avenue NW, is the quarterback of the Redskins. But if that quarterback was going to be Griffin, that order was subject to change.

At first, nobody at the large dinner table seemed to notice as Griffin casually rose to his feet and started to remove his green Adidas hoodie—incognito, just the way he had planned for this moment to go down. The kid had a great sense of timing and a flair for the theatrical, and as he peeled off the sweatshirt all eyes suddenly started to pivot toward his chest, where now was revealed a burgundy T-shirt with the familiar Redskins logo on the front— the gold circle with the profile view of a native American warrior, facing to the right, and two feathers hanging down from the left side of the circle.

The room broke into spasms of laughter and applause at Griffin's surprise, and the young man flashed a big smile and sat back down. It was March 20, 2012—less than two weeks after the blockbuster trade, but still some five weeks out from the draft— and Griffin, his fiancée, and his parents were out at dinner in a private back room at the 135 Prime Steakhouse in Waco, Texas, with the top brass of the Redskins: Snyder, Allen, and Mike and Kyle Shanahan.

The next day would be Baylor's Pro Day—a school-organized showcase of its draft-eligible players for the benefit of any interested NFL teams. It would also be the first time the Redskins had watched Griffin throw passes in person; at the combine two weeks earlier, Griffin had declined to throw—a common choice made by top quarterback prospects—preferring to do so under the more controlled conditions, with his own handpicked receivers, at Pro Day in Waco. The fact that the Redskins' top executives had made the trip personally underscored how important the day would be.

At the dinner table that night, Snyder and his lieutenants seemed genuinely shocked by Griffin's premeditated gesture. It still seemed premature—to everyone but Griffin, that is—for such symbolism. The Colts, who still hadn't made a firm declaration of their intentions with the first overall pick, had also sent a contingent (including head coach Chuck Pagano) to Waco for Baylor's Pro Day, and nobody could be certain they wouldn't veer away from the conventional wisdom and choose Griffin over Luck.

"What if you had gotten the days mixed up," Snyder leaned over and asked Griffin, "and worn a Colts shirt by mistake?"

Griffin laughed at the question, but he was dead serious about the message he was trying to send: I want to be a Redskin.

"I wanted to show them where my mind was, where my heart was," he said later. "I knew my Pro Day was going to go extremely well, [but] I didn't want to make the Colts want me. I wasn't going to play that game."

While Griffin plowed through a filet mignon, Liddicoat, who had grown up a Broncos fan outside of Denver, chatted up Mike Shanahan about the John Elway/Terrell Davis glory days. Meantime, Snyder was quizzing Griffin's father about the young man, perhaps trying to get a better read on his character.

"What kind of car does he drive?" Snyder asked.

"Chrysler Pacifica—the whole time he was at Baylor," the elder Griffin replied.

"Good, because guys in our parking lot drive Bentleys," said Snyder.

The father laughed. "If Robert shows up there driving a Bentley," he replied, "you call me."

Finally, as the dinner was breaking up, Snyder handed the younger Griffin a gift: a book about the history of the Redskins franchise. Griffin thanked him and vowed to read it cover to cover.

The next morning Griffin showed up at Baylor's indoor practice facility—the same place where he had proposed to his girlfriend a year and a half earlier—sporting neon-yellow Adidas sneakers and a lime-green Adidas pullover, which he removed to reveal a black Adidas T-shirt reading, NO PRESSURE, NO DIAMONDS. (He had already signed an endorsement deal with the sports apparel giant.) For thirty minutes, as the coaches and executives from twenty-five NFL teams watched and took notes, Griffin and his teammates put on a show. He flew around the field from sideline to sideline, unleashing a series of cannon-shot deep balls (one of them estimated to have flown sixty-five yards on the fly) and laserlike short-range throws—from the shotgun, from under center, on seven-step drop-backs and rollouts. A sound track handpicked by Griffin blasted from the speakers (tracks included Michael Jackson's "Thriller," Eminem's "Lose Yourself," and Gorilla Zoe's "Look Like Money"—with a refrain that went, "Everywhere I go, I'm looking nice / I look like money").

For his final play, Griffin had scripted a surprise: a trick play, the exact one that had ended every one of Baylor's practices the season before—and that had even worked its way into games a handful of times. After taking the snap, Griffin lateraled to Kendall Wright, his favorite receiver, then bolted down the sideline and hauled in a deep pass thrown by Wright (a former high school quarterback himself, as well as an accomplished collegiate receiver who would wind up going twentieth overall in the draft). Afterward, Griffin and all his receivers converged for a silly end-zone celebration, signaling the end of the show.

(Evidently, the trick play made a lasting impression on Mike and Kyle Shanahan—because some seven months later, in Week 8 of Griffin's rookie season with the Redskins, they would dial up a very similar play against the Pittsburgh Steelers, with near-disastrous results.)

"It's not stressful when you don't feel like you have to prove anything," Griffin, obviously confident about the Redskins' intentions, told a gaggle of media members numbering more than one hundred. "The game tape speaks for itself. [That's] going to tell everybody who you are. Today is just [about] coming out and confirming it."

Standing off to Griffin's side that day, overseeing his workout, was a middle-aged man with the weathered face and hard squint of an NFL coaching lifer. Terry Shea has spent forty years coaching in the collegiate and professional ranks, specializing in quarterbacks, and since 2009 he has worked as a consultant to top draft-eligible quarterbacks heading into the NFL combine and the draft.

For nine weeks over the winter, Griffin worked out under Shea's tutelage in Phoenix, focusing on everything from footwork to balance to throwing mechanics to strength training. Griffin wasn't the first future NFL star to train under Shea—who had also worked with Matthew Stafford and Sam Bradford prior to their drafts—but he was undoubtedly the first to bring his mother along for the whole time. Jacqueline Griffin accompanied her son to each workout, standing off to the side with a video camera, then sent the footage back to Texas for Big Robert to watch.

Here, in Waco, Shea whispered to Griffin just before the workout started, "This is your moment. You go out and grab it now," then watched with a satisfied look as Griffin wrapped up his Pro Day performance. The Colts and Redskins contingents were both headed to California that evening to watch Luck go through the same exercise in Palo Alto.

"Well," Shea told a group of reporters, nodding in the direction of the Redskins' bigwigs, "I can't believe they'd have any questions after that."

So who was the better quarterback, or more specifically, the more deserving No. 1 draft pick: Luck or Griffin?

It was, in one sense, a matter of taste, and in another, perhaps more important, sense, a matter of risk acceptance. NFL history was littered with examples of No. 1 overall picks who wound up as epic busts (Tim Couch and JaMarcus Russell come immediately to mind), and the GMs and coaches responsible for the disastrous picks can never live down their mistakes. Putting aside the relative abilities of Griffin and Luck, the latter was widely seen as the safer choice, as being more polished and more experienced in running a pro-style offense. Maybe it was true, as some argued, that Griffin had a higher ceiling, but Luck was perceived as less likely to wash out or get hurt, and in the risk-averse world of the NFL the safer pick was usually the right pick.

That, essentially, was the Colts' rationale for choosing Luck at No. 1 overall, with owner Jim Irsay, who made the final call, privately expressing worry over Griffin's long-term health.

Still, the differences between Griffin's and Luck's relative abilities were slight, and the army of former star quarterbacks and coaches who populate the various television networks as NFL analysts seemed unanimous in predicting great things for Griffin.

"He's the complete package—plus," said Steve Mariucci, the former 49ers and Lions head coach now working as an analyst for the NFL Network. "There are a lot of different ways we measure quarterbacks on and off the field, [and] this guy seems to have an 'A' grade in all of them."

"He helped put the Baylor Bears on the map of college football, [and] I think he can do the same thing for the Redskins," said Jon Gruden, the former Raiders and Buccaneers coach and current ESPN analyst. "He can revive the Redskins, as long as he stays healthy."

Still, some analysts questioned whether Griffin could make the transition from Baylor's wide-open, spread-style offense to a complex, pro-style passing game. The Baylor offense was unique in that it didn't require an actual playbook—relying on multiple variations on the same handful of base formations and plays—but Griffin was quick to defend the offense to anyone who suggested it was simplistic.

"I'd like to sit down with them and show them how simple it is," Griffin said to one such question at the combine. "It's not a simple offense. It's a good offense. It's a really great offense, and it's a quarterback-friendly offense. 'Simple' would not be the word to describe it."

There was undoubtedly some stereotyping going on in the way Griffin was frequently described as "athletic" and in the suggestion that he would have trouble transitioning to a pro-style offense. He was certainly athletic, of course, but he was also an accomplished passer, as comfortable in the pocket on a straight drop-back as he was on the edges. When he was compared to other quarterbacks, it was always Michael Vick or Randall Cunningham or Cam Newton or, frequently in Texas, Vince Young—you know, because a black quarterback couldn't possibly play like a white one. But in reality, Griffin's father modeled his son largely on white passers of earlier generations, such as Joe Namath, Roger Staubach, Kenny Stabler, and Fran Tarkenton.

"People always talk about Randall Cunningham [as a comparison]," the elder Griffin said. "But when I developed Robert, I looked at guys like Namath, with his deep ball. Stabler—I liked his ability. I liked the calmness of Joe Montana. And Roger Staubach—what did they call him? 'Roger the Dodger.'"

For his part, Griffin always shrugged off the stereotypical comparisons; he only bristled when it was suggested he was a run-first quarterback rather than a pass-first one, or when it was suggested his game wouldn't translate to the NFL.

"Don't let anybody tell you that your game doesn't translate," he said once. "I just try to make sure I don't listen to too much and hear people say, 'His game doesn't translate.' . . . It's not a matter of the pro-style system only [fitting] a certain [type of] quarterback. Everybody's got to make the same reads, and last time I checked I was able to throw the ball a little bit. So it's not a problem to me. I don't want teams to just entirely focus on my running ability and say, 'He can't throw'—because they'll be mistaken."

At the heart of the matter, where the issue of risk-aversion intersected with the differences of playing style, was a critical question: could Griffin—smaller and more mobile than Luck—survive a full NFL season without injury? Obviously, every quarterback faces the possibility of injury every time he receives a snap, but some in the league apparently saw a red flag in Griffin's penchant for scrambling and the temptation that would be there for a team to call a bunch of designed runs for him.

"As for how much [Griffin] runs, and gets exposed to big hits, that's going to be a balancing act in the NFL," *Sports Illustrated*'s Peter King, the dean of American pro-football writers, opined the week of the draft. "Mike Shanahan would be foolish to tether to the pocket a man who was a semifinalist in the 400-meter hurdles at the 2008 U.S. Olympic Trials. But the one aspect that worried two personnel men last week was Griffin's ability to protect himself outside of the pocket [from] the kind of scary hits that mobile quarterbacks often absorb. It's a game of roulette."

"There is that susceptibility when you're a more mobile quarterback," said NFL Network analyst and former Redskins quarterback Joe Theismann—still revered for having taken the franchise to two Super Bowls—"that you could wind up taking that one shot that takes the best-laid plans of an entire organization and puts them on the shelf."

One segment of the American star-making machine that had no worries about Griffin was Madison Avenue. Far from it. Companies—major ones—were lining up to get a piece of him almost as soon as he declared himself for the draft. His agents at Creative Artists Agency (CAA) sifted through the offers and steered him toward a handful with large, national reach and strong brand awareness: Subway, Gatorade, Adidas, Nissan, EA Sports. Well before he had taken his first NFL snap, Griffin was starring in four major, nationwide commercial campaigns—a level of exposure believed to be unprecedented for an athlete before his pro debut.

"It is rare, especially considering the caliber of endorsees he was able to obtain," said Dan Kozlak, manager of analytics for Navigate Research, a Chicago-based sports and entertainment marketing firm. "There have been certain can't-miss superstars who will naturally garner such endorsements before they play professionally, i.e., LeBron James, but for someone to go somewhat under the radar for most of his college career, then sign all these endorsement deals, is pretty special."

Typically, agents try to limit a new superstar's exposure prior to his rookie season, in part because of the potential backlash from veteran teammates once the player arrives for training camp. But few rookies had come along quite like Griffin—in terms of both his popularity and his ability to handle the backlash. As a pitchman, Griffin was darn-near perfect—blending Michael Jordan's natural magnetism, Peyton Manning's ease in front of the camera, and Derek Jeter's pristine image—except, of course, for the fact that he had yet to throw one NFL pass. The strategy of heavy exposure that Griffin's agents chose for him so early in his career served to heighten the expectations and the pressure on the young man.

"If he comes out after doing all that marketing and the team goes 2-14 and he has an average year, people will say, 'Holy cow, maybe the guy should've taken a few more snaps and done fewer takes in front of the camera,'" said David M. Carter, founder of the Los Angeles–based Sports Business Group and executive director of the Marshall Sports Business Institute at the University of Southern California. "The perception can be, 'Man, this guy is everywhere.' That would put a burden on anybody."

(Meantime, it did not escape anyone's notice that Luck, who of course was about to beat out Griffin for the coveted No. 1 overall pick, could barely get a sniff from Madison Avenue—although that could have been a conscious decision by his management. Still, a sports marketing expert named John Stone was quoted on ESPN.com before the draft as saying, "Luck is awkward in the way he speaks. RG3 is a rock star.")

By mid-April—after the Heisman ceremony, after the combine, after the Pro Day—Griffin had answered just about any question anyone could have had of him. But then, all of a sudden, someone raised a new one—and curiously, they waited until a few days before the draft to do so. On April 19, one week before the draft, the *Milwaukee Journal-Sentinel* quoted two unnamed NFL scouts as tearing into Griffin, one of them saying he had "a little bit of a selfish streak" and didn't "treat anybody good," and the other saying his game was little more than "just running around winging it."

The word "selfish" jumped off the page. Was Griffin really selfish? To anyone who knew him well, the question was puzzling and irritating—but also so absurd as to be laughable.

"When that came out, we kind of laughed about it, because we know who our son is. He knows who he is," Jacqueline Griffin said. "For someone to think he's selfish? That's hilarious to us. I remember when he got hurt [tearing his anterior cruciate ligament while at Baylor in 2009], he cared more about the fans and coaches and teammates that he didn't want to let down, than about himself. His concern was for everybody else.

"So we just chuckled about [this story], and we just figured that whoever that is [saying those things], in time they'll figure out that they put their foot in their mouth. I can't say as a mother I wasn't a little upset, but I had to let it go, because I know who my son is."

"It didn't make any sense at all," said Lanear Sampson, one of Griffin's receivers at Baylor. "When I heard that, I figured whoever wrote that must not know Robert, because he's one of the most outstanding people I've met in my whole life."

Perhaps someone had mistaken Griffin's competitiveness and confidence, mixed in with a dollop of aloofness around people he didn't know, for selfishness. Maybe some scouts were taking out their own frustrations over whiffing on Griffin—he wasn't anywhere near the first round on most draft projections heading into the 2011 college football season—on the kid himself. Maybe they were just big meanies.

Whatever the case, the bizarre "selfish" episode was the backdrop as the Griffin clan all headed to New York for the anticlimactic event known as the 2012 NFL draft—where the Redskins, apparently unswayed by the concerns of the unnamed scouts, indeed selected Griffin with the second overall pick.

Jacqueline Griffin dabbed her eyes with a tissue as her son—looking stylish in a powder blue suit, checkered shirt, purple tie, and specially made (by Adidas, of course) burgundy-and-gold socks that read CATCH YOUR DREAM—took the telephone call from Shanahan, who was back at Redskins Park in Ashburn, Virginia, in the team's "war room."

"Yeah, they're here right now," Griffin said into the phone. "Yes, sir, I can't wait. Yeah, I'll be there tomorrow afternoon."

When NFL commissioner Roger Goodell called out his name to the packed crowd at Radio City Music Hall, Griffin, now wearing a Redskins cap over his trademark braids, strode across the stage with purpose, grabbed Goodell's outstretched hand, and engulfed the commish in a giant bear hug.

Through the hallways and tunnels of Radio City Music Hall went Griffin, ushered along by a Redskins media relations official and trailed by his parents and a phalanx of microphone- and notepad-holding media members. There were hands to shake, hugs to dole out, interviews to give.

On a teleconference with Washington-area media, Griffin suddenly broke into song—"Hail to the Red-skins! Hail vic-to-ry!"—before admitting he didn't know the rest of the words. But there was plenty of time to learn them, he said.

And then he turned serious.

"A team fell in love with me," he said softly, as if in wonderment, "and wanted me for who I am."

TWO

THE CHILD PRODIGY

The man of God placed his hand on the boy's head and suddenly felt something—a surge, an energy. It could only have been the Holy Spirit. And at that moment Bishop Nathaniel Holcomb, leader of the Christian House of Prayer Ministries in Copperas Cove, Texas, knew with certainty that this boy standing before the congregation, ten years old, skinny and doe-eyed, would one day do great things, things that would bring great fame to the boy and great glory to the Lord. It was the kind of feeling a pastor might experience only once or twice in an entire career, or maybe never. What it was, was a prophecy—straight from God.

"The hand of God is upon your son," Holcomb told the boy's parents, Jacqueline and Robert Griffin Jr. "God wants to shoot him, as an arrow from a quiver."

Holcomb had recently seen the boy play basketball in a church youth league, and the boy was electrifying with the ball in his hands. But it wasn't merely his athletic skills that had caught the pastor's attention. It was the way other people were drawn to the boy—kids and adults alike. He radiated something, a magnetism that wasn't easily defined.

"His character—there was something unique about him," Holcomb recalled. "At the time, you couldn't put your finger completely on it."

Standing at the front of the church that day, Jacqueline Griffin's eyes welled up with tears. She had always felt her son, little Robby, was destined for greatness—this boy who could walk at eight months and who could dribble a basketball like a point guard at age three—and so the pastor's words were simply confirmation that she wasn't just another mother who dreamed of such things for her child. This was real. At that moment, she was convinced her son was going to revolutionize the world of sports.

The Griffins had joined Christian House of Prayer, a five-thousand-member church with sanctuaries in Copperas Cove and neighboring Killeen—working-class military towns that straddle Fort Hood, the massive Army base where Jacqueline and Robert Jr. had recently been assigned after a stint in Korea—just a few months earlier. The Copperas Cove sanctuary of CHOP, as the church was known locally, sat at the corner of Highway 190 and Pecan Cove Drive on the western edge of town, and the Griffins would become pillars of the congregation, with young Robert eventually joining the church choir—first as a boy soprano and then, after his voice changed, a tenor.

"The family has been just upright, just meek and humble," Holcomb said of the Griffins. "They are a family that has been very faithful."

Not long after he had placed his hand on the boy's head and prophesized over him, Bishop Holcomb pulled him aside and told him what the prophecy meant: that young Robert was now bound by the responsibility that came with it, to work hard to fulfill the bishop's words and carry the glory of God to the world.

The word of God, which had flowed through the bishop that day, was not to be taken lightly. The boy nodded—he understood.

"I always say that God has a plan," Griffin told the *Killeen Daily Herald* in 2011, "but it's our job to live that plan. So when [Holcomb] said I was destined for great things, greatness doesn't just come to you. You have to go get it. You have to work for it."

Some twelve years later, the boy would play every game of his rookie season in the NFL with a chain around his neck. On the chain was a dog tag, and on the dog tag was a single Bible verse, Jeremiah 29:11, which echoed the words the bishop had spoken to him all those years ago.

"'For I know the plans I have for you,' declares the Lord," the verse reads, "'plans to prosper you and not to harm you, plans to give you hope and a future.'"

It was going to be another girl—Jacqueline Griffin was fairly certain of that. In her husband's family, it was an ironclad rule: all the Griffin girls had boys, and all the boys had girls. Robert and Jacqueline had done their part to perpetuate the pattern, delivering Jihan and De'Jon, and now, in the spring of 1990, stationed at Torii Station in Okinawa, Japan, they were preparing for the arrival of number three.

"The whole time I was pregnant, all my sisters-in-law, my grandmother—everyone was telling me, 'You're going to have another girl,'" Jacqueline Griffin recalled. "They said I even looked like I was having another girl, the way I was carrying. I secretly prayed that I'd have a boy. I'm traditional—I wanted to give my husband a son."

Robert Jr. never said anything when all the women in his family told him he was having another girl, because he had an entirely different hunch. "The only thing that was different was the heartbeat," he said. "This time, the [baby's] heartbeat was just racing the whole time my wife was pregnant. The girls' was slower. So from my standpoint, it was just grand anticipation."

Jacqueline and Robert Griffin Jr. were both New Orleans natives, and they started dating in 1984, not long after he joined the Army straight out of Kennedy High School. It was a long-distance romance in the beginning, with Jacqueline, a graduate of the all-girls St. Mary's Academy, attending Southern University for two years before enlisting in 1987. That same year, at Fort Carson, Colorado, where they were stationed, Jacqueline and Robert were married. Daughters Jihan and De'Jon were born in Colorado, and their third child was conceived there as well, but by the time Jacqueline was ready to deliver, the family had been transferred to Okinawa. In the pre-Internet, pre–cell phone era, it felt as if they were light years from home.

Lo and behold, when the baby came on February 12, 1990, it was a boy. "Outside of God," Robert Jr. said, "I was the first to see his anatomy."

Joy swept over the stoic, hardened Army man, and after a good, long while of gazing at his new son and marveling at God's blessings, he set off in search of a pay phone. After finding one, he set about lighting up the 504 area code with collect calls from a small island in the Pacific.

"I called my entire family," he said. "I called every cousin I knew. Every uncle, every aunt, and all my siblings—collect. I was on the phone for twelve hours."

No one needed to ask the elder Griffin what his son's name would be. There were things that were negotiable in the marriage of Robert and Jacqueline, such as names for their daughters, and there were things that were not, such as the name of their first boy.

"That," the elder Griffin said, "was not a question."

His own father and namesake, Robert Griffin Sr., a foreman for a construction company, had suffered from serious health problems, contracting glaucoma in his thirties, which forced him to stop working, and eventually dying in 1984 at the age of forty-three from an aneurysm in his brain. But before he passed, he made a request of Robert Jr., his firstborn son: name your first son Robert, he told him. Keep the line going.

"He said he wanted to have a bunch of Robert Griffins—for generations," Robert Jr. said.

And so the firstborn son of Robert Lee Griffin Jr. and Jacqueline Griffin was given the only name he could have possibly been given: Robert Lee Griffin III.

Robert Griffin Jr. joined the Army because he wanted to see mountains.

He had grown up in the Iberville Projects of New Orleans, just west of the French Quarter—almost within the late-afternoon shadow of I-10, with its busy lanes stretching from Los Angeles to Jacksonville—the third-oldest of Irene and Robert Griffin Sr.'s eight children. In the interproject sandlot football games that seemed to go on continuously around the city, twelve months a year, he was a legend for the Iberville Chargers: a left-handed quarterback with a cannon for an arm. He was renowned as a trick-play artist who could throw a pass behind his back forty yards down the field.

But at Kennedy High (a school that would be torn down and never rebuilt following Hurricane Katrina in 2005), his football coach didn't want any left-handed quarterbacks, and Griffin didn't want to play anywhere else, so he never did. He focused on basketball and was good enough to draw the attention of some college recruiters, but none offered him a scholarship. Paying for college himself and trying to walk onto a hoops team didn't much appeal to him at the time, he recalled, after seeing one of his older sisters enroll and "nearly bankrupt us."

He had seen mountains in a book once, and that was what Robert Griffin Jr. wanted.

"I look up, and all I see is skyscrapers," he said. "I wanted something different. I wasn't really restless, but I felt too contained there. I needed to be somewhere where I could really express my intellect. I wanted to see the mountains. I wanted to see the world. So I said I'd go into the military and have a way to pay for college."

His first stop was Fort Sill, Oklahoma. He was an artilleryman in his early days, but he eventually found a career as a petroleum-supply specialist. (A nondrinker—"How can you be from New Orleans," he is often asked, "and not drink?"—he was usually tabbed as the designated driver in any social situation.) In his first years in the Army, he was so homesick, he would drive home to New Orleans on the weekends—first from Fort Sill, then later from Fort Carson, Colorado, some sixteen hours away—just to spend half a day there before turning around and driving back.

But perhaps Jackie filled his longing for home, and anyway, once they were shipped to Okinawa in 1989, the opportunity to drive home on the weekends was gone. They spent a little more than three years in Okinawa—enough time for Jihan, their oldest, to become nearly fluent in Japanese.

Finally, in 1993, the Griffins received transfer papers sending them to Fort Lewis, Washington, so they packed up their three small children and crossed the Pacific Ocean to Puget Sound.

The Griffins were determined to expose their children to as many places and cultures as they could in their military travels, bleeding all they could from the experience. In Okinawa, they had made sure to explore Japan's mainland, and at Fort Lewis they made frequent weekend trips to Oregon and across the Canadian border to British Columbia. Little Robert III, three years old when the family moved to Washington, was soon enrolled in karate classes, reaching the brown-belt level before the family moved again.

But the next move was going to be a tricky one. In 1996 the Griffins received orders deploying them to Korea, but this time it would be an unaccompanied tour—in other words, without children. Jacqueline would be stationed on one side of Korea, and Robert Jr. on the other, and they would need to make other arrangements for Jihan, De'Jon, and Robby.

"We understood it, because that's the military, and we signed up for it," Jacqueline said. "We couldn't complain."

What do you do with three small children when you have to be away from them for a year or more? You lean on your extended families, and luckily for the Griffins, both of their families were in the same place, the place they both still considered home. And so they loaded Jihan, De'Jon, and Robby into the family car and headed south, to New Orleans.

· · ·

The boy was called "Ponytail" around the neighborhood, in honor of his most distinguishing feature. Already asserting his individualism at the age of seven, Robert Griffin III loved his ponytail and wore it proudly, but in the Iberville Projects it pegged him as an outsider—as soft—and when the other kids teased him about it, he cried.

But Ponytail was a natural athlete—faster than the other kids, and with serious game for a seven-year-old when he ventured onto the same basketball courts his father grew up on. The teasing usually went away after they saw him run or shoot a basketball.

"He used to sleep with that basketball," recalled John Ross, Griffin's maternal grandfather. "He used to challenge me [to a game of basketball] when I stepped out of the house: 'C'mon, old man!' No one could have guessed he'd be a football player."

The reality of their parents' deployment and the modest means of the families back in New Orleans meant the Griffin children were going to have to be shuttled around a little bit during their time there. They started out with Ross, Jackie's father, on Desaix Boulevard in the City Park neighborhood, then moved out to Alabama for a spell with one of Jackie's brothers, and finally wound up with Irene Griffin in the Iberville Projects for the last six months of what became a fourteen-month stay.

Each time they moved, the Griffin children had to change schools, which means, when you factor in Fort Lewis, that little Robby attended five different schools between kindergarten and first grade.

It was Uncle Shane Griffin who decided to sign up Little Rob, as he called him, for football—after all, Robert Jr. had told him to get the boy signed up for some organized sports, and in Louisiana "organized sports" meant football—and it was Uncle Shane who all of a sudden changed his mind while en route, turning the car around and taking the boy to get some snowballs instead.

"I said to myself, 'Man, these project kids are gonna tear him up, and Jackie would never forgive me if something happened to him,'" Shane Griffin recalled. "And I look back now—I was driving around with the future Heisman Trophy winner. And I didn't even sign him up! Can you imagine that?"

Little Robert's time in New Orleans did him plenty of good, instilling in him an appreciation for family, a tolerance for humidity, a foolproof recipe for beignets, and a healthy dose of street smarts. He encountered rats for the first time there, and once, when he had a toothache, a cousin attached a string to the tooth and another to a doorknob and slammed it shut. End of toothache.

When Jackie and Robert Jr. picked up their kids at the end of the Korea tour, after a total of fourteen months away, they noticed something different in their youngest: a newfound toughness.

"I think it was good experience for him, because he got to see a side of life he had no idea about," Jacqueline said. "It was good that he could appreciate—that all of my kids appreciate—what we, his mother and father, sacrificed, so he would never have to see that type of lifestyle. I'm not saying it was a bad thing. My mother-in-law and her family, they eventually got out of [the projects]. But for him and for my daughters to see and experience that, it made them stronger and matured them, but it also made them more grateful."

Not long after the Griffins had settled into their new home base—a town of some thirty thousand in central Texas called Copperas Cove—young Robby, full of stories about his father's legendary exploits on the basketball court back in New Orleans, informed his dad he wanted to be the best hoops player in the world and wondered if his dad could help him do it.

Copperas Cove sits in almost the exact geographical center of Texas, which means it is either close to everything or close to nothing—depending on whether your sense of distance is that of a Texan or not. It is an hour and change from Austin or Waco, two hours and change from Dallas or San Antonio, and three hours and change from Houston. But is only eight miles down Highway 190 from Fort Hood, a proximity that defines the town's economy and culture. Before Fort Hood came along in 1942, "the Cove," as it is known, was a tiny ranching community of fewer than five hundred residents, but its population would double in each of the next four decades, ultimately checking in at 32,032 in the 2010 U.S. census.

In March 1997, Jacqueline and Robert Griffin Jr. bought an 1,800-square-foot brick rancher and five acres of land on the out-skirts of town—where the daily sound track was the bleating and baying of farm animals and where the road to this day is made of dirt—and started the next phase of their family's life, only this time they were intending to be there awhile. The Griffins believed strongly that, while the itinerant life of the military is good for young kids—exposing them to different cultures and geography during those formative years when everything revolves around

Mommy and Daddy—by the junior high years it is important to put down some roots.

"Young kids, they adjust so easily," Jacqueline said. "Our main concern was the junior high years and the high school years. We figured, once we got here to Fort Hood, we were probably going to be here awhile. We weren't going to uproot them during their junior high and high school years, [when] they're forming relationships, they're getting used to things. Once [Robert and De'Jon] started playing sports, we said, 'That's it. We're going to be here for a while.'"

Jacqueline and Robert Jr. immersed themselves in the duties of parenting, with Jacqueline—who received a medical retirement from the Army in 1998 following hip surgery—taking on the role of shuttle driver, ferrying everyone around from school to sports and everything in between. "We decided that once we had kids, it wasn't about us anymore," she recalled. "Everything we did was going to revolve around what was best for the kids."

The Griffins were on the same page in their philosophies of parenting. The household was run with the strict discipline of the military: Homework was to be done before any fun activities were permitted. Back talk was not acceptable. Direct questions were to be answered with "Yes, ma'am," and "No, sir."

"None of this, 'Mmm hmm,' or 'Naw,'" Jacqueline recalled. "That's disrespectful in my book. And if someone is talking to you, you look them in the eye."

Robby was allowed to have his various action figures—he loved Teenage Mutant Ninja Turtles, Dragonball Z, and Power Rangers—but his parents removed all the toy knives and guns. "He got his action figure," Jacqueline said, "but he did not get any weapons. We taught him that weapons are bad. You don't need a gun or a knife in order to settle disputes. He was brought up with a nonviolent mind-set. That was important to us." Robby would lose himself for hours in his own imagination, sometimes staying so quiet for so long, his mother would have to go back to his room to check on him, just to make sure he was still there.

None of the Griffin children had cars while in high school (Robert got his first driver's license midway through his freshman year at Baylor), and there would be no dating permitted. The Griffins didn't only preach the importance of education—they taught by example, both of them eventually enrolling in college themselves to work toward the bachelor's degrees they had put aside when they joined the Army. (Robert Jr. eventually got a master's in psychology as well.) For the kids, an incentive system was put in place, with toys and cash payments for good grades—but little Robert was threatening to make his parents go broke, so good were his grades. On the rare occasions he got anything less than an A, he would badger his teacher to let him do extra credit to make up the difference.

"He was especially great at math," Robert Jr. said. "We used to drive between Texas and New Orleans all the time to go see family, and my daughters weren't that good at math, so I would quiz them on things. Algebra, stuff like that. We would use landmarks as we went along—time equals distance divided by speed. All of a sudden I'd hear answers coming from the back. I'm like, 'Who's that?' And it was Robert. He was maybe seven or eight years old, already understanding algebra concepts."

It was during that first summer in Copperas Cove, 1997, that little Robby told his father he wanted to be the best basketball player in the world. What followed would test the unity of Robert Jr. and Jacqueline as parents and provide one of the critical formative lessons of their son's athletic career.

"I watched Michael Jordan, and I'm a seven-year-old kid, I've got an imagination, so I wanted to be great," the younger Griffin recalled. "I didn't know what it was going to take—but he showed me a couple hours later what it was gonna take."

Out behind the middle school in town was a basketball court with four goals. Robert Griffin Jr. took his son there and made him dribble around in a huge circle—using only his left hand—from one goal to the next, shooting layups, also left-handed, until he had made 120. When they went home, the boy went straight to his mother in tears.

"Dad's being mean!" the boy sobbed. "I'm not left-handed!"

Jackie confronted her husband about whether such an intense layup drill was really necessary—but only in private, never in view of Robby, since the sight of parental discord, she felt, could weaken their authority.

"It was a house divided," Robert Jr. recalled. "I wanted to prepare him to be well balanced and able to shoot with either hand. I knew I was pushing him, but he and my wife weren't in athletics, so she didn't understand and he didn't understand."

"He said, 'Jackie, just let him work through it,'" Jackie recalled. "'He's going to understand why when he gets in the game and he uses that left hand instinctively without thinking.' . . . I would question him, but when we started seeing the results, I stopped questioning."

The next day little Robby told his dad he wanted to do the drill again, and so they did, eventually getting to the point where the

boy was nearly ambidextrous. One day the father bought a basketball goal and installed it in the driveway; it lasted until the boy, by
then in high school, brought it down with a thunderous dunk.

Nowadays Robert Jr. almost never tells the story of the 120
left-handed layups, and of the tears and the house divided, without
adding the kicker:

"His freshman year in high school, he started for the varsity,"
he recalled. "And his first goal was a left-handed layup against a
six-foot-ten defender. He ran up the court smiling."

The boy was an expert mimic—like, could've-been-on-*Star-
Search* good. He had all the essential Michaels down pat: he
could do Michael Jackson's lilting voice or Michael Johnson's
straight-backed sprinting style or Michael Jordan's tongue-
wagging drives to perfection. And when Denver Broncos quarterback John Elway, in Super Bowl XXXII on January 25, 1998,
launched himself into three Green Bay Packers defenders in order
to get a critical first down late in the game—getting spun around
in midair in the process, a play that went down in Super Bowl lore
as "The Helicopter"—little Robby went out in the front yard the
next day and tried to imitate Elway's move, sans the tacklers.

Elway was Griffin's favorite quarterback, and the Broncos his
favorite football team (not the Cowboys, he is quick to point out
these days), and when he played by himself in the yard, he was
Elway when he threw a pass in the air and Rod Smith when he
caught it. At one point, when Elway-to-Smith needed a higher degree of difficulty, he decided that Elway ought to be on one side of
the house and Smith on the other—and therefore he would need to

be able to throw the ball over the roof and run around to the other side and catch it before it hit the ground.

"He worked on it for two months, throwing the ball over the house and running around, over and over and over, but he finally did it," recalled De'Jon. "He figured out the key was to throw it really high."

But Robby's first love in those days was basketball, and he told his mother he hoped he grew up to be as tall as Jordan (who was six-foot-six), before correcting himself: "No," he said, "I want to be taller. I want to be six-eight." (The fact that he eventually topped out at six-two was a major factor in his choosing football over basketball as a career.)

People were starting to take notice of how good Robby was on the court, not least of all his father. Once, in a church-sponsored youth league game when the boy was nine and playing against kids as old as thirteen, he came in toward the basket from the right side, sailed over a couple of taller opponents, and finger-rolled the ball into the hoop.

"It was like Dr. J against Kareem and Magic," Robert Jr. recalled. "Everybody was like, 'Wow!' I said to myself, *How did he do that?*"

Realizing he might have something special on his hands, the father dialed up his son's training. When he got off work at Fort Hood in the evenings, he would have Jacqueline bring the boy to the gym on base, where, right off the bat, he would put him through a drill he called "hot shot," in which Robby would have to hit twelve shots in one minute from various designated spots on the floor. An average kid might hit seven or eight, Robert Jr. figured, but the boy soon got to where he could hit all twelve.

In almost every drill the father put his son through, he used a stopwatch, so the boy had to work fast—against the clock. The father would call out the time remaining: "Thirty seconds! Fifteen! Ten! Five, four, three, two, one!"

"What I was teaching him," Robert Jr. recalled, "was how to play under pressure."

The father was also a devotee of video study and would tape Chicago Bulls games off television, or go to the library and check out Jordan's highlight videos, so young Robert could study the master's moves.

With plenty of examples out there—famous examples, as well as ones you can witness on any Little League field or youth basketball court on any given day—of fathers who push their sons too far and too fast in sports, it is easy to be skeptical of Robert Griffin Jr.'s motives and methods with Robert III. But Jacqueline was the ultimate counterbalance, always making sure she watched her son carefully for signs that her husband was taking it too far. And there were none. The boy wanted it. His drive to be great was all his own.

"I always wanted to make my dad proud, but he never made me feel like I was obligated to do anything," Robert III recalled. "He didn't want to be that dad that pressures their son to do sports just because they want them to. . . . [But] I wanted to be the best. He pushed me because I wanted to be pushed. I had the want-to, and he had the know-how."

They would play one-on-one, of course, and sometimes the father would let the son win—"I wanted him to have the confidence to perform," Robert Jr. said—until eventually there was no more letting. Robby could beat the old man on his own, legitimately.

Track entered the picture when Robby was eleven years old and joined an AAU track and field team for the summer, thinking it might be a fun diversion until it was time for basketball again. He wound up becoming one of the top preteen hurdlers in the country, qualifying for the AAU Junior Olympics in Norfolk, Virginia. But in the championship heat of the 80-meter hurdles, he finished second, losing by seven-hundredths of a second to a boy named Frank Wainwright from Brookhaven, Pennsylvania—a result that infuriated the boy, as well as motivated him.

"I'm never coming in second again," he told his mother.

"And he never did," recalled Jacqueline.

To the best of anyone's knowledge, only one other person on either side of the Griffins' family had ever run track before— Jacqueline's grandmother, Evelyn Thomas. But maybe it was a skill that skipped a generation. Robert Jr. certainly didn't know anything about hurdling, but he took to the Internet for a crash course on its basics and its intricacies so he could coach his son. And then one day Robby's coach moved to San Antonio, and Robert Griffin Jr. became a track and field coach.

"Track brought a different dimension," the father recalled. "Track makes you focus on what you're doing because everybody's watching you. We feel track really helped Robert, more than anything because of the stage. . . . When you're used to being under a lot of pressure, you develop a tolerance for it, and with him running track and playing basketball—a lot of times he was rated No. 1 and had to perform with everyone expecting him to win, and that helps his approach to playing at [the NFL] level."

Track resonated with Robby because it was simple and pure: everyone lined up, and the fastest guy won. Every race had a defined outcome, with a time that was measured down to the hundredths of seconds, and once he crouched in his starting stance, nobody could affect that outcome or that time but him.

He tried it all—long jump, high jump, even the shot put. But something about the hurdles suited him—perhaps the metaphorical challenge of each hurdle laid out in front of him, perhaps the run-run-run-run-jump, run-run-run-run-jump rhythm and the perfection of technique it required. In any case, he had a new love now, a new obsession. But its place at the top of his list was short-lived.

Little Robby was her baby, Jacqueline Griffin's precious baby, and yeah, she was protective of him. Of course she was. She didn't need a bishop's prophecy to tell her how special he was. Yes, if you want to be truthful about it, he was a mama's boy, and when people called him that, neither mama nor child protested much.

Even now, "he's a mama's boy," Jacqueline said, "and he's proud of being a mama's boy."

For a while there, she had been able to keep him away from organized football, steering him toward other sports, always keeping him too busy to dwell on what he was missing. But this was Texas, and Robby came to understand that here, football was king. There were three seasons in Texas: football season, spring football season, and recruiting season. In most folks' minds, the other stuff just filled in the gaps.

As his seventh-grade year approached at S. C. Lee Junior High, one of two junior highs in town that fed into Copperas Cove High, the two Robert Griffins—father and son—were starting to turn up the heat on Jacqueline to let the boy play football. Around here, even junior high football was big. The uniforms worn by the S. C. Lee Cougars were the same as the ones worn by the big boys—the Bulldawgs—at Cove High. The coaches even wore the same polo shirts. The junior high team was like a minor league team, a feeder team, for the Bulldawgs. If Robby was going to play one day for the Bulldawgs—and he *had* to play for the Bulldawgs—he first needed to play for the Cougars.

"Our first love was track. And basketball was what we played the most," recalled Troy Vital, Robby's best friend in grade school. "But we knew football was what was going to take you places. That was the way to make it."

The Pinkie Promise, then, was less a hard-and-fast vow than a coping mechanism for mother and a message for son. It was a way to let the boy—and his father—know that she wasn't totally on board with this, that she would be watching closely, and that he had better be careful out there. *Think about the promise when you have to decide whether to take a hit to gain three more yards, or duck out of bounds.*

"Mama, they'll never catch me," the boy had said, and for that season at least, he more or less upheld his end of the promise. In his first game, Robby threw for three touchdowns, ran for three others, and the Cougars won, 60–6. He got tackled of course, but more times than not, either with his speed or his moves or his smarts, he made the other kids miss.

And the boy had the huge heart of a champion, right from the start. In one game that season, a hard-fought slog on a rainy, muddy field in which the Cougars had squeezed out a narrow victory, Robby came walking off the field toward his father. His uniform, his helmet, even his chin were all caked with mud. But he was holding his head high. *The boy left it all on the field,* the father thought. *He really gets it.*

Robby was a quarterback of course. That's just who he was. His father had already been training him as a quarterback, and he was the best athlete on the team—not just the fastest, but the kid with the strongest arm—and so the coaches lined him up behind the center, and that's the way it always was and always would be.

People took notice of the young Griffin boy, whether it was football, basketball, or track. There was something special about this kid, and tales of his ability began to circulate.

"I've known him since I was nine or ten," said Vital, "and he's always been the best athlete I've ever seen. No stage was ever too big for him."

David Windham, a longtime family friend of the Griffins whose daughters ran track for Robert Jr., recalled meeting their youngest for the first time when the boy was twelve years old. A former Jackson State University lineman who went on to play briefly in the NFL as a replacement player during the strike-shortened 1987 season, Windham could recognize supreme athletic ability, and after seeing the boy in action he immediately called his friends and said, "I just saw the next World's Greatest Athlete."

"This kid was destined for stardom," Windham recalled. "He was doing all the events back then—high jump, long jump, hurdles—and was winning all of them. I asked him, 'Son, what do you want to be when you grow up?' He said, 'It's not about what I want to be, sir—it's what I *will* be. I will be an NFL quarterback, and I will be a lawyer.'"

t was 11:30 P.M. on February 12, 2003—Robert Griffin III's thirteenth birthday—when the call came in to the Griffins' home phone. Sergeant First Class Robert Griffin Jr. was being stop-lossed—deployed to Iraq, where the United States, under President George W. Bush, was preparing to open a new front in the war on terror. He would be leaving the following morning, off to run a refueling operation for tanks and helicopters. It was stunning news to the Griffins, since Robert Jr. was on the verge of retirement—in fact, he already had his retirement papers in hand. But when you get a call like that, you don't argue. You say, "Yes, sir," and you pack your bags.

The kids were asleep, so Jacqueline and Robert let them sleep until 5:00 A.M.—an hour before he had to depart for the airport— before waking them to tell them the news. Robby cried, and now the father was the one comforting him.

"Daddy's going to be okay," he said.

Robert Jr. had scribbled down a workout regimen for the boy to follow while he was gone, and he looked him in the eye and told him things would need to be different now. "You're the man of the house," he told the boy. "You're going to have to take care of your sisters and your mom."

Sudden deployment was an accepted part of life around Fort Hood and Copperas Cove. Everybody, including young Robby, knew friends whose fathers or mothers had been shipped out. And some of them had not come back.

"We knew there was a chance my dad would be stop-lossed," the younger Griffin recalled. "But none of us expected it to be on my birthday. At such a young age, it was kind of tough. But they called him that night and told him he was going out the next day. So there was not much of a building-up period to get ready. I was pretty devastated. It was the worst birthday I ever had."

Before he left for the airport, the father gave his son one more order: keep everyone away from the television. Nobody was going to be helped by seeing war footage on the news. Robby took his role as man of the house—and as the TV police—seriously. More than once in the months that followed he caught his mother or one of his sisters watching war coverage on TV and walked over and turned it off. But in a roundabout way, it was news coverage of the war that helped Robert Jr. stay in touch with his family: Ted Koppel, as it turned out, was embedded with Griffin's platoon, and he borrowed cell phones from Koppel's crew to call Jacqueline and the kids.

One of those calls came shortly after the start of the war, in March 2003. Out of view of her little man-child, Jacqueline had snuck a peek at the news on the night of the first U.S. maneuvers and saw a line of trucks moving across the desert. Immediately, she had what she described as a vision from God and knew it was her husband's platoon.

"Did you see that line of trucks?" her husband said over the phone.

"Yes," she said. "That was you."

"How did you know that?" he asked.

The Army had tabbed Robert Griffin Jr. in the first place, despite his pending retirement, because they valued his leadership. "The commander told him it was because he believed that my husband was the one they felt could make the platoon believe in him and the best man to get those boys home alive," Jacqueline said. "And he did. Not one of them died or was even injured."

Once, SFC Griffin's platoon was crossing a desert expanse in the middle of the night when he sensed something—a looming danger. He radioed to the base to scramble an Apache helicopter to light up the night sky, and sure enough, there was an enemy cell hiding in the distance, waiting to ambush Griffin and his platoon. The helicopter took out the threat and the platoon proceeded; Griffin's actions may have saved his platoon from multiple casualties.

Griffin Jr. was gone for six months, and when he returned, his son ran into his arms. Robby had grown some, physically, but he had grown even more emotionally. The period during his father's deployment was "a pivotal moment for him," his mother recalled, teaching him a lasting lesson about leadership and sacrifice. His father had put his duty to his country ahead of himself and his own family.

The lesson was this: "Sometimes," Jacqueline said, "you have to take one for the team."

THREE

THE SAVIOR ARRIVES

A vast and beautiful new landscape revealed itself to Robert Griffin III early in the afternoon on April 27, 2012, out the window of Daniel Snyder's private jet—tail number N904DS, but better known as Redskins One. It was a perfect day for flying, with nine miles' visibility. Had he looked carefully, Griffin might have been able to make out the outlines of MetLife Stadium in New Jersey and Lincoln Financial Field in Philadelphia, two buildings not far from the plane's flight path that would bear stark witness to his talents later that fall.

A shuttle bus had picked up Griffin and his family—his fiancée, his parents, his two sisters, and his four-year-old niece, Jania—at their New York hotel that morning and driven them to an executive airport in Teterboro, New Jersey, where Redskins One was waiting for them on the tarmac. Griffin, wearing a black Redskins T-shirt, a black military-style jacket, a black Adidas cap, and (somewhat incongruously) red Santa Claus socks, ascended the seven steps of the drop-down stairway and settled into one of the plane's leather seats.

As the great East Coast megalopolis passed by outside the window, that day's *Washington Post* sports section—featuring above the fold a giant picture of Griffin striding across the stage at Radio City Music Hall the night before, under the headline "Dawn of a New Era in D.C."—sat on a table. A flat-panel television on one wall was tuned to the NFL Network, with footage from the night before—of smiling, fresh-faced draft picks, Griffin included, striding across the stage to shake the commissioner's hand—playing on a constant loop.

When the plane landed in suburban Virginia, a convoy of limos met the Griffin clan on the runway and spirited them all to Redskins Park in Ashburn, the team's headquarters. Entering the building through the front doors, Griffin stopped to gaze at the three Lombardi Trophies encased in glass in the lobby, representing the Redskins' Super Bowl titles in 1982, 1987, and 1991. A tour of the building led Griffin, finally, to the locker room, where he found his locker and took note of one spine-tingling detail: he had been placed next to London Fletcher, the fourteen-year veteran linebacker and spiritual leader of the Redskins' locker room.

"To me that was a big moment," Griffin said later, "because it means I get to sit next to the guy who is the leader. For me to be next to him is an honor."

In just seven days, Griffin and the team's other rookies would report to Redskins Park for a brief rookie minicamp, but the magnitude of what he was walking into was only then beginning to hit him. Before going to sleep in his hotel room in New York the night before, Griffin had surfed around on YouTube and Twitter and found himself blown away by the thousands of celebratory missives and well-wishes from Redskins fans everywhere. Shortly after landing in Virginia, Griffin was whisked off to an autograph-signing event in nearby Chantilly, where fans waited in line two and a half hours for his signature and where he had counted seven different T-shirt designs featuring his name.

But even that had not prepared him adequately for what awaited him the next afternoon, April 28. The Redskins had planned a public unveiling of Griffin at FedEx Field—their sprawling, charmless stadium in the dreary Maryland suburb of Landover—and it was becoming clear by late morning that when the gates opened, the crowd was going to be huge.

(Coincidentally, that same night, in Los Angeles, nineteen-year-old outfielder Bryce Harper, the No. 1 overall pick of the 2010 Major League Baseball draft, would make his big league debut for the Washington Nationals, launching a memorable rookie season that would end in his winning National League Rookie of the Year honors and the Nationals winning their first division title. Had one city ever been blessed with two such high-voltage phenoms at one time? Perhaps New York in the spring of 1951, when Willie Mays and Mickey Mantle debuted within a month of each other?)

By the time Griffin, wearing a charcoal-gray suit and burgundy tie, was introduced to the crowd, jogging through a gauntlet of cheerleaders to chants of "R-G-3! R-G-3!" some 19,880 fans— more fans than attended most home games of the Washington Wizards or Capitals—had packed onto the field and in the lower bowl of the stadium to get their first in-person glimpse of the new savior of the franchise. Many of them were wearing brand-new Redskins replica jerseys with Griffin's name and number (10) on the back—the Redskins having conveniently put them on sale in the stadium gift shops that morning, at $130 a pop. Others held up signs reminiscent of the iconic HOPE signs that had become ubiquitous during Barack Obama's first presidential campaign in 2008, only with Griffin's pixelated face in place of Obama's. For Redskins fans, this was change they could believe in.

Oh my goodness, Jacqueline Griffin said to herself. *All this for my baby?*

At the sight of Robert Griffin Jr., the crowd broke into chants of "R-G-2!," which brought tears to Jacqueline's eyes.

Oh my gosh, she thought. *They've accepted my whole family.*

At a news conference down the hall from the Redskins' game-day locker room, the younger Griffin posed for the cameras while holding up his new jersey—with GRIFFIN III above his number 10. (The "III" on Griffin's jersey was the result of a conveniently timed rule change instituted by the NFL: beginning that season, players would be permitted to use surname suffixes such as "III" or "Jr." on their uniforms, something that had been banned before then. Though the league never said as much, it was widely believed that Griffin's arrival in the NFL was the impetus for the rule change.)

The assembled media seemed just as taken with Griffin as the fans were—with good reason. As some reporters already knew, and as others would soon find out, Griffin was press-conference gold, whether you were aiming for short-and-sweet sound bites for the six o'clock news or long, expansive answers for a flowery feature. Down in front, the staccato *click-click-click* of still-photographers filled the air every time Griffin flashed his prize-winning smile.

"A lot of people can look at this as a bad side [to stardom], but it's all a part of the gig," Griffin said to a question about the attention he was getting. "The one thing people have said is [that] it's only going to get worse. But if it gets worse, that means I'm doing my job. When you're successful, people are going to want a part of you. They're going to want to talk to you and see what's going through your mind. So I plan on being successful. And I hope the teammates that I now have will join me in that battle and hopefully the spotlight and all the cameras, all the flashes will get worse for everybody—because that means we're doing what we're supposed to do, and that's win football games."

Asked what he knew about his new teammates, Griffin rattled off a comprehensive list of every receiver and running back on the roster, adding with a wink, "I've been doing my homework."

The only remotely sour note came when Thomas Boswell, the venerable *Washington Post* columnist, asked about Griffin's ability to slide in order to avoid tackles, and Griffin sheepishly admitted his lack of skills in that area. "When it comes to sliding, I'm not the best slider," he said. But he quickly added, "I do know when to slide and when to keep running, just in case people were wondering."

Maybe it just came out wrong. Maybe it was a misguided attempt at being cute with an answer. In any case, if this had been act 1, scene 1 of an Italian opera, the "sliding" quote would have been accompanied by a loud, scary leitmotif going up from the violins, foreshadowing the gruesome ending in the final scene.

Mark Rypien. Rich Gannon. Cary Conklin. Heath Shuler. John Friesz. Gus Frerotte. Jeff Hostetler. Trent Green. Brad Johnson. Jeff George. Tony Banks. Shane Matthews. Patrick Ramsey. Danny Wuerffel. Tim Hasselbeck. Mark Brunell. Jason Campbell. Todd Collins. Donovan McNabb. Rex Grossman. John Beck.

Twenty-one men: every quarterback who started games for the Redskins between the franchise's last Super Bowl title in 1991 and the arrival of Griffin in 2012. Twenty-one men who couldn't hold the job down for more than a couple of years, many of them not lasting even one—a wasteland of squandered talent, stopgap journeymen, ill-fated acquisitions, and disastrous draft picks. That was something else Griffin was getting himself into—a whole lot of ugly history.

"I try not to take the weight of the past twenty years on my shoulders," Griffin said at his introductory news conference, when that history was tossed in his face.

No offense to solid, accomplished quarterbacks such as Rypien and Doug Williams, who had won Super Bowls in Washington, but the fact was, the Redskins hadn't had a franchise quarterback since . . . well, when exactly? Joe Theismann in the 1980s? Sonny Jurgensen in the '70s? Sammy Baugh in the '40s?

At any rate, it had been a long, long time, and the Redskins' decades-long desperation to land a franchise quarterback informed virtually every media report about Griffin's arrival. Before he had even been fitted for a Redskins helmet, before he had signed a contract, before he had been introduced to the fans, Griffin was already shouldering the burden of all that history and all those hopes.

Even Snyder, the Redskins' owner, was heaping shovelfuls of the stuff on his new superstar. In a meeting with Griffin at Redskins Park on the morning of the FedEx Field unveiling, Snyder had told him point-blank, "We're relying on you."

Griffin's response was classic: "I like to be relied on."

That day was also the third and final day of the NFL draft,

starting with the fourth round, and in their meeting that morning Shanahan informed Griffin that the team was preparing to select Michigan State's Kirk Cousins, another quarterback, with their fourth-round pick. Shanahan reassured Griffin that the team considered him their franchise quarterback, but explained that they had Cousins rated as a second-round-caliber talent and felt he was simply too good to pass up in the fourth round.

It was an odd choice, to say the least—and one that was widely panned around the league. It had been twenty-three years since any team took two quarterbacks in the first four rounds of the draft, and it brought to mind nothing so much as the Redskins' 1994 draft, when the team took Shuler out of Tennessee with the third overall pick of the first round, then turned around and chose Frerotte out of Tulsa in the seventh round. And as any Redskins fan could tell you, Shuler—the most heavily hyped Redskins quarterback draftee before Griffin—turned into one of the biggest busts of all time, losing his job in 1996 to Frerotte, who reached the Pro Bowl that season.

So why exactly had the Redskins felt they needed Cousins?

Shanahan offered several explanations—that he couldn't pass up a guy who had rated so highly, that he wanted to improve the team's overall depth, etc.—but when pressed, he acknowledged that it basically came down to one issue: Griffin might get hurt.

"There are injuries," Shanahan said. "You're always one or two plays away being the starter. If you see a guy who is a quality player that you can get in the fourth round, that is one or two plays away from being the starter—hopefully it doesn't happen, but you want to be prepared if it does."

Cue the scary-violin-foreshadowing leitmotif again.

This had been a particularly rich draft for quarterbacks, with some calling it the best batch of signal-callers to hit the NFL at the same time since the 1983 draft that produced John Elway, Jim Kelly, and Dan Marino. Besides Luck and Griffin at Nos. 1 and 2 overall, two other quarterbacks went in the first round—Texas A&M's Ryan Tannehill (Miami, eighth overall) and Oklahoma State's Brandon Weeden (Cleveland, twenty-second overall)—and in the third round the Seattle Seahawks took a chance on a dynamic but diminutive quarterback out of Wisconsin named Russell Wilson.

Still, imagine being in Cousins's shoes and looking forward to the draft for months, poring over rosters to see which team might have a need for a quarterback in the middle rounds—then hearing your name called by the Redskins, who only two days earlier had acquired the franchise quarterback they intended to lead their offense for the next ten years.

"It is a little surprising," a dumbfounded Cousins told reporters on a conference call after the selection. "I was trying to forecast which teams would be in need of a quarterback, and I didn't see the Redskins thinking along those lines."

Still, Cousins professed his gratitude for the Redskins' belief in him and vowed to be a loyal teammate, and as the year went on his graceful handling of what was undoubtedly an awkward situation—not to mention his inspired play when called upon—was one of the best sidebar stories to Griffin's amazing rookie season.

That night, following the head-spinning introduction at FedEx Field, Griffin and his family once again dined with the Redskins' top executives, along with the entire Snyder family—this time at the tony Café Milano in Georgetown. At one of the other tables, someone spotted actress Reese Witherspoon, who was in town to attend the White House Correspondents' Dinner the next night. When it was determined that Griffin and Witherspoon shared the same agency, introductions were promptly made, and Witherspoon wished Griffin well in his rookie season.

When he boarded his flight back to Texas at the end of the draft weekend, Griffin had a new possession in his black Adidas duffel bag that he carried onto the plane. It was the Redskins' playbook, presented to him during the morning meeting with the team's top officials the day of the FedEx Field unveiling, and it would become Griffin's constant companion over the ensuing weeks.

Mike Shanahan told Griffin that he would have input on the playbook's final shape, and that they wanted him to be vocal about what he liked and didn't like about the offense they would be installing. Shanahan also said something that resonated deeply with Griffin: "We see you as a throwing quarterback who happens to be fast"—not the other way around. Griffin had gone to great lengths to rise above the stereotypes confronting African American quarterbacks, and that was exactly what he wanted to hear.

The playbook itself was massive—a three-ring binder, five inches wide ("The biggest you can buy," Griffin marveled), stuffed nearly full with pages. The white cover had the familiar Redskins logo on it, and the playbook was divided into chapters and tabbed for easy flipping: cadences, snap-counts, formations, pass protections, receiver routes, red-zone offense, two-minute offense, etc. It was, in essence, the owner's manual for the Redskins' offense.

"That playbook is Coach Shanahan's vision," said Robert Griffin Jr., the only person the younger Griffin entrusted to look at it other than himself. "And that's what Robert is going to capture—Coach Shanahan's vision. Understand the architect, and you understand the playbook."

Griffin had only a week between the FedEx Field unveiling and his first official duties at Redskins Park—the three-day rookie minicamp alongside the team's other draft picks, a handful of undrafted free agents the Redskins had signed, and a few dozen warm bodies who theoretically were trying out for spots but whose NFL careers, in the vast majority of cases, would never make it past those five practices over that weekend.

Griffin spent much of that week in between with his nose in the playbook.

"It's not my Bible, but it's what we live by," Griffin said. "I've been shipping some of my stuff to D.C., but I don't ship the playbook. And I don't check it [in luggage] at the airport. If someone is going to jack my playbook, they're going to have to steal all my stuff."

Griffin, remember, had no real playbook at Baylor (where the coaching staff installed plays straight from the film room or the blackboard to the field), so this was like going from not knowing how to read to being assigned *War and Peace* on the first day of kindergarten. It certainly appeared that the Shanahans were trying to test Griffin. Rather than giving him the playbook in pieces, they handed him the whole thing, figuring they could always scale it back if it overwhelmed him. But Griffin was determined not to let that happen.

"They wanted to throw the whole offense at me, just so I could see all the possibilities," he said. "They wanted to confuse me. They wanted to make things hard, to see what I could handle."

Griffin, as it turned out, had a partner, an accomplice in his quest to conquer the playbook, in his fellow rookie Cousins. Griffin had reached out to him by text message soon after the draft, and any awkwardness that could have existed between them was melted away by their shared senses of duty and loyalty. Say what you will about the curious decision to draft Cousins in the first place—and plenty of talking heads on the television networks were blasting it—but it gave Griffin a natural study partner and confidant.

Griffin and Cousins even became roommates during the late-spring series of camps at Redskins Park, sharing a two-bedroom apartment at an extended-stay hotel just around the corner from the complex. There, in the evenings, they worked on their nightly take-home quizzes, devised by Kyle Shanahan, the offensive coordinator, and Matt LaFleur, the quarterbacks coach.

The quizzes were designed to do what quizzes do—to test your knowledge of the concepts being taught and to drill them into your brain. The quiz would present a play-call—say, "Pistol Trips-Right 300 Jet Double-Stick"—and Griffin and Cousins would have to describe what formation (Pistol, Trips-Right), protection (300 Jet), and receiver routes (Double-Stick) the call described. For a kid who always loved school, it felt good to be back in learning mode.

"You want to get it in your brain, so it's stuck there, and you can pull from it," Griffin said. "What's your protection on a certain play? What's your 'hot' [i.e., your quick-react target if you are under immediate pressure] on that play? What's your primary [target]? Your secondary? What are your reads? What do you do against this coverage? What do you do on that coverage? So it's about an extreme attention to detail, and I love it. Some [answers] don't come to you immediately. You have to go look them up in the playbook and write them down, and that makes you learn it."

The quizzes weren't graded and weren't marked up with those angry-looking red pens your elementary school teachers used, but each morning Griffin and Cousins would report to Redskins Park and hand the quizzes over to Kyle Shanahan and LaFleur, and any mistakes would be corrected on the spot.

Out on the practice fields in the late mornings and afternoons, the quizzing continued. Griffin would run a play, then immediately circle back and confer with Kyle Shanahan, who was holding a clipboard filled with notes. What did you see? he would ask Griffin. What coverage was the defense in? Where were the safeties? Did all your receivers run the proper routes?

In lengthy film sessions, Griffin studied clips of other quarterbacks running the same or similar offensive concepts as the ones the Redskins were installing—not only former Redskins quarterbacks such as Donovan McNabb and Rex Grossman but stars from other teams, such as Drew Brees and Matt Schaub—as well as compilations of Shanahan offenses from years past. Kyle Shanahan was the primary instructor, pointing out the important lessons from each clip.

It was becoming clear to the Shanahans that Griffin's aptitude was at least equal to his talent. The rookie blew them away on a daily basis. At the end of the three-day rookie camp in early May that marked Griffin's first on-field drills under the Redskins' scheme, Mike Shanahan marveled at the lack of a single busted play or wrong formation during the entire camp.

"I don't think I've ever had that [happen] in any minicamps I've been involved in," he said. "Very few people can take as much verbiage. It's like learning a new language. Some people are able to pick it up very quickly, and [others can't]. Robert was able to pick it up very quickly, and it showed on the field."

Each evening after practice, Griffin would call his father back home in Texas and fill him in on the day's lessons. "Today it was a grueling one," he told him one time, "but I learned so much. I truly felt I'm elevating my game."

Another time the elder Griffin was watching clips from practice on the Redskins' website and saw something in his son's footwork that he didn't like, so he called him immediately. "Dad," his son told him, "I'm already on top of that." Sure enough, when the father checked some more video clips a few days later, the issue was indeed fixed.

During his breaks between minicamps, Griffin would head back to Texas and inevitably wind up at his kitchen table with his father, talking at length about this new offense, this new world he was absorbing. It was a cherished ritual between them—sitting around talking football.

Griffin and his mother had a different cherished ritual. Every few weeks, she would rebraid her son's hair, a painstaking process that took up to four hours. She would start by undoing the old braids, and then, after he had washed his hair, she would carefully redo them one by one, giving her son his trademark look.

Sometimes he would nap as she toiled away, or he'd munch on

peanut butter sandwiches. Most of the time they just talked. This was "Mommy Time," as she sometimes called these sessions.

But as she braided his hair one day in early May 2012, just a few weeks into Robert Griffin III's professional career, Jacqueline Griffin toiled away in near-silence, while her son kept his eyes—and his focus—fixed on something else: the huge, white, three-ring binder that sat on his lap, with the Washington Redskins logo on the front and the raw materials for a brilliant rookie season inside.

Of all the people who had staked their legacies on Griffin's talents, nobody had more to lose than Mike Shanahan. The Redskins' head coach was still a flinty old cuss at age fifty-nine—his expression rarely changing, but his color veering from a healthy pink to a deep crimson depending on whether he was only moderately irritated or extremely so—but the 2012 season might have been his final chance to prove he could still win in this league. And Griffin was his magic ticket.

At one time Shanahan was among the NFL's coaching royalty—his Denver Broncos teams had gone 224-138 between 1995 and 2008, winning four division crowns and two Super Bowl titles in that span. But Shanahan's best seasons were inextricably linked to John Elway, the quarterback who led Shanahan's Broncos to those two Super Bowls, and as his critics in D.C. were fond of pointing out, Shanahan had won exactly one playoff game in Denver in the ten seasons following Elway's retirement in 1998.

Of course, Shanahan's first two seasons in Washington, with a combined record of 11-21, had only emboldened those who wondered if the game had passed him by. Two years of losing was just about all Daniel Snyder was usually willing to accept from his head coaches (see: Zorn, Jim; and Spurrier, Steve), and while Shanahan's reputation, name recognition, and sparkling Denver résumé had undoubtedly earned him a longer grace period, time was running out on him.

But Shanahan was still among the keenest offensive minds in the game, and with this particular quarterback he saw limitless potential—a blank slate on which to construct his masterwork. Once it became clear that the Redskins were going all-in to get Griffin, Shanahan, and his son, Kyle, to hit the film room hard, pulling together concepts from all over football's ideological map.

The elder Shanahan's first coaching job had been with the University of Oklahoma in the mid-1970s, when the Sooners' triple-option wishbone offense was one of the most brutally efficient offensive machines the game had seen to that point. Now, nearly forty years later, he went back and restudied that offense to see what elements he could pull out and reconfigure for Griffin, who had run variations on the option at Baylor. Shanahan understood that, even in small doses, those option concepts could put a scare into NFL defenses.

"With Robert, the difference is you have a guy that can run under a 4.4[-second] 40[-yard dash] and then has the capabilities of really putting pressure on the defense," Shanahan said. "You only have to run an option or an option scheme maybe two or three times a game. But in the back of their mind, a defense knows you have the ability to do it, so you've got a chance to keep them off-balance even if you don't run it a lot."

During his year away from football—after his firing from Denver and before his hiring by Washington—Shanahan had spent time with Urban Meyer, then the Florida Gators head coach, learning the intricacies of Meyer's spread offense. Now he looked again at that offense, with an eye toward putting some of those concepts to work for Griffin.

The Shanahans watched tape of Griffin's Baylor offense, Cam Newton's Carolina Panthers, and Tim Tebow's 2011 Broncos—Newton and Tebow being two quarterbacks with dangerous running abilities whose teams had molded their offenses to suit those unique talents.

"It's kind of fun to do some of those things you haven't done for a while," Shanahan said of his dip into his coaching past in a search for inspiration. "When you've got a guy like Robert, who has the ability to really keep a defense off-balance with his ability to do a lot of different things, then you've got to make decisions [about] what you think works best with his talents. There are a lot of different directions we can go. . . .

"There's not a throw he can't make. And he can do something you can't teach. He can make plays when everything breaks down. The fun part about Robert is, I believe he can do things no one else has done. The great quarterbacks I've been around, the quarterbacks who win Super Bowls, who give you a chance to make a difference in big games, are the guys who can do things with their legs and make a play happen [when they're] off-balance."

On the afternoon of May 6, after the last of the five practices during the three-day rookie minicamp, Shanahan looked out at a bank of television cameras and microphones—that day's media contingent numbered around fifty, roughly double that of a typical year—and announced that Griffin would be the Redskins' starting quarterback for 2012. It seemed to be a fairly random time to make such an announcement, except that very few things Shanahan does are random.

There hadn't been any great mystery or debate regarding whom the Redskins were intending to start at quarterback in 2012. It wasn't as if they had John Elway or Joe Montana sitting there on the roster. Aside from Griffin, their viable quarterback options were Grossman, the nine-year veteran with fifty-six career touchdowns and sixty career interceptions, and Cousins, another rookie. In naming Griffin the starter, Shanahan was only stating the obvious.

"Anytime you pick a player with the second pick of the draft and you give up another two number ones and number two and you move up four spots," Shanahan said, "you've got a game plan in mind."

So what was Shanahan's motivation in making the starter announcement—essentially answering a question that no one was actually asking—at that particular moment?

A cynical answer suggests itself: is it possible that Shanahan was doing so to drum up interest (and sell tickets) at a time of year when interest in the NFL is typically at a low ebb? After all, part of the rationale for spending all those draft picks to get Griffin in the first place was his potential to reenergize a flagging fan base.

Shanahan, in fact, was doing a lot of public praising of Griffin that spring, in a way that seemed wholly out of character for the grizzled lifer with the poker-faced aversion to self-revelation. At a luncheon the week after the rookie minicamp to celebrate the eightieth anniversary of the Redskins franchise, Shanahan spoke to the attendees and assured them that Griffin was "a franchise quarterback who will be here the next fifteen years."

"It's not going to happen overnight—we'll have some growing pains," Shanahan said. "But I promise you he will do things that you have not seen quarterbacks do."

FOUR

THE BULLDAWG

The hill isn't so intimidating when you're standing at the top of it, near the FARM ROAD 116 sign, on a mild Texas spring day, with an occasional car zooming along and, off in the distance somewhere, a large number of dogs barking incessantly. Heading south from up where it intersects with Whispering Avenue, a couple miles north of Copperas Cove, the two-lane road bends gently to the east through dusty scrubland and descends the hill gradually to a valley near a public works facility.

But now try running up and down this hill a few times. And now try it with an SUV tire tied around your waist by a rope. And now do it in the hot sun of a Texas summer, or in the only slightly less suffocating air of a hot Texas night, when all your friends are vacationing at the beach or playing video games in their air-conditioned rooms. Do it with your father standing there with a stopwatch.

This stretch of Farm-to-Market Road 116, designated by the state of Texas in 1944 to help farmers in tiny Copperas Cove get their goods to Gatesville—the county seat of Coryell County, twenty-four miles to the north—is known around these parts now as Griffin Hill, for it was here, on many an evening in the mid-2000s, where a talented young athlete named Robert Griffin would wind down from football practice by dragging a tire up and down the hill.

The father would tie one end of a rope to the tire, hook the other end to a loop of garden hose, and fasten the hose—less likely to cut into skin than the rope—around his son's waist. He would stand at the bottom while the son went up and down the hill, trailed by an SUV, driven by Jacqueline Griffin, with its lights on and its blinkers flashing. The posted speed limit was 55 miles per hour, and an occasional car or semi-truck would zoom past, but mostly the only sound track was the barking of dogs from the animal shelter at the public works facility, their howls growing louder as the gravely scraping noise of Griffin dragging the tire along drew closer.

"Believe it or not," Robert Griffin III recalled one afternoon in April 2012, standing beside this roadway and reminiscing with his father, "this was a place of comfort, even with all the cars and the dogs."

He would pull that tire up and down Griffin Hill right after practice, or sometimes after dinner, or other times as late as midnight or 1:00 A.M. He would do it on weekend afternoons too, and he would do it on Thanksgiving Day, and later, after he enrolled at Baylor University up the road in Waco, he would do it on his spring and winter breaks.

"When you train, you've got to have something you're confident in," Griffin said. "So this was something we were confident in. It didn't matter what time of season it was. If I needed to get in shape, we came to Griffin Hill."

In 2006 and 2007, folks would spot the young man running the hill in the evenings, and call up the Copperas Cove Bulldawgs football coach and ask why his star quarterback was dragging a tire up a hill at night—after football practice. Who was making him do that?

"I think it's what Robert wanted to do," recalled Jack Welch, the football coach. "His dad didn't make him do it. Robert's his own man. He's going to do what he wants to do. If he didn't feel like doing something, he didn't do it. But Robert was a very focused young man."

The more it became evident the young man had extraordinary, God-given talent, the more dedicated the father became to nurturing and maximizing that talent. On fall afternoons, while her husband was at work at Fort Hood, Jacqueline would sit under an umbrella with a book and a video camera, burying her face in the book while the camera recorded the entire practice. In the evenings, the father would study the tapes and bring Robby in to show him something he had noticed. He tried to look at his son the way a defensive coordinator would, searching for weaknesses, tendencies—only he wasn't looking to exploit them, he was looking to shore them up.

Other times he would bring his son in to sit next to him in the living room, and they would study tapes of NFL quarterbacks. He wanted to show his son all the different styles, highlighting one or two aspects of each quarterback's game he believed to be worthy of emulation.

"I liked Ken Stabler. He was in the pocket, making great runs, great throws. I wanted [Robert] to be able to do those things," Robert Griffin Jr. recalled. "Roger Staubach—the Dodger. He was moving. Fran Tarkenton—always moving. Robert ain't nothing new. He's faster than those guys, but in a sense, this game has been evolving for a long time. Roger Staubach was a running quarterback before Randall Cunningham. I also liked those guys who threw the ball. I liked Steve Grogen at New England. I liked Jim Kelly a lot. Dan Marino. There were a lot of great quarterbacks in that era. Look at their form, their balance, their footwork. I watched those things."

He watched sporting events with an eye toward the lessons each game could teach his son. Once, he had Robert watch a tape of the epic 2006 Ohio State–Michigan football game, start to finish, because he considered it the ultimate example of two great teams refusing to back down, refusing to bend.

Robert Jr. learned about strength training and nutrition from bodybuilding magazines and put Robert on a special diet, which eventually required Jacqueline to drive back to school in midmorning with a snack for her son, go again at midday with a special lunch, and then, of course, make a fourth trip in the afternoon to videotape football practice. The father's motto was: "Train hard, eat right, hydrate."

The boy could eat like a horse—De'Jon, with a laugh, could still recall her brother's usual order from Taco Bell: four half-pound burritos and four soft tacos—but now Robert Jr. had him on a nutrition regimen that he would alter depending on which sport was in season.

"The other kids laughed about it: 'Man, Robert, I wish that was me. You have three meals a day delivered to you,'" Jacqueline recalled. "He would have turkey meat and no bread during track season, and we would add wheat bread during football season.

Lots of cut-up strawberries, lots of water. And [Robert] bought into it. To this day, when he needs to train and eat a certain way, he still does that."

All of this struck some other parents as being over the top, or overbearing, but the Griffins knew where the line was between devotion and suffocation, and young Robert wasn't denied the typical comforts of childhood, such as television and video games. People sometimes misunderstood the purpose of videotaping every practice—that wasn't for the boy to pore over for hours every evening. It was for his father to watch, looking for one or two things to show his son.

"I was still able to be a kid," Robert III recalled. "The fun that I sacrificed was hanging out all the time with my friends. And that's just something that I didn't do."

For the Griffins, who treated their daughters with a similar level of devotion, it never felt like a burden, and it always served a higher purpose.

"I enjoyed it," Jacqueline said. "There's something about being a mom and having that level of devotion. We felt if they saw how devoted we were to them, and the sacrifices we made so they could be the best they could be, then they'd only strive harder."

Bulldawg Stadium sits at the corner of Rodney Avenue and Williams Street in Copperas Cove, a 9,845-seat palace that would be the envy of many small college programs. Need directions to the stadium? Just follow the blue painted paw prints that line the streets of the town's central district and lead straight into the stadium's main parking lot. There is a video scoreboard and a state-of-the-art synthetic track encircling the field. In one end zone is painted the word COVE, and in the other, DAWGS. An adjacent building houses the football offices and training complex, featuring a ten-thousand-square-foot weight room that dwarfs some NFL ones.

In a hallway outside the office of Bulldawgs head coach Jack Welch, a digital-readout clock counts down the days, hours, minutes, and seconds until the start of spring football practice. Framed pictures of past Bulldawgs teams line the walls.

Robert Griffin, as he was known then, appears in three of them.

As a freshman, Griffin was good enough to start for the varsity basketball team, the only freshman to even make the squad. But that was basketball. Football was different. Nobody plays for the Bulldawgs' varsity football team as a freshman, not even a whip-smart, preternaturally talented quarterback who was already the talk of the town in the fall of 2004. And so Griffin went off to play for the JV and bided his time.

In school, Griffin was that rare kid who bridged social cliques—a star jock who also liked poetry, who made straight A's, who wore silly socks and still loved his superhero figurines. Outside of his sports prowess, in fact, you might say the guy was a straight-up dork. "If I didn't play sports," he acknowledged, "I would not have fit in."

As his sophomore year approached, Griffin pushed himself extra hard, hoping to wrest the team's starting quarterback job from a rising senior named Brent Garner. Already, the town was buzzing over the quarterback battle, with one faction supporting the older Garner, an all-district performer the year before, and a growing faction pushing for Griffin, who had already become well known as the best all-around athlete in the area.

When Welch, the head coach, wound up choosing Garner, who is white, the decision sparked a perhaps inevitable backlash that focused on race, with some of Griffin's friends telling him the decision must have been racially driven. But in the Griffin household that sort of talk was not tolerated. Jacqueline and Robert Jr. had made a conscious decision to raise their children in as color-blind a way as possible, and no Griffin was going to pin something like this on racism. Over the ensuing years, as Robert Griffin III's race was frequently turned into an issue or a story line, the pattern would repeat itself: everyone else focusing on race, and the Griffins refusing to do that.

"Clearly in everybody's mind he was the better quarterback, but he didn't get to play that year," Jacqueline recalled. "But instead of coming home and saying it's because of this, that, or the other, we said, 'Continue to work hard. It doesn't matter—continue to work hard.' Next year, when [Garner] graduated and we were told Robert would have to compete for the starting job? Well, competition is never a bad thing. Everything has to be earned. So he went into a competition with two other kids, and he won. Everybody was saying Copperas Cove would never endorse an African American quarterback. We, as an African American family who didn't believe in race, and who didn't raise our kids that way, didn't want him to have that mind-set. So we continued to instill in him that it's not about race. It's about performance on the field. At the end of the day, even if it is about race in other people's minds, the coach will make the right decision because he wants to win. At the end of the day it's about winning."

Robert Griffin Jr. echoed his wife's sentiments, in his own suc-
cinct way: "If [anyone] said the coaches were prejudiced against
Robert, I'd say I do not support that," he said. "I would say the
coaches do things no one understands."

And so Jack Welch, a good football coach and a good man,
may go down in history as the only person who could stop Robert
Griffin III. He could have had him as his quarterback for four
years and chose to have him only for two—but still has no regrets.
Griffin wasn't ready as a freshman, and as a sophomore he sat
behind a senior who had been all-district the year before. Plenty of
coaches would have done the same thing. And according to Welch,
even when Griffin's time finally came his junior year—when Welch
chose him over a kid named Logan Brock, who wound up switching positions and now is a tight end for the Houston Texans—
there was some rawness to his game that had to be refined.

"Some kids grow into their height, or grow into their size—he
had to grow into his talent," Welch recalled. "What I mean by that
is, he could throw the ball a country mile. It just wasn't always
accurate downfield. That's where we tried to work on him and
develop it."

Raw or not, Griffin's two years as quarterback of the Bulldawgs produced the two best seasons in the school's history, with
appearances in the state Class 4A championship game in both
2006 and 2007. Griffin was 25-4 as starter during those two
years, passing for 3,300 yards, rushing for another 2,161, and accounting for 73 total touchdowns.

"There are fast quarterbacks in Texas," the *Houston Chronicle*
wrote in December 2007, "but compared to Robert Griffin, the
rest look as if they're running in quicksand."

He was also a natural-born leader, a critical quality for a quarterback. He would bring doughnuts for his offensive linemen in the mornings, and he was a world-class text-message communicator, firing off encouraging texts at a dizzying pace.

"When we experienced a loss," Welch recalled, "he was always texting to his teammates: 'C'mon, we gotta hang in there. Let's get it together.' It was just like he was a coach."

And Griffin tolerated no losing mentality. Once, in a playoff game their senior year against Waxahachie High, Griffin and Vital, his running back and best friend, sat on the bench late in the fourth quarter, with the Bulldawgs trailing by 14 points and the defense buckling again. College Signing Day was approaching, and with things looking hopeless on the field, Vital wondered aloud how Signing Day would play out.

Griffin looked at him incredulously and barked, "Don't even worry about that. We're about to get back in this game. This is what we live for. This is our moment."

The Bulldawgs scored 23 points in the fourth quarter and came back to win, 37–35.

"All this stuff he's doing now—none of this is shocking to any of us," Vital said after retelling that story. "Not shocking at all. If you had been around him, you'd know."

In 2007 alone, Griffin led the Bulldawgs to the state football championship game, set state records in the 110-meter and 300-meter hurdles (his time in the latter, 35.33 seconds, was one one-hundredth of a second off the national record), served as president of the student body, and graduated seventh in his class with a 4.71 grade point average on a 5.00 scale. (Five years later, he could still name all six of the students who graduated ahead of him, as well as their GPAs.)

He still dreamed of playing in the NBA, but now that dream competed with other ones: running the hurdles in the Olympics, playing quarterback in the NFL, going to law school. The time was coming fast when he would have to start making some choices.

The concept of sacrifice was rarely far from Robert Griffin III's mind, whether it was Jesus Christ's ultimate sacrifice that stands at the heart of the Christian faith, or his parents' sacrifices to give him and his sisters the life they had, or the sacrifice required in one's own life in order to be the best at something.

At Copperas Cove High, on Friday nights during football season, there was a standing party, known as the "Fifth Quarter," where students would gather until the wee hours and do what teenagers do. In four years at the school, including two in which he was the star quarterback, Griffin attended exactly zero of those parties. Instead, he usually went to Coach Welch's house and played pool with a group of teammates. He didn't touch alcohol.

"My parents were stricter than most," he recalled. "I didn't go out much as far as nighttime. It was usually school, then whatever sport was in season at that time, then back home. So I kind of realized once I got into high school that what I was doing was not normal, because everyone was talking about the tire-pulls up the hills and all the extra work. The constant thing that was said was, 'You're not having any fun.' Well, I thought winning was fun, and

I was winning a lot, so I had a lot of fun. The sacrifice I made was to not have what people traditionally thought of as fun. I guess I was goal-oriented at a young age, and I guess my parents realized that and ran with it, and I tried to keep up."

Amazingly, father and son almost never clashed. Asked if he could recall any conflicts from his son's teenage years, Robert Jr. said, "The only conflict I ever had with him was when I'd say [of one of Robert's teammates], 'That guy is not pulling his weight.' He'd defend the guy: 'You don't know what that guy went through to get where he is.' "

The issue of dating, though, was a contentious one. Jacqueline and Robert Jr. didn't allow any of their children to date during high school. "We didn't want Robert to be looked at as a typical jock, jumping from girl to girl," the father explained. But Robert fought them on this one, and perhaps because he fought them so infrequently, ultimately he won.

"I kind of just broke my parents down when it came to dating, and they eventually let me date my junior year," he said. "But that was the only thing I rebelled against. Other than that, to that point everything they told me to do and I did, I was successful at, so there was no point for me to rebel against it."

Football, too, was going to start requiring some sacrifices. It was never his first love—that was basketball—or even his second. That would be track. But it had overtaken the others in terms of his success, his notoriety, and the time commitment it required. He was still a three-sport star through his junior year as he continued to play basketball and run track—drawing interest from colleges in both sports, as well as some early scholarship offers—but that was making some people question his commitment to football, which, of course, was all that really mattered in Texas.

"As a kid growing up, I didn't want to choose one sport, so I played everything—baseball, basketball, track, football. I wanted to make sure I had every door possibly open to go through. But I had to choose. In high school it was hard because I was the starting point guard on the varsity team my freshman year, the starting shooting guard sophomore year, the starting small forward my junior year. So basketball was my thing. I played football for fun. So you're going to tell me the sport I love is getting wiped out by the sport I play for fun, just because I have more success in that sport?"

Increasingly, Griffin was resigned to the idea that basketball was the sport that would have to go. He already had to miss the first part of each season because of football, especially when the Bulldawgs got good enough to go deep into the playoffs. But even more than that, he was simply being a realist: he knew his odds of making it to the highest level were longer in basketball than in either football or track.

"I felt like my height was going to hurt me in basketball," he recalled. "You don't see many six-two guys in the league anymore. There's one here or there, but even most point guards are six-four, six-six guys, so I felt my height would be better suited to football. So I stopped playing basketball—always with the thought that I would play eventually, if I got a chance to. Or say, if football didn't work out, I could still go back to basketball."

Track made the cut because, being a spring sport, it caused less of a conflict with football—and in truth, it was probably his best sport. In the summer of 2007, after his junior year of high school, he won gold at the AAU National Championships in both the 110-meter (13.46) and 400-meter (49.56) hurdles, with the latter time ranking him No. 1 in the nation among high school athletes.

Griffin realized something else important: 2008 was an Olympics year. People, knowledgeable people, were telling him he was good enough to make it to Beijing, and so he concocted a plan to maximize his chances: already ahead of schedule to graduate, he would take summer school classes before his senior season in order to finish at Cove High a semester early, then head off to college, where he could play spring football and run track in preparation for the U.S. Olympic Trials in June 2008.

And so basketball was out. With that decision made, it was time for Robert Griffin to start figuring out where to go to college.

The coaches would plop down on the chair in front of Jack Welch's desk, or call him on the telephone, asking him about his quarterback. It started during the kid's junior year. Plenty of times, these college coaches wanted to know what Welch thought about the kid playing another position. College football coaches love speed, and they are often drawn to high school track stars who also shine on the gridiron, but rarely do those speedsters play quarterback.

"Coach, what do you think about him playing safety?" the college coach would ask Welch.

"He could," Welch would reply, "if he wanted to."

"Coach," another would say, "I think he'd be a great wide receiver. What do you think?"

"He could," Welch would reply again, "if he wanted to."

Finally, Welch would have to deliver the bottom line: Robert Griffin wanted to play quarterback, fellas, and it was non-negotiable. If that didn't suit a particular recruiter, the recruiter might as well just get on up from that chair in Welch's office and make his way to the door.

"A lot of folks saw him as an athlete," Welch recalled. "He was not a polished passer at that point, but he was a great athlete."

Griffin wasn't the bluest of blue chips in his recruiting class, failing to crack any of the coveted Top 100 lists put out by nationwide recruiting websites and magazines. Maxpreps.com had him rated the 232nd-best recruit in the United States, and the 32nd-best in Texas. Rivals.com had him rated No. 42 in Texas, but not within its top 250 in the nation. Ranking him 50th in Texas (33 spots below a quarterback from Stratford High named Andrew Luck), Lone Star Recruiting referred to Griffin as "an elite-level track athlete that still has a long ways to go as a player on the football field" and "a big project with a ton of upside."

Still, plenty of big-time programs sent representatives to visit Jack Welch's office next to Bulldawg Stadium, and plenty of them ignored his warning about Griffin being committed to playing quarterback. The University of Texas, with the biggest and most storied program in the state, famously made a scholarship offer to Griffin that was nonspecific as to his position, simply calling him an "athlete."

"That's Texas for you," Griffin told reporters in 2010. "They get talent from anywhere they want. If they put an offer on the table and you don't accept it, they'll go find some other guy."

Nebraska, UCLA, Wisconsin, and Texas A&M were among

the schools whose recruiting of Griffin was contingent upon him switching to defensive back. "We told them, don't call back. It's not a position he wants to play," Robert Griffin Jr. recalled. Oklahoma, LSU, Miami, Kansas, Illinois, Tennessee, Missouri, Oregon, BYU, Washington State, and Harvard all zoomed into the picture at various times, and then for various reasons zoomed back out.

Along with his parents, Griffin was doing his homework about colleges, studying their academic records and graduation rates as well as their quarterback situations and the types of offenses they ran. Already looking several years ahead, he also wanted a school that had a good law school.

"We went on a college visit to Tennessee," recalled Vital, who was being recruited as a running back, "and that was the first thing Robert asked them about: 'How is your law school?' Anybody we sat down with, he was asking about the law school."

When Jim Harbaugh, at the time the new head coach at Stanford, started recruiting Griffin, it was its law school that initially attracted him. But Harbaugh was proposing something unusual— a co-quarterback system with Griffin splitting time with Luck, who had already committed there. The idea would be to keep defenses off-balance by alternating Luck's more traditional dropback style with Griffin's mobile style.

It was intriguing enough that Griffin made an official visit to the school in Palo Alto, California, where he walked the lush, tree-lined campus pathways with Harbaugh and sat in the coach's office for an hour, listening to his sales pitch. Harbaugh latched onto Griffin's academic bent, introducing him to star professors and talking up the law school. Griffin's father seemed to be particularly smitten with the idea of his son going to Stanford, and by the time they said good-bye Harbaugh thought he had the kid locked up.

"I thought we were doing really well with Robert," Harbaugh, now the coach of the San Francisco 49ers, recalled to the Associated Press in April 2012. "Loved looking at his transcript. His test scores were extremely high. I mean, this to me was a Stanford guy."

There was another school that was coming hard after Griffin, one that kept popping into his head as he mulled over his options. The University of Houston had a decent football history, with a top-10 ranking as recently as 1990, and had produced a Heisman Trophy winner, in quarterback Andre Ware, the year before. It had a law school, and Griffin, if he went there, figured he would have no trouble landing summer internships at law firms, given Houston's size. Most of all, it had a charismatic football coach, Art Briles, who ran a high-octane, pass-oriented offense and who seemed to connect with Griffin in a way other coaches didn't. He also told Griffin that he wanted him as a quarterback and spoke to him about offensive concepts the way a coach would with his quarterback.

"There was just a comfort level with him," Griffin recalled.

Like Griffin, Briles was a man of deep faith who was raised in a small Texas town (Rule, Texas: population 698) by God-fearing parents who taught him the values of hard work and sacrifice. He was straight out of central casting: the Texas Football Coach— a swashbuckling, dark-haired Texas gentleman who spoke in a thick drawl and wore cowboy boots and jeans away from the football field. It would not be at all surprising if actor Kyle Chandler revealed that he based his portrayal of Eric Taylor, coach of the fictional Dillon High Panthers on the NBC television show *Friday Night Lights,* on Briles, so eerie was the resemblance.

Briles's adult life had been shaped by one tragic event: in 1976, when he was a twenty-year-old junior wideout at Houston, his parents and an aunt were on their way to see him play one fall Saturday afternoon at the Cotton Bowl in Dallas when a semi-truck traveling westbound veered and hit their car outside of Newcastle, Texas, killing all three instantly. Briles's coach broke the news to him after the Cougars' win that afternoon over SMU, and Briles spent most of the next year trying to put his life back together.

"I had to decide whether I would fight or falter," he once said of the tragedy. "You've got to pick a road to go down, and I chose one where I tried to build a positive legacy for my family's name. I became determined to honor them in the best way I could."

After college, Briles went straight into coaching and within a decade had established himself as one of the top young offensive minds in the state of Texas at Stephenville High, where he popularized a pass-happy spread offense that would eventually take hold across the state. He joined Mike Leach's Texas Tech staff in 2000 and got the head coaching job at Houston in 2003.

Griffin had attended Briles's football camp for high schoolers at Houston in June 2007, the summer before his senior season, and Briles was well aware of Griffin's track exploits and his athleticism as a football player. But as Briles tells the story, after seeing Griffin's arm for the first time, he turned to his offensive coordinator,

Philip Montgomery, and said, "This guy is incredible. We've got to hide him." When Briles invited him to visit, Griffin brought his mother and sister De'Jon with him, and at one point the four of them sat in Briles's office, watching film together for some ninety minutes.

"I thought, *These people are pretty serious about winning,*" Briles recalled, "because that was pretty unusual to sit there [as a family] and go through the whole tape."

"He treated Robert like he was part of the team," Jacqueline Griffin recalled. "There was just such a strong connection there."

By the end of Griffin's decision process, it was down to Stanford and Houston—but he just couldn't get past the idea of sharing the quarterback position at Stanford. He figured it would never work, and one of the two players—himself or Luck—would ultimately leave.

And so, in October, Griffin called up Harbaugh and delivered the news: he was going to Houston.

"That," Harbaugh told reporters later, "left a bruise."

Griffin played his senior season at Copperas Cove in the fall of 2007 figuring he would be a Houston Cougar by the following spring. Moving forward with his plan to graduate high school after the fall semester, he was already beginning to look at classes and housing at Houston.

But there would be an unforeseen twist: on November 27, Briles, whose Cougars had just accepted an invitation to play in the Texas Bowl the following month, traveled to Waco to interview for the vacant head coaching job at Baylor—which had just fired Guy Morris following a 3-9 season (0-8 in the Big 12), the program's twelfth consecutive losing season.

Briles was offered the job, and the very next day, November 28, he accepted.

A stunned Griffin heard the news of Briles's hiring at Baylor on a television report, and there was a period of twenty-four hours or so when his world was plunged into chaos. Did Briles still want him? Was his commitment to Houston binding?

Just the day before, he had called Briles and asked whether the rumors of his interviewing at Baylor were true, and Briles had told him, "They're just rumors. You just keep playing football." But now, there was Briles, on television, standing before a podium with a Baylor cap on his head, giving the "Sic 'Em Bears" claw sign. He wasn't even going to coach the Cougars in their bowl game. "I am a Baylor Bear," Briles was saying on TV, "as of about eleven o'clock this morning." Griffin tried calling Briles multiple times, with no luck. But finally, he got hold of Briles's wife, Jan, who promised to have the coach call him—which he did that evening.

"I want you to come with me," Briles told him.

Griffin agreed on the spot—which, predictably, set off a firestorm in Houston. "But he never chose Houston," Jack Welch, Griffin's high school coach, recalled. "He chose Briles."

Despite Griffin's verbal commitment to go with him to Baylor, Briles wasn't taking any chances with the kid he considered his top recruiting priority, so he called Jacqueline Griffin and asked if he could come to Copperas Cove to see her son in person and lock down his commitment.

"Coach," she told him, "we already told you we're coming to Baylor. Don't worry about that. Go out and get him some teammates."

And so Baylor it was—and the irony of that choice was not lost on Griffin.

Baylor University had been at the top of his wish list way back when the thought of college first entered his head, and it had stayed there for a good long while. Baylor had nearly all the things he was looking for. It was close to home, Waco being a little more than an hour from Copperas Cove. It had a Christian foundation and a strong academic reputation that kept it a fixture on lists of the top 100 colleges and universities in the country. It had a top-notch law school. It had a storied track program that had produced Olympic sprint champions Michael Johnson and Jeremy Wariner. And even though the football program was more or less a joke, it still played in the Big 12—the big time.

Griffin had been on Baylor's radar as well—at least for track and basketball. Both basketball coach Scott Drew and track coach Todd Harbour wanted him, and Griffin had visited the campus in the fall of 2006 at Harbour's invitation. But when Griffin met with Morris, Baylor's football coach at the time, he was told he would have to walk on if he wanted to play quarterback there. And that was the end of that.

But now, here he was, more than a year later, signing his name to the scholarship papers that would make him a Baylor Bear.

On December 15, 2007, Griffin walked off the football field for the final time as a Copperas Cove Bulldawg following a heart-wrenching 20–14 loss to Jacquizz Rodgers and the Mustangs of Lamar Consolidated in the Texas Class 4A Division I state championship game—a game that turned late in the fourth quarter when Griffin was stopped at the 2-yard line on fourth-and-goal from the 4.

He graduated from high school a week later, and suddenly it was good-bye to the blue-and-white, hello to the green-and-gold. Robert Griffin III—Jacqueline Griffin's baby boy, Robert Griffin Jr.'s lean, mean winning machine—was a college man now, a Baylor man.

FIVE

THE NEW CHAPTER

The headquarters of the Washington Redskins sits atop a bluff in the middle of a 162-acre former dairy farm in the Washington, D.C., suburb of Ashburn, Virginia. A hill behind the white concrete building slopes down to four practice fields below—three natural grass, one artificial turf—and beyond that, through thick woodland, to Broad Run, a tributary of the Potomac River. There is rich Civil War history in this part of the Commonwealth: Union and Confederate forces crisscrossed the region, frequently squaring off for control of a strategically located county that changed hands six times between 1862 and 1864. Standing out on the balcony off the rear of the building and looking out over the practice fields, you might imagine for a moment you are General John Fullerton Reynolds—commander of the First Corps of the Union Army of the Potomac, which passed through here in June 1863, fifteen thousand men strong, on its way to Gettysburg—scanning the countryside from this lookout for any sign of Colonel John Mosby, the famed "Gray Ghost" of the Confederacy, a quick-strike ambush artist who was the scourge of many a passing Union platoon.

Or you might just be Mike Shanahan, checking to see whether your 350-pound defensive lineman had passed his conditioning test yet. Shanahan, whose office at Redskins Park led out to that balcony, fashioned himself a general of sorts, and he waged his own battle against the enemy—of which the media was the only visible one (but in the NFL you never know who else could be lurking in those woods)—with an array of security cameras lining the outside of the building and grim-faced lieutenants patrolling the media ranks (and during the summer, the thousands of fans who attend daily training camp sessions) for signs of an organized attack, or just to make sure no one stepped over one of the lines painted on the grass to corral the great unwashed.

As the Redskins' 2012 season approached, Shanahan was breaking in a young but brilliant new field general, undoubtedly his most talented since the glory days in Denver. Quarterback is a unique position in all of professional sports: in the many tangible and intangible skills it requires, in its involvement in every offensive play and its full integration within the offensive game plan, in the status and leadership responsibilities it carries within the locker room—in summary, in the way in which every aspect of an NFL team revolves around it. And Shanahan, the grizzled general of Redskins Park, knew he might just have one of the best ever on his hands.

Beginning in the middle of 2012—with the minicamp in May, organized team activities (OTAs) in June, and training camp in July—this headquarters became Robert Griffin III's office, his place of work. He decorated his locker with superhero figurines (Incredible Hulk, Spider-Man, G.I. Joe) and pithy mottoes and quotes ("Army Strong," "Be Unstoppable," "Sacrifice," "Conquer Every Obstacle"), and he parked his new jet-black Nissan

Armada—for which he didn't spend a dime (one of the spoils of being a national pitchman)—in the players' lot out front.

Loudoun County also became Griffin's new home as he and fiancée Rebecca Liddicoat took up residence in a four-bedroom, stucco rental home in a gated community in the middle of what, with a median household income of around $115,000, is the wealthiest county in the United States (a designation that would only be bolstered by the arrival of Griffin, who signed a four-year $21.1 million contract with the Redskins on July 18). Each morning he would be out the door shortly after 5:00 A.M., beating the rush-hour traffic to busy Route 7. He would exit Route 7 at Loudoun County Parkway, pull onto Redskins Park Drive, wave at the guard at the gatehouse, park his car, and head into the office. He liked to be the first player to arrive, and at that hour there would frequently be a family of deer munching on one of the grass practice fields below.

For the first part of the summer, before the opening of training camp marked the official run-up to the Redskins' regular-season opener at New Orleans, Griffin was still toggling between Texas and Virginia—tying up loose ends back home and making plans to move his life, and Liddicoat's, to the East Coast, while at the same time taking the first steps toward building a business empire and a brand, with commercial shoots and various public appearances eating into his schedule. For a man who calls himself a romantic at heart, it was a time of deep reflection, a time when he could see the bounty of a dream come true laid out in front of him, but also a time when he understood that with each door closing behind him, life would never be so simple again.

The NFL, he reflected at one point, "is such a business that people don't realize it from the outside [looking] in. But when you're on the inside looking out, you kind of see the freedom you had as a college player is basically gone when you're professional."

As the Redskins veterans started to roll in, Griffin began meeting the men who would be his teammates—the men with whom, in NFL parlance, he would be going into battle. He had already made the acquaintance of many of them via text message, but these first face-to-face introductions were important to Griffin, who understood one critical contradiction facing him: he needed to be the leader of this team—both as a fundamental requirement of the quarterback position and because he had a specific vision and attitude he hoped to instill—but he also needed to show a rookie's proper humility and deference.

He may have come into the organization as a five-star general, but he made a conscious decision to conduct himself like a private.

"I'm not going to be a guy who's all about show, or all about myself," he had said the night of the NFL draft. "I'm going to be a guy who comes into work every day, ready to go."

The deftness with which he walked that line between humility and confidence in his mission in those early days would be a testament to Griffin's upbringing and groundedness. Many teammates who had only known of him as the flashy Baylor superstar and the ace pitchman for Gatorade, Subway, Adidas, and Nissan were surprised to meet a young man so overwhelmingly unassuming and humble.

"Any skepticism was answered the minute he walked in the door," veteran tight end Chris Cooley recalled. "Within a week of being here, he knows everyone's name, he has everyone's phone numbers, he's texting to guys, he's calling guys."

Fullback Darrel Young recalled passing Griffin on the stairway connecting the main floor of Redskins Park with the lower-level locker room and training facility. "He stopped me and said, 'I'm Robert Griffin III. I'm the quarterback they drafted in the first round.' I just looked at him and thought, *Yep, we're going to be just fine here.* This kid is as humble as they come."

"Very humble," added tight end Niles Paul, recalling those early days. "Very willing to prove himself. He didn't come in talking. He didn't say a word. He came in like a regular free agent, a regular draft pick, trying to prove himself."

Of course, everyone was anxious to see Griffin on the practice field—to witness the blinding speed, the arm strength, and the playmaking ability they had heard so much about—and from the very beginning all questions were answered in the affirmative.

"After the first practice or two," recalled long-snapper Nick Sundberg, "everybody was like, 'Oh yeah, this guy is legit.'"

Griffin took the traditional rookie hazing good-naturedly, dutifully carrying a veteran's pads and helmet up the hill to the complex following practices when asked, and once, when he was tasked with bringing in breakfast for everyone, he surprised teammates with homemade beignets (a New Orleans specialty, for which he used his mother's recipe). But everyone went light on the hazing when it came to Griffin. It was almost as if there was an understanding: This kid is our savior. You don't tape your savior to the goalposts and leave him there.

"We knew when we drafted him he was going to bring a different dynamic to this team that we hadn't seen before," recalled left tackle Trent Williams. "So we welcomed him with open arms."

Still, there was no getting out of the rookie variety show, in which all the Redskins rookies were made to perform goofy skits for the veterans and coaching staff. Unfazed, Griffin slayed his audience with a spot-on rendition of the Randy Watson and Sexual Chocolate scene from *Coming to America*—singing a faux-earnest "The Greatest Love of All" in the style of Eddie Murphy's character, with the other rookies as backup singers, a performance that had Shanahan practically in tears. (Griffin was, however, overshadowed that day by Cousins, his backup, who did a drop-dead-perfect impression of Shanahan.)

Underneath Griffin's over-the-top performance, though, was another truth that blew away his teammates: the kid could actually sing—like, he was legitimately good. Was there anything he couldn't do?

They wanted to box everything up themselves, to relive each memory together, and so that's what Robert Griffin III and his fiancée, Rebecca Liddicoat, did. It was July 8, 2012, and the moving truck was coming soon to carry all their belongings to Virginia. Standing in the middle of the now-empty, two-bedroom apartment in Waco, with everything in boxes and the walls now bare, Griffin put his arm around Liddicoat and cried.

"I didn't feel any kind of sadness until it was done," Griffin said later. "When I saw the apartment empty, that's when I knew this chapter was closing."

Before leaving town, he dropped by the football offices on the Baylor campus to say good-bye to staff members and found himself halfway thankful that Briles wasn't around that day—because that particular good-bye would have been extra painful.

"It was tough for me to go to campus and say, 'See you later,' to people I'd been working with for years," he recalled. "That's where I had sweated. That's where I tore an [anterior cruciate ligament] and recovered from it. That's where I won a Heisman and [where] we won ten games [in 2011]. We did so many great things there. To leave that all behind and move on to something new, it was sad. There were a lot of tears."

He had been saying a slow good-bye to Waco all that summer, still using his apartment there as his home base until move-out day. In May and June, when he came back to Waco, his parents would come up from Copperas Cove to visit him, and he would always find time to squeeze in a workout with his dad and a hair-braiding session with his mom.

In early May, Griffin made the drive down to Copperas Cove, and he and his parents joined the other congregants at Christian House of Prayer for Wednesday evening services. Bishop Nathaniel Holcomb had asked Griffin to speak to the congregation, and Griffin brought along the Heisman Trophy as a prop.

"When I was young, you always told me [to] never forget where I came from," Griffin said to Holcomb, as the latter handed him the microphone. Turning to the congregation, he said, "[So] I want to take this time to tell you guys about my parents. . . . We have the Heisman here, and it's so much more than just a trophy. You don't build a house all at the same time, so that trophy came through all those different things my mom and dad had to go through when they were young to give me the life they gave me. One thing my dad always told me was, he would make sure I always had what he didn't have. He couldn't play basketball because he didn't have tennis shoes—so I had five pairs of tennis shoes."

When Griffin was done, Holcomb—who twelve years earlier had stood in that same spot and prophesized over him—placed his hand on the young man's shoulder, bowed his head, and prayed: "We thank you for this mighty oak in the forest of God . . . and [ask] that wherever you take Robert, others will see the love of God, and they will come out of darkness and into the marvelous light because of this young man."

Nothing symbolized the profound transition in Griffin's life during this time better than the last weekend in June. He had taken a chance and invited some of his new Redskins teammates— the wide receivers and tight ends—to spend that weekend in Waco in an impromptu, informal, passing-camp-slash-bonding-session. Griffin fully understood that no matter how much he loved Waco, it wasn't exactly South Beach when it came to desirable off-season vacation spots for rich, young athletes. But to his surprise, most of them accepted.

"That was a big deal for me, to get [stars like] Pierre Garcon and Santana Moss down there," Griffin recalled later. "They said, 'We're coming to Waco to work out with our quarterback, because we believe in him.' It really meant a lot to me."

Temperatures climbed close to 100 degrees all weekend, but Griffin and his receivers went through two workouts a day, and Griffin would say later that he was keeping a close eye on distinguishing "who's truly dedicated and who you have to continue to stay on." In the evenings, he took the group bowling and out to eat at some of his favorite restaurants in town. (Veterans Garcon and Moss usually picked up the check.)

Griffin's worlds were colliding—his old Baylor stomping grounds and his new Redskins teammates—but it was a cathartic experience for him, and an educational one for his teammates, who got a glimpse of where their quarterback had come from.

"That was impressive for him to invite everybody. He didn't have to do that," recalled second-year receiver Aldrick Robinson. "Just to build that chemistry, that camaraderie—working out, going out to eat. That went a long way with everyone."

But now here Griffin was, barely a week later, turning in the keys to his apartment and preparing to say a final good-bye to Waco—closing one amazing chapter of his life and starting another. He was feeling philosophical, his emotions needing an outlet, and so, the day after boxing up his apartment, he took to Twitter. Using the hashtag #KnowYourWhy, he asked teammates individually, "Why do you grind? Why do you play the game? Why do you sacrifice?" In case anyone was confused by the questions, Griffin tweeted out his own answers: "I play because I love the game & God has a plan for me. My story is his message. I sacrifice everything for my family & my team."

Griffin later explained to the website RantSports.com that he was just "having a moment" and that the tweets were intended as much for Redskins fans as for his teammates. "I was kind of just feeling like, this part of my journey is over," he said. "It really hit me hard. I just wanted to tell the fans that I was going to bring the same passion. . . . I think it was a great platform for all those guys—for the fans to see why these guys do what they do.

"I know my why. I sacrifice for my teammates. I want to make my family proud. So I know my why. I just want [the teammates] to know theirs."

Griffin had always been a frugal kid, a trait he inherited from his father. As a child, he would save all his allowance money and the reward money he earned for good report cards and stash it away, while his sisters went to the mall and blew theirs on clothes. As a college student, he once called his father from an airport, astonished at the prices for airport food and vowing to go hungry rather than be gouged an extra dollar or two for a sandwich.

Now, as a young adult who had gotten used to the central Texas cost of living, he was suffering from a severe case of sticker shock as he went house-hunting in Loudoun County—which, come to think of it, made him no different than most other new transplants to the area. He wanted to rent rather than own in his first season, just to streamline his rookie year and keep himself as free from distractions as possible, and the Redskins had found a handful of rental houses for him to choose from. But getting him to pull the trigger on a rent payment in the $3,000-plus-per-month range was no easy task.

"He was shocked" at the prices, his father said. "He called me—they were looking at a place, following the [team's] suggestions. [It was a] harsh reality. Everyone who knows him knows he's not going to be some guy spending wildly. But he had to make a choice, and he felt it was important to be close to the [Redskins] facility, so he did it. I want him to live at middle-class. Now, the rent he's gonna pay is not middle-class, but his expenditures away from the rent will be. And that's important to me. If I see something I don't like, he's gonna get it from me."

Griffin settled on a four-bedroom town house in the exclusive Leesburg community of River Creek, a Hail Mary heave from the banks of the Potomac. Diving into their new suburban life, he and Rebecca loaded up on provisions at Costco and Wegman's, and Griffin, who was about to become a multimillionaire, allowed himself one big splurge purchase: a new Tempur-Pedic bed. As for cars, his national marketing deal with Nissan and a local endorsement with an Audi dealer took care of that.

The new house had a mantel over the fireplace—the perfect spot, Griffin thought, for a certain decorative item that none of his neighbors could ever hope to procure. The only problem, he figured, would be prying his Heisman Trophy away from his parents' house, since Jacqueline Griffin liked to display all her children's trophies and awards in her living room.

He called his mother and said, "Mom, I know it's a family tradition to keep all our trophies at the house, but—"

"Yes, it's okay," she cut him off, knowing exactly where this was going. "You can have it."

And so, on a subsequent trip to Virginia to visit her son, Jacqueline Griffin carried onto the plane a specially designed case that held inside the 2011 Heisman Trophy, which upon her arrival took its place in its new home—on the mantel of Robert Griffin III's rental home.

It wasn't long before Griffin's neighbors realized who was living in their midst—perhaps it was the sight of him pulling an SUV tire around the neighborhood that gave him away. Before long, the neighbors started tying balloons to his mailbox after victories, and

Griffin would venture out to the lawn once in a while to throw a football around with neighborhood kids. Sometimes people would leave items on his doorstep, asking that he sign them and leave them, and so he would, and the next morning they would be gone.

But Griffin and Liddicoat, for the most part, were homebodies. They joined a nearby church that had a Wednesday night service (since, starting in September, his Sundays would all be spoken for) and found a convenience store that had a Redbox DVD-rental dispenser, which became their outlet for entertainment.

Besides, going out had started to become a problem. He was instantly recognizable—even when he tried to hide his hair in a ponytail or under a hat—and he also had a difficult time saying no, fully aware what his presence meant for the people of the "DMV" (as the D.C./Maryland/Virginia area is known locally). Once, he and Rebecca had gone to a nearby shopping/restaurant complex and thought everything was going swell—not too many people recognizing him, and the ones who did for the most part giving them space. But then they saw a large group converging on them, and they knew the jig was up. Griffin posed for a few pictures and signed some autographs, but he made sure he and Rebecca kept moving toward the parking lot, where, once in their car, they sat for a moment in silence. He understood that mindblowing celebrity was part of the game—and he took seriously his status as the new face of the Redskins franchise—but it was still astonishing to experience its full force.

"You'd rather have people wanting to have a piece of you than talking bad about you behind your back," he said later. "I don't mind signing autographs or taking a picture here or there, whenever I do go out—just to show the fans that [the players] do care."

Senior quarterback Robert Griffin in action for Copperas Cove High in the 2007 Class 4A Texas high school championship game. Griffin didn't make the varsity team as a freshman and served as a backup as a sophomore, but in his two years as starting quarterback, he led the Bulldawgs to back-to-back state title game appearances. Griffin's Bulldawgs lost both times, including here, 20–14, to Lamar Consolidated. On the game's pivotal play, Griffin was stopped at the 2-yard line on fourth-and-goal from the 4 in the fourth quarter. (*KILLEEN DAILY HERALD*)

With his right knee heavily taped, Griffin celebrates a first-half touchdown pass during Baylor's 68–13 win over Northwestern State on September 26, 2009. Griffin had been forced out of the game briefly in the first quarter with a knee injury, but he returned to throw for 226 yards and three touchdowns in the first half. At halftime, he was benched when it was determined the injury was serious, and an MRI the next day confirmed a tear of the anterior cruciate ligament, requiring surgery that would cost Griffin the remainder of the 2009 season. (*Baylor Marketing and Communications*)

In the opener of his junior season, Griffin unleashes a pass during Baylor's 50–48 upset over TCU on September 2, 2011. He threw five touchdown passes in the win, which announced the Bears' arrival as a college football power and launched his campaign for the Heisman Trophy. "He's as good a quarterback as there is in the United States, at any level," Kansas State coach Bill Snyder would say of Griffin four weeks later. "He's Jim Thorpe all over again—but with a heck of a lot more speed." (*Baylor Marketing and Communications*)

Freshman Robert Griffin competes for Baylor at the 2008 Midwest NCAA Regional Championship in Lincoln, Nebraska. In his only full season running track as a collegian, Griffin set a meet record in the 400-meter hurdles with a time of 49.53, qualifying him for the NCAA Championships, where he finished third and earned All-American honors. He also qualified for the 2008 U.S. Olympic Trials, where he advanced to the semifinals before being eliminated. He eventually quit track to focus on football, but coaches and other observers believe he would have been an Olympian, and perhaps an Olympic medalist, had he continued. (*Jon Brown*)

Standing beside his girlfriend, Rebecca Liddicoat, Baylor's Griffin is engulfed by jubilant fans on October 23, 2010, after the Bears' 47–42 win over Kansas State. The victory made Baylor bowl-eligible for the first time in fifteen years. Later that same night, Griffin would propose marriage to Liddicoat in an elaborately planned ceremony in front of both their families, complete with a song Griffin wrote himself and sang to Liddicoat on bended knee. (*Baylor Marketing and Communications*)

Griffin conducts the Baylor University marching band after the Bears' 67–56 win over Washington in the Alamo Bowl on December 29, 2011. He had received the Heisman Trophy three weeks earlier, and after the Alamo Bowl victory he broke down in tears in the locker room, deciding then to forgo his final season of NCAA eligibility and turn pro. (*Baylor Marketing and Communications*)

Less than twelve hours after guiding Baylor to its season-opening upset of TCU in 2011, Griffin visited the set of ESPN's *College GameDay* in Arlington, Texas. The four-minute interview with hosts (*left to right*) Chris Fowler, Lee Corso, and Desmond Howard introduced Griffin's easygoing charm to millions of viewers. "Great ambassador for the Baylor Bears football program!" Fowler exclaimed. (*Heath Nielsen*)

Griffin gets into the Halloween spirit on October 31, 2011, wearing a *Friday the 13th*–style hockey mask and wielding a fake knife during a television interview. Baylor's media relations officials took full advantage of Griffin's charisma and camera-ready magnetism, and by November he was doing thirty to thirty-five interviews a week. (*Heath Nielsen*)

Griffin and Baylor teammate Isaac Williams flash the "Bear Claw" hand sign with assorted guests at a birthday party for one-year-old Griffin Polnick in Waco in July 2010. The boy's mother, Kimberly Polnick (yellow shirt, in front), didn't know RG3 but invited him to the party out of the blue, and to her surprise, he showed up with three teammates and mingled with guests for about ninety minutes. (*Kimberly Polnick*)

Griffin celebrates with his mother, Jacqueline Griffin (white jersey), and fiancée, Rebecca Liddicoat (green sweater), and his Baylor teammates on December 5, 2011, as he is announced as a finalist for the 2011 Heisman Trophy—along with Stanford's Andrew Luck, Wisconsin's Montee Ball, Alabama's Trent Richardson, and LSU's Tyrann Mathieu. (*Heath Nielsen*)

Griffin poses with the 2011 Heisman Trophy, awarded to him in New York City on December 10, 2011. He became the first Baylor athlete to win the Heisman, presented annually to the nation's top collegiate football player. "This moment right here," he told the audience in his acceptance speech, "is unbelievably believable. It's unbelievable because, in the moment, we're all amazed when great things happen. It's believable because great things only happen with hard work." (*Baylor Marketing and Communications*)

Posing with Bishop Nathaniel Holcomb and the Heisman Trophy at the Christian House of Prayer Ministries in Copperas Cove. Griffin addressed the congregation at his home church in May 2012. Twelve years earlier, soon after the Griffins joined the church, Holcomb prophesied over the young boy, telling his parents, "The hand of God is upon your son." (*Christian House of Prayer*)

With his father, Robert Griffin II, Griffin shows off his flashy socks and new jersey at New York's Radio City Music Hall after being selected as the second pick overall by the Washington Redskins in the first round of the NFL 2012 draft. The Redskins had given up four draft picks to the St. Louis Rams in order to move up four spots in the first round and take him. "A team fell in love with me," Griffin told reporters, "and wanted me for who I am." (*AP Photo/Mary Altaffer*)

Griffin with fiancée Rebecca Liddicoat outside the team's practice facility in Ashburn, Virginia, in the summer of 2012. "He has two sides," she has said of him. "What everyone sees is the serious, football side. But really, he's kind of goofy." (*AP Photo/Alex Brandon*)

Jacqueline Griffin gets a hug from her son after a preseason NFL game against the Buffalo Bills. Griffin's parents, both retired Army sergeants, have never missed one of his games, at any level. "He's a mama's boy," Jacqueline Griffin said of her son, "and he's proud of being a mama's boy." (*AP Photo/Bill Wippert*)

Griffin confers with Redskins head coach Mike Shanahan before Washington's Week 2 game against the Rams in St. Louis. Griffin grew up a fan of Shanahan's Denver Broncos teams in the 1990s and 2000s, but Shanahan had won only one playoff game since the retirement of quarterback John Elway in 1998, and his first two seasons in Washington produced a combined 11–21 record. (*AP Photo/Tom Gannam*)

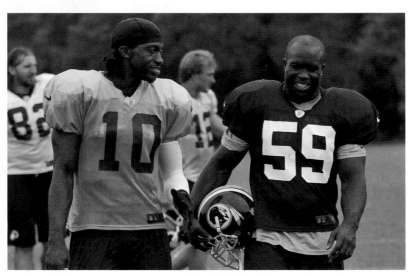

Rookie Griffin chats with fourteen-year veteran linebacker London Fletcher after a Washington Redskins practice. Before Griffin's arrival, Fletcher, a defensive captain, was the unquestioned leader of the Redskins' locker room, and team officials decided to place Griffin's locker next to his. "For me to be next to him," Griffin said of Fletcher, "is an honor." Fletcher became a mentor of sorts to Griffin during the season, and eventually Griffin assumed a more vocal leadership role with the team; he was named an offensive captain at midseason. (*AP Photo/Pablo Martinez Monsivais*)

Although the Redskins lost to the Rams 31–28, Griffin threw for 206 yards and a touchdown and ran for 82 yards and two more scores; he would be named NFL Offensive Rookie of the Month for September. Here, Griffin bounds into the end zone on a five-yard touchdown run in the first quarter.

(*AP Photo/*ST. LOUIS POST-DISPATCH, *Chris Lee*)

In the first half of a preseason game against Chicago, Griffin was sacked three times and was outplayed by backup Kirk Cousins. The Redskins limited Griffin's exposure during the preseason, keeping their modified, zone-read offense under wraps until the regular season began.

(*AP Photo/Charles Rex Arbogast*)

Griffin's knee buckles after a bad snap in the fourth quarter of the Redskins' loss to the Seattle Seahawks in their NFL playoff game on January 6, 2013. From their 3–6 nadir in early November, the Redskins reeled off seven straight victories to clinch their first NFC East division title since 1999 and make the playoffs for the first time since 2007. (*AP Photo/Richard Lipsky*)

The handling of Griffin's knee injury at the end of the season produced a firestorm of criticism from media and fans, much of it directed at Coach Shanahan. Three days after the Redskins' playoff loss to Seattle, Griffin had surgery to repair a torn lateral collateral ligament and a torn medial meniscus, and to reattach his anterior cruciate ligament. Here, he writhes in pain after his knee buckled in the fourth quarter of the Redskins' 24–14 loss.

(*Getty*/THE WASHINGTON POST)

Let's also be clear about this: Loudoun County was not Washington, D.C., either demographically, culturally, or geographically. On a good day, it might take you forty-five minutes to get from Griffin's home to the heart of D.C., and with D.C. traffic, there was rarely a good day. And so his forays into the actual city were few. However, Liddicoat had never even visited the city by the time they moved there (Griffin had been there a few times as a child), and so they spent one full day that summer—with a video crew from Gatorade tagging along—doing the tourist thing.

On the top deck of a double-decker tourist bus, they toured the monuments and the National Mall. At one point Griffin commandeered the microphone and gave a fake-tour-guide spiel.

"There's the White House," he deadpanned. "Looks kind of beige now."

Griffin's relationship with superstardom was a complex one. He was comfortable in the spotlight, but wasn't one to seek it out. He accepted the public duties that came along with his growing celebrity, but cherished his time alone. He had been dealing with notoriety, to one degree or another, since he was eleven years old and started making a name as a track phenom, but not even as the top college football player in the country had he experienced anything like this.

Along with his management team at Creative Artists Agency, Griffin had mapped out an aggressive endorsement portfolio that filled his schedule with numerous commercial shoots and sponsor-mandated public appearances for much of the summer, cutting into his downtime between the draft in April and the start of training camp in late July. He spent much of that summer jetting from one event to another—always traveling with his Redskins playbook and an official NFL football stashed in his carry-on duffel bag.

So difficult had it become to carve out time with his family that, on a stopover in Houston for an autograph-signing session, he coaxed his parents into driving there, some three hours each way, to spend the day with him—which, of course, they did— before he had to go back to the airport.

"I've definitely been busy," Griffin said in July, "but I've found my pockets of time to chill out and relax for three or four days and make sure I can spend some time with my family before I have to go off. I usually ask myself, 'Am I doing too much?' And usually when I ask myself that, I am. And I haven't asked myself that."

But from the outside it appeared as if Griffin was everywhere that summer. He did *The Tonight Show with Jay Leno*—showing off, at Leno's request, his prodigious beat-boxing skills. He posed for pictures with Snoop Dogg at an Adidas event. He, his mother, and Liddicoat attended the ESPY Awards in Los Angeles, where he won an award for Best Male College Athlete and hung out on the red carpet. His first Adidas commercial—a brilliant, dark, futuristic spot titled "Do What Light Does"—immediately went viral on Twitter.

It was essentially unprecedented for an unproven rookie to have this type of marketing penetration so early—Griffin had major advertising and commercial campaigns with Subway, Gatorade, Adidas, and Nissan before taking his first NFL snap—but the idea behind the aggressive schedule was simple: CAA felt it could position its new client as the future face of the NFL. For Griffin, too, there was a good reason to do it: true to his frugal nature, he hoped to live off his endorsement earnings while banking his entire Redskins salary.

The Redskins and Griffin's agents at CAA helped maximize his downtime by limiting his media availability. He did almost no one-on-one interviews between the draft and the start of training camp, other than those arranged by sponsors, who traded access to Griffin for exposure for their products. Once the Redskins took over Griffin's media schedule in July, the same limitations held: Griffin did almost no one-on-one interviews for the entire 2012 season, other than league-mandated ones with the NFL's TV broadcast partners and an occasional one-day, sponsor-driven blitz of interviews in conjunction with a product release. When star sports journalists such as Peter King and Rick Reilly showed up at Redskins camp, they had to ask their questions in Griffin's once-weekly group sessions.

It was during this busy run-up to training camp that Griffin witnessed firsthand the dark side of celebrity. On June 18, a man claiming to have derogatory information about Griffin contacted his lead agent, Ben Dogra, and demanded $1 million to keep him from revealing the information publicly. Dogra went to the FBI, and a few days later authorities arrested a twenty-five-year-old former Baylor walk-on basketball player named Richard Khamir Hurd and charged him with attempted extortion. He pleaded guilty in September and in November was sentenced to eighteen months in prison.

At the time of the arrest, Griffin was in Berea, Ohio, attending the NFL's rookie symposium—where new players learn about the many dangers confronting them as newly rich, newly famous young men—and, to his credit, managed to turn the harrowing episode into a teachable moment for his fellow rookies.

"There are vultures out there," he cautioned, "people looking to climb on top of all your money."

Griffin's family was understandably shaken by the episode— because of what it said about the dark side of fame—but Jacqueline Griffin more or less dared any other extortionists who might see her son as a target to bring it on.

"We have nothing to hide," she said. "So we're not worried. It just seems like high-profile people, whether athletes or actors or whatever, they come under a lot of scrutiny. I'm not saying he's perfect or we're perfect. But there's nothing you're going to find. I mean, good luck."

For Griffin's parents, too, this was a time of transition—their last child was now out of college, which in a sense meant that their life's mission, or at least the most meaningful part of it, was complete. They had raised three successful, college-educated offspring. Jihan was a teacher's aide and mom who lived in Killeen, Texas, the next town over from Copperas Cove. De'Jon was a department-store manager and budding fashion designer who lived in the suburbs of Philadelphia. And Robert III was a professional quarterback. Whatever the future held for their youngest, Jacqueline and Robert Griffin Jr. had done their part.

One day in June 2012, the father sat in the living room of his house in Copperas Cove. It was late afternoon, but the heavy curtains were drawn, giving the room a deep amber glow. *SportsCenter* played on the television, the volume low. The Heisman Trophy his son had been awarded seven months earlier sat behind him, but was hidden from view by the doors of the tall wooden cabinet that housed it.

For the elder Griffin, this house was a symbol of a life well lived and a career well executed. He had entered the Army as an eighteen-year-old who dreamed of mountains and had exited it twenty years later—he retired from active duty in 2003 but stayed at Fort Hood as a counselor for soldiers returning from war—as a successful family man who owned five acres of land. Once, when Robert III was in college, he heard the young man bragging to some friends about having grown up poor. "Robert," he told him later, "you weren't poor. Look where we live. We have five acres. You had all the shoes you needed for basketball, all the spikes you needed for track. We may have *trained* like we were poor, because we wanted you to stay hungry. But we weren't poor."

Now, in the summer before his son's professional career would start, the father was asked how he felt about sending the young man out into the world. In response, he joked that maybe now he could finally get Robert taken off his cell-phone carrier's family plan. But then he turned serious.

"We gave him as much as we could give him with us, and now he has to go out there and face the world," Griffin Jr. said, with typical hard-assed honesty. "I'm not his mother. I'm not in protective mode all the time. He needs to get out there in different situations. That's how you mature and grow. I feel we equipped him. And he doesn't have to face anything by himself. It doesn't matter if he was a janitor of a tall building or the president of a tall building. He's still our son. That's never going to change.

"I look at the man he's developing into. That's what I'm interested in."

By the end of the summer, the Griffins would move to the D.C. area, too, settling in Gaithersburg, Maryland, about an hour from their son—close enough to be available should he need them (and also "to keep an eye on him," his father added), but far enough away to give him space. Robert Jr. refused to move to the area without having a job first—freeloading off his son was absolutely out of the question—but soon landed one at the Department of Veterans Affairs as a management analyst, which amounted to a promotion: instead of counseling veterans returning from war, as he had been doing at Fort Hood, he would be helping administer the counseling program.

"I think Robert and my wife cornered me a little bit," Robert Jr. said about the move. "My wife said, 'We're moving. We've got no kids in the house anymore.' There was nothing preventing us."

And so RG2, as he was sometimes called, became the quintessential Montgomery County federal worker, waking up at 6 A.M. every day, five days a week, to catch the Red Line Metro train downtown, getting off at the McPherson Square stop, and walking the two blocks to his office, which was only about three blocks from the White House. On those rare days when he drove himself in to work, he would spend the whole time fuming about the Beltway traffic. As the Redskins' season played out and the entire region fell in love with RG3, most Red Line commuters probably had no idea that the man who had done more than anyone else to make the quarterback what he is today was right there in their midst.

Jacqueline, meantime, began volunteering with the Wounded Warrior Project and a local literacy program and started a side gig as a motivational speaker, launching a spiffy new website (rg3mom.com) and marketing herself as "the woman responsible for raising up" RG3. Her schedule still left her plenty of time to visit Robert, but her federal-worker husband would sometimes see his son only on game days.

She loved the region; he simply tolerated it.

Once, Jacqueline attended a Wounded Warriors function at the Supreme Court, intending to keep her identity as RG3's mom under wraps. But word got out anyway, and next thing you know she had Justices Clarence Thomas and Elena Kagan fawning over her. "Oh, I am in love with your son!" the latter told her.

As the Griffins were beginning to understand, that was a sentiment shared by an overwhelming majority of the populace in their new adopted hometown.

Rookies, the NFL saying goes, are supposed to be seen and not heard, and Griffin did his best to adhere to that mantra. But it was difficult not to be heard when your teammates could look at any television set, at any time of day—at Redskins Park, in their own homes, or at any bar or restaurant in town—and hear your voice pitching foot-long sandwiches or sneakers.

At one point that summer, Santana Moss, the Redskins' veteran receiver, was lying in bed half-asleep when one of Griffin's

Subway commercials came on TV, and he bolted up in bed, wondering, *Is RG in my house?* Another time, the Redskins were on the team bus coming back from a preseason game when two Griffin commercials aired back-to-back on the vehicle's television, inducing a round of good-natured groans, faux-disgusted shrieks, and threats of a hefty fine from his teammates.

Griffin was by far the highest-profile member of the Redskins, weeks before he would take his first NFL snap—which might have been a problem in the hands of a lesser-skilled craftsman in the art of human relations. But by this point in training camp, Griffin, who had become well known around Redskins Park as the first to arrive each morning and the last to leave each evening, had earned the full respect of the team's veterans. Wisely, he shied away from speeches in those early weeks, instead making a point of sitting down with his offensive teammates individually and talking about the playbook, or that day's practice, or how much weightlifting they were doing. He would also pick the brains of the team's defensive leaders—primarily veteran linebacker London Fletcher, whose locker was beside his—to ask what they had seen from their perspective. Was he tipping any plays? Were his cadences varied enough?

And very subtly, Griffin was doing something else—infusing the Redskins' practices with a different, more gamelike atmosphere than his teammates had been used to in years past. One day, when he threw an interception—a point at which, in practices, the play is usually whistled dead—the defensive back who picked him off made a beeline for the end zone and Griffin turned on the burners to catch him and deny him the satisfaction of a pick-six. Some practices grew feisty, with plenty of chirping back and forth between the offense and defense and even an occasional shoving match.

"I brought a different type of attitude to practice than they were used to, [a feeling that] every day is a game day," he said.

Perhaps aware of the growing hype around Griffin and the growing belief on the part of fans that he would alter the franchise's fortunes immediately, the Shanahans began to make what appeared to be a calculated effort to lower expectations on him. (Not that expectations weren't already low enough, at least based on some of the preseason predictions made in the national media. Pete Prisco, the respected NFL writer at CBSSports.com, picked the Redskins to go 3–13; *ESPN The Magazine*'s NFL preview issue thought that was a little too optimistic and predicted a 2–14 record for them.) Mike Shanahan dug up the records of some Hall of Fame quarterbacks in their rookie seasons in the league—Peyton Manning, for example, went 3–13, while Troy Aikman went 0–11—and showed them in private to Griffin, then took his findings to the media.

"A lot of people don't understand how hard it is for a young quarterback coming into the National Football League and playing his first year," Shanahan said. "First of all, you have to be lucky enough to have a little bit of a supporting cast. . . . Some of these Hall of Fame guys had tough first years."

Over the previous decade, as Shanahan pointed out, only five quarterbacks had led their teams to winning records in their rookie seasons—Ben Roethlisberger, Joe Flacco, Matt Ryan, Mark Sanchez, and Andy Dalton—and most of them had the benefit of a highly ranked defense or an elite running back, or both, to help ease their load.

Shanahan spoke frequently of a three-year growth model for Griffin, implying there would be growing pains in years one and two.

"We're only doing things Robert is comfortable with [at first]," Shanahan told NFL.com. "He's a rookie. You have to do that. So we put the offense in over the first two weeks of OTAs . . . and we saw what he was comfortable with. Over a time frame of about three years, we'll put everything in, and he'll really be able to branch out. But initially, we're gonna do what he does well."

The zone-read option—in which the quarterback "reads" the defense (typically focusing on the defensive end or linebacker) and makes a quick decision whether to hand off to the running back or pull the ball back and keep it—was a natural tool for the Redskins to use to exploit Griffin's unique skill set. Although the offense had become a staple of college football, the NFL, with its faster defenders and smarter defensive coordinators, had been reluctant to adopt it. However, the zone-read had gained some traction in the last couple of years with teams such as the Denver Broncos and Carolina Panthers that had mobile quarterbacks—Tim Tebow and Cam Newton, respectively—who didn't mind contact, and the Redskins spent much of the summer of 2012 installing a hybrid offense that fused elements of the zone-read with the more traditional West Coast offense that was a Shanahan hallmark.

Griffin seemed to be all-in with the idea—"The option won't work," he said, "unless you buy into it wholeheartedly"—but there was an undercurrent of danger running through the offense. Griffin wasn't Tebow or Newton, who were substantially bigger than him, and the basic equation that came to define the Redskins' offense was how much risk the Shanahans were willing to take with their franchise player for a potentially huge payoff.

"Coach promised me he's not going to get me killed," Griffin said in July. "We're going to do whatever we have to do to help this team move the ball. The guys in this league are a lot bigger and a lot faster. So we'll be smart. Whatever we have to do, we'll do it."

Plus, as the Redskins were beginning to see, Griffin's acute competitiveness—and perhaps a subconscious belief, honed at Baylor, that he was simply faster than anybody else on the field—made him an even bigger risk. To put it simply: Griffin seemed to think he could run the ball as aggressively as he wanted to, a common problem with young quarterbacks.

"Everybody [thinks that] until they get drilled," Shanahan said on the league's website, pointing out that Elway had been the same way. "What we have to teach him is you don't have to run—sometimes it's better if the [running back] does. When he was in college, he was so fast, that chances are if he gets in the open field, he's gone. Here, sometimes, it needs to be [gain] ten to twelve yards and then slide. And there's nothing wrong with that."

Still, for the most part, the Redskins were downright giddy about Griffin's quick development as the summer wore on. His aptitude and work ethic were both off the charts, and the coaching staff didn't have to spend nearly as much time as it had budgeted to teach him the playbook.

"He's being exposed to stuff he's never done his entire career," said Matt LaFleur, the Redskins' quarterback coach, who had worked under Kyle Shanahan with the Houston Texans before both came to Washington following the elder Shanahan's hiring.

"He's done such a great job of not only picking it up, but retaining it. We won't revisit something we did until a week later, and he's still able to retain what we talked about, whether it was five practices ago or three practices ago. He's incredibly sharp."

Training camp was a revelation in one other way: it marked the first opportunity for Redskins fans to see their new messiah in action firsthand, as the team opened thirteen practices to the public, and it is probably no exaggeration to say there was more interest in Griffin than in the other eighty-odd players in camp combined. He got the full rock-star treatment from the crowd—spontaneous chants of "R-G-3! R-G-3!," shrieks from female fans whenever he walked by, and scrums of autograph-seekers as he came off the field.

After each practice, he would hand his helmet to a Redskins security man, who in turn would hand Griffin a Sharpie pen, and he would walk toward the crowd—always careful to stop a few feet in front of the rope that separated him from the masses—and sign as many autographs as he could, with the security man standing sentinel at his side.

There was a comforting rhythm to training camp—a walk-through practice in the indoor "bubble" each morning, then meetings and film study, then a spirited practice in the afternoon. Even the suffocating D.C. heat didn't faze Griffin, for whom 95 and humid is just another pleasant Texas afternoon.

But there was one thing that bothered him greatly. As much as he had tried to prepare himself for the cold, hard, business-side aspects of the NFL, he found himself shaken by the experience of seeing some of his new friends and teammates cut from the roster

as training camp rolled on. It wasn't something he was used to seeing, and his reaction bordered on disillusionment.

"You see guys' dreams taken away from them," he said. "That's
tough to see."

A s the first Washington Redskins players boarded their bus at
the team hotel in Buffalo, New York, on the afternoon of
August 9—on their way to Ralph Wilson Stadium for their first
preseason game of the year—they encountered a solitary figure in
the front row. It was Robert Griffin III, their rookie quarterback,
and how long he'd been there nobody knew. But as each of his
teammates walked past, he looked them in the eye, nodded, and
held up his fist for a fist-tap.

Even with the understanding that Griffin would be limited to a
few offensive series that night against the Buffalo Bills—and that
the Shanahans would almost certainly not be revealing much of
their regular-season offense—the anticipation was palpable for a
fan base that had now endured more than two decades without a
Super Bowl title. It would be Griffin's first time in game action
wearing a Redskins uniform—and damn, didn't he look good in
it? White jersey, "gold" pants (actually, more like a mustard yellow), and black cleats shiny enough to have been patent leather.
On his left (non-throwing) arm he wore a white sleeve and white
glove, a fashion statement (inspired, he would admit later, by Michael Jackson) that would become a common sight on youth football fields around the area in the coming months.

Beginning with the Bills game, we began to see Griffin's pregame ritual. He came onto the field at five o'clock sharp, two hours before kickoff, sporting white Beats By Dre headphones, and took two laps around the field—one at a walk, one at a jog. ("Marking my territory," he would later explain.) He would stretch meticulously, make dozens of throws—short, deep, and long—then goof off a little, sometimes throwing some left-handed passes, sometimes attempting some dropkicks. He was disconcertingly good at both.

The Redskins' first two drives of the Buffalo game were three-and-out misfires—the most notable moment coming when Griffin, not realizing that a fumble by running back Evan Royster had been whistled dead, chased down Bills safety George Wilson and leveled him at the 2-yard-line with a sliding tackle.

But on the third offensive series, Griffin offered a tantalizing glimpse of his abilities—leading the Redskins on an eight-play, eighty-yard touchdown drive, capped by a twenty-yard touchdown pass to Pierre Garcon, who took a screen pass and did the rest himself. Griffin had his arms pointed toward the sky before Garcon was even halfway to the end zone. Then he ran in a giant circle out toward midfield, took a quick knee, crossed himself, and pointed quickly to the sky—a celebration ritual that would become familiar over the next five months. Finally, he sprinted toward Garcon in the end zone and engaged his receiver in a flying chest-bump.

The touchdown was pretty, but what really had the coaching staff buzzing was the completion before that one—when Griffin had to check-down to his third option, Garcon, before firing an eighteen-yard strike for a first down.

"That was like, wow. That was pretty impressive," LaFleur said. "To be able to check-down like that, and do it so quickly, that's something not everybody can do."

For the players, too, Griffin's play was a revelation. He could do all he wanted in practice, but until you get out there against hostile defenders and make the same plays, there is still a kernel of doubt.

"I don't think anybody really knew until he played," veteran tight end Chris Cooley said, "and then it's like, 'Holy cow!'"

When the local television ratings in D.C. came back the next day, Griffin's preseason debut had clocked in as the highest-rated show in the history of *Comcast SportsNet,* topping a 2010 Capitals/Canadiens NHL playoff game and more than doubling the next-highest rating for a Redskins preseason game.

And so, around the DMV, the regular season couldn't get here fast enough.

The Redskins would bump up Griffin's preseason playing time to a full half against the Chicago Bears (a game most notable for the three sacks he took and the way he was outplayed by backup Kirk Cousins), then two and a half quarters against the Indianapolis Colts (a game most notable for the Griffin–Luck matchup it featured, with all the attendant hype, much to the annoyance of Griffin and Luck themselves).

But per tradition, the Redskins held Griffin out of the preseason finale, and so by the end of the preseason he had attempted only thirty-one passes in game action—the fewest of any of the five rookie quarterbacks who were set to start in Week 1. As for the zone-read option offense the Redskins had been running in practice, it was pretty much nowhere to be found during the preseason.

There was a distinct feeling that the Redskins were holding something back, and that the full RG3 experience would only be unleashed in New Orleans on September 9.

SIX

THE BEAR

Baylor University was established by the Baptist Church under a charter of the Congress of the Republic of Texas on February 1, 1845—exactly twenty-seven days before the U.S. Congress authorized the annexation of the Republic itself, eventually making Texas the twenty-eighth state in the Union. For most of its existence, Baylor—named after a Baptist judge who was once a roommate of Davy Crockett's—has been a very bad place for anyone who likes good football or any sort of dancing. The Baylor football team existed mostly for the purpose of giving other Texas schools a suitable homecoming opponent; at one point, the Bears went fifty years between championships in the old Southwest Conference. But that's nothing compared to how long a hypothetical couple of God-fearing Baylor students had to wait to enjoy a little Texas two-step within the leafy confines of the campus.

It wasn't until 1999, 144 years after its establishment, that the school lifted its ban on dancing, which was considered sinful under church orthodoxy. (Which brings to mind an old joke popular among Southern Methodists: Why don't Baptists have sex? Because it might lead to dancing.) On the Day the Dancing Lived, dozens of national reporters and television news crews descended upon campus to chronicle the moment when Baylor president Robert Sloan Jr., clad in a tuxedo, danced with his wife, Sue, in the middle of Fifth Street to Beethoven's "Minuet in G"—before breaking out in a jitterbug for Glenn Miller's "In the Mood." (The school's current president, Kenneth Starr, has done his part in the battle against the prurient interests as well: in the 1990s, as independent counsel, he famously led the investigation into the Bill Clinton–Monica Lewinsky affair, leading to Clinton's eventual impeachment.)

A man who enjoyed both his football and his dancing, Robert Griffin enrolled at Baylor in January 2008—having graduated high school a semester early in order to get a jump-start on college—and came to understand one thing quickly about his new surroundings: there apparently existed a "Baylor Bubble" that insulated the campus from the rest of Waco. It tended to be the first thing anybody said to him by way of a welcome.

Waco itself was a gritty, dusty, working-class town of 120,000 along the Brazos River perhaps best known as the birthplace of Dr Pepper—at least until 1993, when the U.S. Bureau of Alcohol, Tobacco, and Firearms, attempting to execute a search warrant on the Branch Davidian religious sect outside of town, instead touched off a deadly firefight and a subsequent fifty-day siege that ended in the deaths of seventy-six people in a massive fire. Now, two decades later, the "Waco Massacre" is still the first thing most folks think of when the town's name is mentioned.

Something about the notion of a Baylor Bubble bothered Griffin from the moment he got there, and in later years he would write academic papers on the phenomenon, as well as do his best to singlehandedly burst it by volunteering with as many as five different Waco-area charities, frequently coaxing his teammates to tag along with him to events and appearances. (In his speech upon winning the Heisman Trophy in December 2011, he would thank the people of both Copperas Cove and Waco, in essence equating them as his co-hometowns.) But in those early days, he was in no position to knock down any long-standing, metaphorical walls.

Heck, the kid didn't even have a car—or for that matter, a driver's license.

At the time, Griffin's father was working a night shift at Fort Hood, and so many days he would drive Robert from Copperas Cove to Waco, a little more than an hour away, then kill a few hours while his son went to class before driving him back home. Other days, Jacqueline would handle the drop-off and pickup duties. This system lasted for about a month, before it became obvious the kid was going to need a place to live on campus—and eventually a driver's license and some wheels.

And so, after settling into a freshman-housing dorm room, Griffin was alone and on his own for the first time in his life—the sense of isolation only worsened by the fact that the rest of his freshman class wouldn't arrive until fall semester—and he retreated into his natural-loner mode, mostly staying in his room and studying (he took an aggressive course load of sixteen hours that semester) or downloading music.

"I was a little weirdo," he recalled. "I built a playlist of three-hundred-something songs that hadn't even come out yet. I'd find music that hadn't hit the radio yet. The responsibility I learned from my parents helped me in college, because I wasn't easily pressured into anything. Other kids might have gone to college and just lose their minds because they've got so much freedom. But I didn't do that."

The monotony was soon broken by the start of track and spring football practice in February. For a brief time in the beginning, Griffin tried to do both simultaneously, but there were problems with that. For one thing, the overlapping schedules sometimes made it impossible to attend both practices—and the conflicts would only get worse once the track team started competing in meets. And for another thing, the football coaching staff was asking him to put on weight, which wasn't exactly going to help him get over those hurdles and down the track.

Bulking up "was something we talked about since he came in," recalled Kaz Kazadi, a former NFL linebacker who has been Baylor's assistant athletic director for strength and conditioning since 2008. "When he walked in, I think we caught him at a hundred ninety-three [pounds] one time. We told him, in a perfect world, we'd love to get two twenty-five out of him."

The football coaching staff was trying to walk the fine line between encouraging their young quarterback's outside pursuits and still keeping him focused on football—which, after all, was what he was there for, and where his scholarship money was coming from. The midpoint was this: Griffin could pursue track to his heart's delight, but only at the end of spring football in early April. "The best thing about Robert is he never pushed to do more than that," Baylor offensive coordinator Philip Montgomery recalled. "He understood, 'I'm here to play football. I'm here to be the best quarterback that I can be.' That was the extent of it. It was never, 'Hey, Coach, do you mind if I do this?'"

It was a statement about the status of the Baylor football program in the spring of 2008 that, on April 5, only 3,500 fans attended the annual Green and Gold Scrimmage—the culmination of spring football practice—at Floyd Casey Stadium, the aging 50,000-seat stadium a couple of miles down I-35 from campus, despite the fact that no admission was charged. (By comparison, Nebraska, one of Baylor's Big 12 rivals at the time, claimed an attendance of 80,149 for its spring game, despite ticket prices ranging from $4 to $8.) But if there was one takeaway from Baylor's scrimmage, it was the dynamism of the eighteen-year-old freshman quarterback, Robert Griffin. Five quarterbacks saw action in the game, but Griffin was the only one to lead his squad on three scoring drives, with one of the scores coming at the end of a seventeen-yard keeper.

"He's a guy you've got to watch," Art Briles, Baylor's new head coach, said of Griffin after the game. "If you don't watch him, the next thing you know you'll be looking for him—because he's gone."

Precisely two weeks after the spring football game, Griffin was digging his spikes into the starting blocks of Lane 2 of the Hart-Patterson Track and Field Complex, just next door to the football stadium, for the start of the 400-meter hurdles at the Michael Johnson Invitation—named, of course, for the four-time Olympic gold medalist and Baylor alum who was Griffin's childhood track idol.

To that point, Griffin hadn't competed in a track event since the previous summer, as a rising high school senior some eight and a half months prior. He also hadn't had much experience at this distance, since most high school meets featured hurdle races of 110 and 300 meters. Combine that with the extra pounds he had packed on for football at his coaches' urging (he was above two hundred pounds for the first time in his life), and expectations were not all that high—at least not for anyone besides Griffin. He went into the race expecting to win, and when he finished second with a time of 50.14 seconds—losing by just twenty-six hundredths of a second to Baylor teammate Justin Boyd, a senior—he was devastated.

"You don't understand," he told a football teammate who had come to the meet and thought Griffin's second-place finish was good. "I've never lost a race."

Track season was nearly over by the time Griffin got going, but for the rest of the spring he poured himself into the sport, streamlining his training to focus on just one event—the 400-meter hurdles. And the results were breathtaking. In the Big 12 Championships on May 18 in Boulder, Colorado, he posted a time of 49.22—the third-fastest in Baylor history, and still Griffin's personal best—to win the 400-meters by nearly half a second. Twelve days later, at the NCAA Midwest Regional in Lincoln, Nebraska, he set a meet record with a time of 49.53, finishing first and qualifying for the NCAA Championships.

Though he ran a 49.55 to finish a disappointing third at the NCAAs in Des Moines, Iowa, it was good enough to qualify him as an NCAA All-American in track. And there was one other honor to digest: the 49.22 that he ran back at the Big 12 Championships had qualified him for the U.S. Olympic Trials. Yes, Robert Griffin was suddenly one step away from running in the

Olympics. Okay, well, it was actually three steps—three massive steps—because he would have to advance through the quarterfinals, semifinals, and finals on three successive days, against an experienced field of accomplished hurdlers, to actually qualify for Beijing.

Still, that realization had folks back at the Baylor football offices going straight to their calendars. Hold on a minute now, when are the Olympic Trials? When are the Summer Games? You mean to say this stud freshman quarterback, the plum of Coach Briles's first recruiting class at Baylor, might have to miss pretty much the whole month of August—including (gulp!) the Bears' season-opener, August 28 against Wake Forest—to go to China?

"There was a point in there where he almost made the Olympics," Montgomery, the offensive coordinator, recalled. "We were wondering, 'Is he going to make it back by the time the season starts? How do you tell an eighteen-year-old kid, 'You have a chance to make the Olympics, but, uh, you need to come back'?" The only choice they had, really, was to let Griffin compete at the Trials—with each football coach having to decide privately and individually the degree to which he was rooting for the kid to qualify, or not, for Beijing.

At the same time, somewhere deep down, the success he was having in track was making Griffin question whether he had made the right decision to focus on football as his primary sport—or at least whether he couldn't devise a more equitable split. After all, his track coaches were telling him he could go all the way in the hurdles—to not just qualify for the Olympics but someday to make it to the medal stand—if he devoted himself to it.

"It was an eye-opener to go out and not just compete, but to

win against some of the best in the world," Griffin told Yahoo
.com a few years later. "It showed me how world-class I actually
was [and that] I could compete at the next level."

Was he a track athlete who also played football or a football
player who also ran track? It was getting harder to distinguish, but
on June 27, 2008, it was almost certainly the former. On that day,
he found himself in Eugene, Oregon, for the start of the U.S.
Olympic Trials. He was eighteen years old and could look around
the track and see the likes of Tyson Gay, Jeremy Wariner, Lolo
Jones, and Allyson Felix. It was the big time, no question about it.
That afternoon, in the quarterfinals of the 400-meter hurdles, he
ran a 49.74 to finish third in his heat, barely qualifying for the
semifinals the next day—but qualifying nonetheless. He had studied the history of the event enough to know what he was up against:
He figured he would have to get well below his personal best to
have any hope whatsoever of making the finals, as anything above
a 49-flat was unlikely to get it done. And he knew he could do it
too, with a flawless race.

For the semis, he drew Heat 2, Lane 2, and to his benefit, it
wound up being the slower of the two heats. But when he hit the
finish line, his peripheral vision told him—and the scoreboard
confirmed—that he had narrowly missed. The first four times in
each heat qualified for the finals, and Griffin, at 49.38 seconds,
had finished fifth in Heat 2 by a mere thirteen hundredths of a
second. Both the runner who won his heat and the one who edged
him out for fourth place were twenty-five years old, seven years his
senior.

And so young Robert Griffin's Olympic dream had died—at
least for the moment. After all, who knew where he would be in

2012, when he would be twenty-two years old and just entering his prime athletic years?

In the meantime, he was going to see what he could accomplish on the football field. Baylor's opener was exactly two months away. He figured he would give it one year, then reevaluate. Track or football? Football or track? At that very moment, it was more or less a toss-up.

There was nothing quite like game day. It was still the greatest rush Robert Griffin had ever known—and remains so to this day, even as game day itself has slowly shifted from Friday to Saturday to Sunday. The slow burn as the week builds toward it, then the violent explosion of energy and chaos when it finally arrives. The smoky smell of burgers grilling. The band playing. The feeling of slipping that uniform over your head and buckling up your chinstrap. The confident, shared sense of mission between you and your teammates as kickoff approaches.

By the time Griffin ran onto the field at Floyd Casey Stadium on the evening of August 28, 2008, dressed in the green and gold, he was back to feeling like a football player again. Even though the stands were barely half full for that night's opener against visiting Wake Forest—the twenty-third-ranked team in the nation—it would be more people than he had ever played in front of before. Even as the seven o'clock kickoff approached, it was still a balmy 94 degrees outside.

He scanned the family cheering section, looking for his parents. Griffin had a surprise for them, particularly for his dad. On the back of his green jersey, above the number 10, was a new moniker, a new bit of self-identity: GRIFFIN III. He would have loved to have seen the expression on his dad's face when he saw it. Until then, no one really had ever referred to the young man as "Griffin the Third" or any version thereof. ("Trey" was the only name that was expressly forbidden as a nickname, with the elder Griffin deeming it condescending.) And it wasn't as if the young man had all of a sudden started asking more questions about his namesake—his paternal grandfather, the original Robert Griffin, whom he never got the chance to meet. There were no hints. He just showed up on the field that day sporting the roman numerals on his back.

Up in the stands, the elder Robert Griffin saw the jersey, smiled in disbelief, and all of a sudden was hit by a realization: his son had become his own man. It was no longer enough to just be Robert Griffin—he needed to individualize it, to carve out his own space within that family history.

But at that moment, the son was also dealing with profound disappointment. Coach Briles had waited until a few hours before kickoff to reveal the answer to the question that had been on everyone's minds—players, fans, and media alike—all summer: who would start at quarterback for the Bears?

There had been three candidates, all of them with strong claims to the starting job, but none of them so strong as to be a lock. Blake Szymanski was the incumbent, a junior who had played valiantly, if not particularly effectively, during the Bears' ugly 3-9 season the year before, which had featured an 0-8 record in the Big 12. Kirby Freeman was a senior who had transferred to Baylor from Miami the previous December. And Griffin, of course, was a true freshman—one of only three on the team, the rest of the 2008 recruiting class having been redshirted. Even if he was the most inexperienced of the three, there was little doubt he was the most talented.

Finally, in the locker room a few hours before kickoff, Briles had revealed his choice to the team: "I'm starting Kirby Freeman," he told the players, "but you're going to see Robert Griffin too." Despite the promise that he would get in the game, it was a decision that devastated Griffin, who had been working primarily with the first team in practice, and it quietly disappointed plenty of his teammates as well.

To the extent that any Baylor freshman football player could be a household name in Waco in 2008—back when the program was still a laughingstock, unable to fill its fifty-thousand-seat stadium—Griffin was. Waco High School was a top rival of Copperas Cove, so folks there were already plenty familiar with his gridiron talents. His showing in April's Green and Gold Scrimmage had only increased his profile, and his track exploits that spring had added another level of notoriety and made him arguably the most exciting player on the Bears' roster.

All that may explain why, when Griffin was sent into the game in the second quarter—after Freeman had thrown two early interceptions and put the Bears in a 17–0 hole to the Demon Deacons—he was greeted by a standing ovation from the crowd of 30,633.

"When Robert came in," recalled Lanear Sampson, a receiver who was redshirting that season and watched the Wake Forest game from the stands, "people just went crazy."

The rest of the game was mostly forgettable, from Baylor's perspective. Griffin played well, leading the Bears on two scoring drives and taking one of the touchdowns himself on a five-yard run in the fourth quarter. He passed for 125 yards and ran for another 29, but the Bears were demolished, 41–13, by the visitors. At one point during the final moments of the bludgeoning, with the stands now almost empty, Griffin sat on the bench next to a teammate, receiver Romie Blaylock, and said, "Man, I've never lost a game like this. We can't let this happen again."

But one play in particular had Baylor's players and fans buzzing, a play amazing enough to have coated the entire ugly evening with a layer of optimism and hope. On a second-quarter keeper to the left side, Griffin approached the sideline pursued by several Wake Forest defenders. All of a sudden, he stopped on a dime, sending one Demon Deacon hurtling past him face-first into the turf and fooling the others, leading to a twenty-two-yard gain. It was an astonishing show of athleticism, awareness, and body control, and it made all the highlight shows the next day, including ESPN's *SportsCenter*.

"You knew at that point—your eyes just brightened up," Montgomery recalled. "It was an unbelievable-type play. He has those types of abilities [and] that was probably the first time you felt in a game situation he had it—and it was the very first game he played in. You knew you were going to have some more moments like that."

The next week, Briles named Griffin his starter—making him at the time the youngest starting quarterback in the country—and his Baylor teammates gave him the honor of leading them out of the tunnel before that week's game against Northwestern State. "When I lead the team out of the tunnel," he told reporters afterward, "that's [another way of] saying, 'He's the leader, and we're going to follow him.'"

Griffin passed for three touchdowns, ran for another, and amassed 336 yards of total offense in a 51–6 romp over the overmatched Demons. A week after that, he set a Baylor record with 217 rushing yards (on only 11 carries) in a 45–17 win over Washington State.

The most important stat, in Griffin's mind, was the fact that he was 2-0 as a starter. But the good times would not last. The Bears lost seven of their final nine games, including six of their eight Big 12 conference games, to finish at 4-8. Griffin had been spectacular as a true freshman, throwing for 2,091 yards with 15 touchdowns against only three interceptions and rushing for another 843 yards and 13 touchdowns—good enough to earn him freshman All-American honors, as well as the Big 12 Freshman of the Year—and there was little doubt in anyone's mind that the program had taken a major step forward in terms of its competitiveness, largely because of the presence of Griffin.

It was a 4-8 season, but it was a solid 4-8, highlighted by a 41–21 win over Texas A&M in the final home game of the season—just the second time in twenty-three years the Bears had beaten the Aggies.

And it was enough to erase from Griffin's mind any notion that he might be ready to give up football. The question soon became something different: how much was he willing to sacrifice for it?

His new Baylor teammates loved Robert Griffin the quarterback, but they still weren't quite sure what to make of Robert Griffin the young man. He was an enigma wrapped in a hair-braid wrapped in a Teenage Mutant Ninja Turtle sock.

"He was the poster boy," recalled Kazadi, the strength coach, "for guys who don't quite fit in."

Nobody at Baylor could say they really knew Griffin at that point, even as the Bears went through an entire season with him piloting the team's offense. Everything about him seemed to have the purpose of keeping others at arm's length. You couldn't get him to socialize with his teammates, and his quiet confidence was disarming to some, off-putting to others—easily mistaken for aloofness or cockiness.

"He was kind of quiet and standoffish—not intentionally, but just how his personality was," recalled Sampson. "He kind of did his own thing, and off the field he didn't have too much contact with people. That's just how he is, and I didn't judge him or anything. We all stayed in the same apartments, and everybody would be hanging out at one another's apartment, and he'd just be up in his own world all the time."

What was clear was that the young man had an intense drive to succeed, which was fine, even admirable, on its own—except that it also seemed to be accompanied by an expectation that others would share that drive, and a disappointment in those who didn't. In later years, Griffin would be able to hone that drive into a power to lift others to success—the very essence of leadership. But as a college freshman, Griffin had an intensity that sometimes just seemed over-the-top.

"When he was younger," Kazadi said, "he rubbed people the wrong way."

There is a word for what Griffin was at eighteen years old: a perfectionist. At one point in his freshman season, the coaching staff was baffled as to why Griffin couldn't add any weight, despite the extra calories they were giving him. Come to find out, the kid was practicing the hurdles at night.

"The number one problem we had with him was, we needed him to pull back a little bit," recalled Kazadi. "He was working way too much. He was a perfectionist. We told him, 'Griff, that's your weakness.' So we showed him the bad side of being a perfectionist."

Kazadi, a former All-American linebacker at Tulsa who played briefly in the NFL for St. Louis in 1997, quickly developed a special connection with Griffin, one of the few young athletes he had come across who could match his own intensity and keep up with him in any test of conditioning. If Griffin felt a particular workout session wasn't intense enough, he would look at Kazadi and inquire, "Are you feeling okay today? Are you sick?" A native of Zaire whose family came to the United States when he was eight, Kazadi also had a unique appreciation for the struggles of a young man to fit in.

"The first thing you see [is] the socks," Kazadi said. "That's going to introduce you to him. You see the hair. That's just him. He took flak for that his freshman and sophomore years. The guy is a nerd. But the thing is, the way he does it is cool. Then you go watch him compete, and you go, 'Okay.' If you don't fit in, just do what he did and force-feed people your brand."

On November 4, 2008, a Tuesday, Griffin uncharacteristically missed the team breakfast—something Kazadi had insisted was mandatory every morning. Offenders were typically punished by having to run three "bear-claws" (shuttle-runs on all fours) the length of the football field. When Griffin finally showed up, Kazadi immediately got in his face.

"Where were you?" he asked.

"I had to go vote," Griffin replied.

Kazadi wasn't sure what to do. It didn't seem quite fair to punish someone for casting a ballot on Election Day, particularly such a historic election as the one in 2008, with Barack Obama vying to become the first African American to be elected president.

"You're putting me in a tough spot," he told Griffin.

"Coach," Griffin replied, "I'll just do the punishment."

The kid had let Kazadi off the hook. Griffin went off to run the bear-claws so everyone could see it, thus allowing the coach to maintain the appearance of a zero-tolerance policy. It would be, to the best of Kazadi's recollection, the only time he ever punished Griffin.

Griffin's teammates began trying to coax their reclusive quarterback into hanging out with them, but he was inclined to turn them down, not realizing that such a stance was contributing to the perception of him as standoffish, a goody-two-shoes. Eventually, though, they wore him down, and he began accepting an invitation here or there. It took him most of his freshman year to come to understand that socializing with teammates was not only about wasting time and goofing off, but also about team-building. It served a purpose.

"I could sit in my room and go to class and go back to my place and not hang out with anybody and be fine," Griffin recalled. "They kind of broke me out of that—my teammates. They wanted to see more of me. They just thought the quarterback needed to be around. I'm still the same way. I don't really have to be around people to have fun. But I definitely like being around people, so they kind of broke me out of that mold, [and] once I broke out of that loner stage, I became a better leader. People need to see you. They need to see that you're the leader, that you're all for them."

Even at age nineteen, Robert Griffin was good at denial, in the way most brilliant athletes are capable of bending time and space to their will and tossing aside adversity. It was especially true when it came to injury, such as the one he was telling himself he did not suffer on September 26, 2009. The pop he heard in his knee, the sharp pain—he willed it to be gone, and it was (or else that was the painkiller drugs). When the trainers said he should come out of the game, he held them off, saying, Let's look at it at halftime. The examination, the diagnosis of a "possible" anterior cruciate ligament tear, the MRI exam—hey, there was still a chance it could be good news.

Until finally the jig was up, and only then did Griffin concede defeat, and when he did he started to cry. It was Sunday, the day after Baylor's 68–13 win over Northwestern State—in which Griffin, playing on what was now known to be a torn ACL, threw for 226 yards and three touchdowns in the first half before being pulled. He was in a room with his parents and his girlfriend when he got the news, and he saw the concern on their faces. It reminded him of how many people had been counting on him, and the tears rolling down his cheeks were more for all of them than for himself.

"I just felt like I let everyone down," Griffin recalled.

The play had been "Speed Option Right," a staple of the Baylor offense: Griffin, out of a shotgun snap, sprinted to the right and had the option to keep the ball or pitch to the trailing running back, depending on what he saw from the defense. It was fourth-

and-2 on Baylor's first possession of the game, and Griffin saw too late that the defense had a safety in tight. The safety hit him just as he planted his right leg and tucked the ball—and he crumpled to the ground in pain.

After he was helped to the sideline, the pain subsided quickly—those mind-tricks of his—and when the medical staff told him he would have to sit out until halftime, he begged them, successfully, to tape him up and let him go back in the game. Back on the field, he led Baylor to its highest-scoring first half in fifteen years, but at halftime doctors took a closer look at his knee and said he couldn't go back in. After watching the rest of the game from the sideline, with his knee heavily taped, Griffin told the media the knee was "hyperextended"—and maybe that's what he believed himself. But the MRI the next morning delivered the truth.

The news devastated Griffin. His season was over—the Bears were 2-1 at that point and would go 2-7 the rest of the way without him—and he would be facing a long, grueling rehabilitation just to make it back for the 2010 season.

There was also a cruel bit of irony that gnawed at Griffin. That spring, after plenty of discussion with his football coaches and his family, he had decided to quit track—at least temporarily—and focus all his efforts on football. And now, what had all that sacrifice gotten him? A busted knee, a spot on the sidelines, and an eight- to twelve-month rehab.

"I felt like the team needed me to stop running track, and I stopped," he recalled. "And then I got hurt. That sucked, because now you're saying, 'Look, I stopped doing the thing that I loved. I stopped running track—for football. And now I got hurt in football.'"

There was a two-week period there when Griffin more or less disengaged from life—a "dark period," he calls it. He quit going to classes and stayed cooped up inside his apartment except to get treatment on his knee.

"I had to think, 'What do I want to do?'" he recalled. "'Do I want to come back and play football? Do I want to go do track? Or do I just want to be a lawyer [and] give up on sports altogether?'"

The answer, he soon came to realize, was that he needed to keep playing football. To have stopped playing then would have been to quit, and he wasn't a quitter. This was a setback, but a temporary one. It didn't change anything fundamentally. He still had the same dreams and the same goals, and now he was just going to have to take a lengthy detour through a knee rehab to get to them. He vowed to throw himself into his rehab as completely as he did everything else.

"I didn't want to make it a sob story—'Robert Griffin stops running track, dedicates all his time to football, gets hurt in football, never plays again,'" he recalled. "I didn't want it to be that. I was going to work hard to come back—and not just come back and say, 'All right, I'm going to run track, and I'm done with football.' No, I'm going to come back and I'm going to be a great football player. So it was partly me wanting to be great, partly me wanting to prove everyone wrong, and partly me not wanting it to be a side note—great player, boom, injured, career's over."

Kazadi recalls an "infuriated" Griffin funneling all his anger into an intense focus on his rehab. "He held a grudge every single day for getting hurt," he said. "You could call it determination. You could call it extreme focus. I think he was just mad. He channeled it into the recovery process. He channeled it into making sure he was going to be ready for the next season. He just really pushed himself and worked dang hard."

Griffin's father saw the injury as an opportunity. People still regarded the young man as a run-first type of quarterback, and truth be told, he was still probably more dangerous with his legs than with his arm at that point. Robert Griffin Jr. vowed to use this time, with his son's leg immobilized, to work on his arm.

Driving up from Copperas Cove in the evenings and on weekends, he had his son sit in a chair at the Baylor practice facility, or sometimes even in the parking lot of the basketball arena, and throw passes—from 10 yards, 20 yards, 30 yards, 40 yards, over and over.

By the following spring, he had improved both his arm strength and his accuracy, and teammates were stunned when he started letting balls fly.

October 23, 2010, in Waco, Texas, was a gray, foggy, rainy Saturday. Great black storm clouds were gathering over the plains to the west, taking aim at Floyd Casey Stadium, where the Baylor Bears were hosting Kansas State for homecoming. No place does a thunderstorm quite like central Texas, with all that warm air providing it sustenance and all that open space giving it room to stretch out its limbs, and it struck with full might four plays into the game—brilliant javelins of lightning, booming claps of thunder, raindrops the size of silver dollars.

This was an important day for Robert Griffin, Baylor's sophomore quarterback, on two different fronts:

In the afternoon, the Bears would be seeking to become bowl-eligible for the first time in fifteen years.

And in the evening, he would be asking for the hand in marriage of Rebecca Ann Liddicoat.

The rain was causing problems with both pursuits.

The game was delayed for nearly two hours, until the thunder and lightning could move out of the area, and when it finally resumed, Baylor put up a school-record 683 yards of offense in a 47–42 win, with Griffin passing for 404 yards and 4 touchdowns. When it was over, the student section stormed the field to celebrate a win that cemented Baylor's arrival as a football program.

As the rain continued, however, Griffin had to find a new place to make his proposal, his original choice having been an outdoor locale—a sentimental spot, under a tree on campus where he and Liddicoat used to sit and talk for hours.

Liddicoat was a senior biology major from Boulder, Colorado, the president of the Baylor CHIS (Clasped Hands In Service) organization, and a pretty, petite brunette who barely came up to Griffin's chest when she hugged him. When they first met, in 2009, she took one look at his goofy socks and figured, "He must have a girlfriend—he's wearing her socks." But not only was he single, he was also the mother of all good catches—a star athlete who wrote poetry and spoke of becoming a lawyer someday. Once, not long after they had started dating, he had showed up outside the balcony of her apartment, serenading her with a song he had written for her.

For his wedding proposal, Griffin had mapped out an elaborate ceremony. He had not only asked Liddicoat's parents for permission to propose to her but had also asked them to come to town to witness the moment. And he had enlisted his own parents to help with the logistics—which now had become much more compli-cated by the rain. He was going to need a new venue. But where?

Jacqueline Griffin was driving around campus, frantically looking for a new spot for her son's proposal, when she saw the lights on in the indoor football practice facility. Running inside, she found a Baylor assistant coach giving a tour to a group of high school recruits and asked for permission to use the facility for a very important matter that she could not at that moment dis-close. Somehow the coach agreed, so she called Robert with the new location, and they set a time: midnight. She took care of the rest.

At the appointed hour, the Griffin and Liddicoat families were standing in a circle, in the dark, near midfield. A Baylor teammate, offensive lineman Taylor Douthit, was perched on a hydraulic camera-lift above the turf, with a guitar. At the appointed time, Griffin entered with Liddicoat, and after first saying he needed to go to the bathroom—where his father slipped him the ring—he walked her to midfield. There all the family members suddenly switched on battery-powered candles, Douthit started to play, and Griffin dropped to one knee and launched into the song he had sung to her on her balcony all those months earlier. (Neither Grif-fin nor Liddicoat will reveal any details about the song, other than to say it was inspired by the Romeo and Juliet story.)

When he slipped a princess-cut diamond ring on her finger and said, "Will you marry me?" there wasn't a dry eye in the building. She said yes.

"He's that kind of guy," Liddicoat recalled. "He's always been that kind of person. I always knew if he proposed to me, he would make it something special. It wasn't out of character for him. He calls himself a hopeless romantic."

*S*o *let's get this straight,* Flint Harris thought as he contemplated the eighteen-year-old kid sitting in his office at the Baylor Athletic Department in the spring of 2008. *You want to take full loads every semester, plus go to summer school, so you can finish your degree in three years, then enroll in law school and take a full load of law classes in what would be your senior year of NCAA eligibility—all while serving as the starting quarterback of a Big 12 Conference football team?*

Well, that's a new one, thought Harris, who, as Baylor's director of student-athlete services, advised athletes on their academic paths. This kid, Robert Griffin, just might be a special one—or he might be insane.

"He had a goal," Harris recalled. "He always told me when he was younger that law school was plan A and football was plan B. People who didn't know him laughed at him, but then when you saw how serious he was about academics, you'd say, 'Wow, that may really be him.' You could easily see him in a courtroom, winning over a jury. And then football progressed and progressed, and as much as he may have had law school on his mind, he couldn't pass up his potential in football."

The end-goal of Griffin's law school dream had taken different forms over the years. He had a strong interest in human rights and the U.S. civil rights movement and harbored a strong desire to make a difference in some undefined but profound way. There was always politics, certainly, and that could be a possibility at some point, but it was never the end-goal itself. As he learned more about the business of sports, he started to think about trying to use his law degree to start an agency to represent athletes.

But at least in practical terms, the young man's dream of becoming a lawyer meant one thing was certain around the Griffin family: "With Robert," his father recalled, "you'd better have your facts straight."

Harris did as Griffin asked, and set him on an aggressive course toward early graduation. That first semester—spring 2008, when Griffin should have still been a high school senior—he took sixteen hours of classes and wound up posting a 3.65 grade point average.

The knee injury in the fall of 2009 had given Griffin even more options. He petitioned the NCAA successfully for a medical redshirt season: those three games in September 2009 wouldn't count toward his NCAA eligibility and he would still be a sophomore, in terms of football, in 2010. Thus, at the academic pace he had set for himself, he might even be able to finish two full years of law school before exhausting his eligibility.

With his interests and career goals, it was a natural that Griffin would become a political science major at Baylor—not a field that saw a lot of athletes in its ranks—and he eventually added a minor in communications.

In Prof. Joseph S. Brown's Minority and Ethnic Group Politics class, Griffin was the kind of student who sat near the front and led class discussions. "He was very competitive, very assertive," Brown recalled. "If he disagreed with something an author had written, or even with me, he would give his perspective on an issue. It made the class lively, in an intellectual way. He took his work very seriously. When he submitted his research paper, it was well done. And he actually knew the literature. He knew the subject he was writing about."

Communications professor John Cunningham, who had Griffin in an upper-level Interviewing class—and would later have him again for a graduate-level Communication Training and Development class—recalled the young man walking up to him before the first day of class to introduce himself, even though that, of course, was unnecessary.

"You think he's too good to be true, but nope," Cunningham recalled. "I've been teaching for twenty-four years, and he's in the top two or three percent of all the students I've taught. He got high A's in both my classes, and it wasn't just the book-work that stood out, but the way he carried himself in class. Some kids do well, but they sit in back and just write good papers. Robert also added to the discussion in class."

In 2011, when Baylor's in-house magazine put Griffin on its cover, Griffin personalized an autographed copy for Cunningham: "Thank you for teaching me my interviewing skills."

"I thought to myself, *No, that was a God thing*," Cunningham recalled. "*You were born with those*."

True to his goals, Griffin completed his bachelor's degree and graduated in December 2010, with a 3.67 GPA and three dean's list honors. On the same day, his father graduated with a master's degree in psychology from Texas A&M University–Central Texas, but skipped his own graduation to attend his son's.

Ultimately, Athletic Department officials talked Griffin out of starting law school immediately—arguing that the intense demands of both law school and football were simply incompatible—

so instead he enrolled in a master's program in the Department of Communication, specializing in film and digital media, a field he had just discovered in an undergraduate course the previous semester. By the end of the 2011 football season, he was a thesis away from completing his master's.

The thesis that Griffin proposed dealt with a concept known as "augmented reality"—similar to virtual reality, except that data are added to real-world applications, as opposed to simulating an entirely imaginary realm. The idea has long been a staple of military training for pilots and other combat personnel, as augmented-reality data are projected into, say, the helmets of pilot trainees to help prepare them for actual battle. Griffin's idea was to create an application of the concept for football or other sports.

"Say I want to go against the Ravens' defense," he explained. "I could type in 'Ravens defense,' and, boom, I've got eleven animated Ravens defensive players to go against. It's possible, and some people say it's going to be here in five to ten years, but it's going to take funding."

When he declared himself eligible for the 2012 NFL draft, thereby forgoing his senior year of NCAA eligibility, he was forced to put aside the master's thesis—but only temporarily, he vowed.

"When we left it, he said, 'I'm finishing this,'" recalled Dr. Michael Korpi, the Baylor professor supervising Griffin's master's program. "I said, 'Why? You know you don't have to do that. You could just start law school.' He said, 'No, I started this, and I'm going to finish it.'"

When he wasn't scoring touchdowns, acing exams, or building augmented-reality worlds, Griffin was often following through on his mission to burst the Baylor Bubble that separated the students on campus from the denizens of Waco proper. With the help of Harris, the academic adviser, he started volunteering with a handful of local charities—including the Special Olympics; an elementary school reading program called One Book, One Waco; and Friends for Life, an organization for senior citizens and disabled adults.

"He was like a rock star around Waco," Cunningham recalled.

Griffin almost never showed up for a day of community service without at least one teammate tagging along. In the beginning, he might have had to drag someone with him, kicking and screaming. But before long teammates were fighting each other to accompany him, according to Harris.

"The one thing that sets him apart is his ability to relate to everybody," Harris said. "Friends would tag along, just because they wanted to be around him, and around that aura. People just migrated to that."

A true story: In July 2010, a young Waco couple named Benji and Kimberly Polnick were planning a birthday party a few weeks down the road for their one-year-old son, who, not coincidentally, was named Griffin. Kimberly Polnick decided—what the heck?—she would invite Robert Griffin III to the party, and so she reached out to him in a message via Facebook, and he replied. Details were exchanged, but no promises given. It was a Baylor football–themed party at the Polnick residence, and they figured there was little chance he would actually show on what would be the last free weekend before football practice got under way.

But then—what do you know?—who should come strolling up the street, flanked by three Baylor teammates, but Robert Griffin III. For the next ninety minutes or so, the quartet posed for pictures, signed autographs, tossed little toy footballs around with the kids in the backyard, ate a plate of hamburgers and chips—the only compensation any of them received—and helped sing "Happy Birthday" to little Griffin Polnick.

"He's such a real person," Kimberly Polnick recalled of Griffin III. "What he says is who he is. There's not a lot of people like that in the world. I met his parents sometime after that and thanked them for raising him like they did. We loved him and what he did for our city."

By the end of Griffin's time in Waco, one word kept popping up to describe his status there: "ambassador." Baylor president Kenneth Starr has used it in regard to Griffin, and it is there in the second sentence of his official Baylor football bio: "Became not only face of Baylor football program but ambassador of Baylor University in four years in Waco."

All that was needed was a catchy nickname for Griffin, something short and snappy that you could build a marketing campaign around and that could define his era at Baylor. In 2010 a sportscaster for a local Waco television station wound up coining the nickname that stuck: from that point on, Robert Griffin III would be known as RG3.

SEVEN

THE DEBUT

When the NFL released its 2012 schedule in April, just one week before the draft, Robert Griffin III's eyes went straight to the Washington Redskins' opponent for Week 1: "September 9, at New Orleans." That little nugget of information stopped him cold, then brought a smile to his face. It couldn't have been a coincidence, could it? The team that was preparing to select him with the No. 2 overall pick in the draft would be opening the season, Griffin's rookie year, in his ancestral hometown—the city where both of his parents were born and raised, the place where he and his family traveled for Christmas most years—and in a building, the Mercedes-Benz Superdome, where his father had sold popcorn as a kid and where Griffin himself used to run the surrounding ramps and steps during his visits there.

God, he thought to himself upon seeing the schedule, *works in mysterious ways.*

In New Orleans, though, they were wondering if God's opposite number might be responsible. Because what in the devil were all the assorted Griffins and Rosses—the extended families of Robert Griffin Jr. and the former Jacqueline Ross—supposed to do now? This was Saints country, and the bonds of blood and fanhood were going to be tested by the arrival of young Robert Griffin III in a rival uniform. Uncle Rodney Griffin was a longtime Saints season-ticket-holder in section 344. Uncle Shane Griffin was an unabashed Saints face-painter. Grandpa John Ross wore Saints paraphernalia head-to-toe and never missed a game with the fellas down at Smokin' Jo's, his hangout on Frenchmen Street.

For a while, the Griffin family didn't even want to talk to the media about the Saints–Redskins game, so raw were the emotions. "The Saints are our hometown team," Robert Griffin Jr. explained to me. "My brothers and I, we lived through all the bad years, the bags-on-your-head days, the 'Aints. We don't need to go in there and stir up any antagonistic issue with the Saints and motivate them. It's almost a conflict."

But when the day finally came, blood won out over fanhood, and it wasn't even close. There were Griffins and Rosses everywhere in the Superdome on September 9, nearly fifty of them in all. They came in from the Fourth Ward, the Seventh Ward, and the Upper Ninth, from up in City Park, over in Gentilly, and out in Old Aurora. Irene Griffin, grandmother of the Redskins' quarterback, skipped Sunday services at St. Mary of the Angels Church to be there. Even the displaced ones who had scattered to the wind after Katrina, they came back—including great-grandmother Evelyn B. Thomas, eighty-six years young, who had lost her house on Music Street in the storm, but who flew in from her new home in Altadena, California.

And on this day, they were all Redskins fans.

"We are from New Orleans, born and raised and went to school here," explained Rodney Griffin, son of Robert Griffin Sr., brother of Robert Jr., uncle of Robert III. "But that's a Griffin [on the Redskins]. This is one of ours."

What do you suppose folks were saying about "Ponytail" now—all those playground toughs and hardened project kids whom Uncle Shane figured would tear his nephew to shreds if he signed him up for football as a seven-year-old?

Fifteen years after destiny was delayed by the conscience of a loyal uncle, Ponytail was finally going to make his football debut in New Orleans. He was known as RG3 now, and at twenty-two he was already a man in full—with a fiancée, a $21 million contract, a Heisman Trophy on his mantel, four major television commercials in heavy rotation nationwide, and the hopes of the Redskins' beleaguered fan base on his shoulders.

"When he started to gain notoriety, all my buddies are like, 'Wait—that's not Ponytail, is it?'" said Shane Griffin, now the uncle of a superstar. "And I'm like, 'Yep, that's him.'"

Here he was, maybe twelve blocks from the Iberville Projects, where he lived for those six months while his parents were in Korea, where he bounced a basketball everywhere he went and fancied himself the next Michael Jordan, where he had arrived a little soft and departed a little tougher. New Orleans held a special place in his heart: though he was born in Japan and raised mostly in Texas, New Orleans was where he was *from.*

"Home," Griffin said in the days leading up to the Saints game, "is where you go for Christmas, and for me that was New Orleans." One old family photo shows the Griffin family standing in front of their long, white sedan with the Superdome rising majestically in the background. Little Robby, who looks to be around five, is wearing a Saints letterman's jacket and sneakers. Big Rob is sporting the same high-and-tight flat-top haircut he wears today.

When September 9 arrived in New Orleans, sunny, warm, and breezy, Griffin was the first Redskins player on the Superdome field, strolling out of the tunnel and onto the field, still in street clothes, some three and a half hours before kickoff—as soon as the Redskins' bus arrived. He wore a sport coat and tie, sunglasses, and Beats By Dre headphones. (His game-day mix is heavy on Michael Jackson.) He walked the circumference of the field once, taking it all in, then disappeared below the stands. When he returned to the field an hour or so later, he was wearing a white undershirt with the word HEART scribbled across it. (It later came to light that the handwritten word was purposely obscuring the Nike swoosh on the shirt, for which Griffin, a loyal Adidas man, was later fined by the NFL.)

And finally, as kickoff approached for his regular-season NFL debut, he emerged after yet another costume change, this time in the gold pants and burgundy jersey of the Redskins, with the name on his back carrying extra meaning on this day, in this building, in this city: GRIFFIN III.

You either have to be with someone who knows where he is going or else stop at the small cemetery office for directions if you're looking for the grave of Robert Griffin Sr. There's not much in the way of landmarks to give it away. Some New Orleans cemeteries are tourist destinations—famed for their above-ground tombs with ornate gravestones and for the legends of the voodoo queens and ghosts said to inhabit them. But Resthaven Memorial Park is not one of them.

A few weeks before the Saints–Redskins opener, I drove out to Resthaven, east of New Orleans, with Shane and Rodney Griffin, two of Robert Griffin III's uncles. We parked off to the side of Old Gentilly Road and walked along the northern edge of the cemetery, through marshy grass that sucked at your shoes. Rodney knew where he was going, having visited once a year or so since his father's death, but Shane figured he hadn't been there in sixteen or seventeen years.

"I don't do that emotional stuff," he explained.

The gravestone is little more than a simple plaque, partially covered in a layer of dust and grass clipping: IN LOVING MEMORY / HUSBAND AND FATHER / ROBERT L. GRIFFIN / SEPT. 17, 1941 / SEPT. 27, 1984.

They stood and looked at the gravestone. He was a tough man, a hard man, with big hands that could seemingly put together or tear down anything. I asked Rodney Griffin: did the old man give preferential treatment to Robert Jr., by virtue of his being the namesake? "No," he said, "he was equally hard on all of us."

Robert Griffin Sr. was a construction foreman whose brightness of mood was in direct proportion to the proximity of payday. "When he said he was going to the bank," Robert Jr. recalled, "that's when you knew life was about to be grand." He loved his football, and at the house in the Iberville Projects where he and wife, Irene, raised their four girls and four boys, everyone would pile into the parents' big old bed to watch games on the only working TV in the house. Once his eyesight started to go from the glaucoma he contracted in his thirties, he was ultimately forced to quit work and would rely on the kids to tell him what was going on in the game.

And when the old man died from an aneurysm at age forty-three, Robert Griffin Jr. was among those who simply couldn't believe it. Despite the health problems, his father had been the strongest man he ever knew.

They were all Saints fans, of course, but in those days the Saints were so bad, it was permissible for everyone to pick a secondary team to root for. Robert Sr., for instance, rooted for the Rams, because Eric Dickerson was his favorite player, and Irene rooted for the Redskins. "There was something about the way they were called the 'Over the Hill Gang' that I liked," she said. One time, years later, Shane Griffin challenged his mother to name one player from those Redskins teams, and she said, "I know they were coached by Vince Lombardi."

"Vince Lombardi?!" he said in disgust, assuming she was wrong. But then he Googled the great coach and learned that his final coaching job, in 1969, had been with the Redskins.

The four Griffin boys—Robert Jr., Rodney, Shane, and Michael—all worked Saints games at the Superdome, selling popcorn. You'd fork over $20, and they would hand you a tray full of boxes of popcorn. You got to pocket the profits. "After the third quarter, you didn't have to sell any more," Shane recalled, "and you could sit and watch the game."

Out on the playgrounds of the projects, the Griffin boys staked their claims to athletic greatness, with Robert Jr. and Rodney becoming legends of sorts—until their dreams of athletic glory petered out and each joined the Army on his eighteenth birthday, roughly a year apart.

"If these walls could talk," said Rodney Griffin, now a sergeant first-class who works as a recruiter for the Army, as he stood
in the grassy courtyard between the brick houses, beneath the
shade of a Southern live oak, "they'd still be talking about the
battles we had on those playgrounds."

Every Mardi Gras, the Griffins would stake out their spot at
the corner of Bienville and Basin, waiting for the Zulu parade to
bend off Canal Street and head down Basin. Even though the Griffins haven't lived in the Iberville Projects for years, that's still their
Mardi Gras parade spot, and everyone around the neighborhood
knows not to encroach on it.

After their father's death, the Griffin children worked hard to
get their mother out of the projects, and eventually they did, moving her to a house on Alvar Street in the Upper Ninth Ward. She
now has eighteen grandchildren (who call her "Mami") and, thus
far, four great-grandchildren. Like everyone else in the family, she
knows with certainty that her husband would be overcome with
pride and joy at the success of young Robert III, the namesake he
never got a chance to meet.

"He would have been extraordinarily proud of what this young
man is doing," said Irene Griffin. "Even though he couldn't see,
he'd be there watching and having people telling him what Robert
is doing."

That day 72,180 revelers—Griffins and otherwise—packed into
the Superdome, dancing to "When the Saints Go Marching In"
and hollering "Who dat?" There were 72,180 eyewitnesses to what
may have been the single greatest NFL debut by a rookie quarter-

back in the history of the league. Robert Griffin III was handed one of the most difficult assignments imaginable—on the road, Week 1, NFL debut, in one of the loudest, most inhospitable buildings in the league, against the defending NFC South champions, a team that didn't lose a single game at home the year before—and he pulled off a shocker: a 40–32 Redskins victory in which he out-played both Drew Brees and history itself, and in the process cap-tured the cold, cynical hearts of any Redskins fans back home who had yet to succumb to his charms.

"He's a sight for sore eyes," veteran linebacker London Fletcher said, speaking for all those fans, and also for every player in that locker room who had played behind Rex Grossman and John Beck the year before. It was no slight against those men, merely the cold truth, to say a win like this simply would not have been possible with either of them at quarterback.

One game into his career, Griffin had given Redskins fans an improbable victory, a hopeful future, and an indelible image seared into their brains (and captured on the front page of the next day's *Washington Post*): a picture of Griffin, still seated on the Super-dome turf following a vicious hit, raising his index fingers to the sky as Pierre Garcon sprints to the end zone at the end of an eighty-eight-yard touchdown pass. Somewhere, the silly, invisible people who turn such impromptu moments into Internet memes gave a name to the pose: Griffining.

The stats: 19-for-26, 320 yards (plus another 42 yards rushing), two touchdowns, no interceptions, a 139.9 passer rating—including a perfect 158.3 rating in the first half of his first NFL game. The historic context: it was the first time in league history a rookie quarterback had thrown for more than three hundred yards in a victorious NFL debut. The present-day context: four other rookie quarterbacks made their NFL debut that same day—Andrew Luck, Ryan Tannehill, Brandon Weeden, and Russell Wilson—and they combined to throw eleven interceptions and only two touchdowns, with all four losing. That was how a rookie quarterback is supposed to play in his NFL debut. They weren't supposed to be able to do what Griffin did.

"I'm proud of you," Brees whispered in Griffin's ear when they met at midfield after the game for the traditional quarterback bro-hug.

In the victorious Redskins locker room, Coach Mike Shanahan tossed Griffin a gift—the game ball, the same one Griffin had used for the touchdown pass to Garcon, the first of his NFL career. For the next hour or so, as Griffin moved through the bowels of the Superdome—still in his Redskins uniform—he kept the ball tucked safely under his arm, refusing to surrender it. He juked around reporters and slipped through holes in the tangle of bodies in the locker room, following the lead block of the Redskins media official charged with leading him from one interview to another, and the ball stayed with him. Someone offered to hold it for safekeeping, and he said, "No, I got it."

He tossed it back and forth from his left hand to his right as he spoke, and he twirled it idly, and at one point it slipped from his grasp and fell to the floor. A half-dozen people stooped to recover Griffin's fumble, but he beat them to it, scooping up the ball, tucking it back under his arm, and flashing that increasingly famous smile.

In the summer of 2012, some seven years after Katrina blew through, you could still see the watermark about six feet up the outer wall of John Ross's house, where the floodwaters had crested. Ross, Robert Griffin III's maternal grandfather, had bought the house in 1976 and had raised his kids there, but when the water came rushing down Desaix Boulevard that day in August 2005, he knew it would be a long time before he lived in it again. Now, in the summer of 2012, he was finally getting around to fixing it up.

That's how it was with the best contractors in New Orleans after Katrina—they fixed everyone else's houses before they finally turned to their own.

"I've probably done forty, maybe fifty, maybe more," Ross said, standing outside the gutted shell of his house in August 2012. "I helped mostly elderly people, because after the storm these contractors were ripping off people. It made me sick."

Whatever musical ability Robert Griffin III possesses—his pretty voice, his songwriting chops—he probably inherited from his Grandpa Ross, a drummer who gigged around New Orleans for years and then ran sound for the great vocalist Irma Thomas, the "Soul Queen of New Orleans," for a while. When he played drums, it was usually with the Batiste Brothers, but in his heyday you would find him behind the kits for Ernie Vincent, Joe Tex, and Joe Simon. He did it for the money, gigging at night to supplement his income as a truck driver for Popeyes Fried Chicken.

Like anyone who was in New Orleans when Katrina came up the Gulf of Mexico and slammed into New Orleans, the lives of the Griffin and Ross families are divided into pre-Katrina and post-Katrina periods. The storm scattered members of the extended family everywhere—to Shreveport, Nacogdoches, Birmingham, Houston. In Copperas Cove, where Robert Griffin III at the time was fifteen years old and a rising star in track and field and football, the Griffins took in a dozen family members who had been forced to evacuate, with some of them staying for a year or more as the insurance claims were sorted out and their houses rebuilt.

Most of them eventually went back, but John Ross's mother, Evelyn B. Thomas, who lost her house in the Ninth Ward, never did go back but moved instead to California to live with her oldest son.

"She just couldn't go back," Jacqueline Griffin, her granddaughter, said. "It was more than she could bear."

For Robert Griffin III, the coming of Katrina also marked a change in his connection to New Orleans. He and his sisters were getting older, and their summers were filling up with sporting events and other obligations, and so the family trips to New Orleans had already been getting more and more infrequent. After Katrina, it would be a while before he made it back to New Orleans, and even then it would never quite be the same.

"I remember New Orleans after Katrina, and just the devastation that occurred and how many of my family members ended up having to move to Texas with us, or to homes and shelters for a little bit, before they went back," he recalled. "And then just to go back and see the devastation, how many of them lost their houses and had to start over—it was extremely sad. I do have great memories of [New Orleans] from my childhood, but as of lately, I haven't been back as much. The last image in my head is from Katrina."

When he thought about the circle coming full—his being back in New Orleans as an NFL quarterback, surrounded by family—Griffin got goose bumps. He managed to carve out some time the night before the game to visit with family members, and it was just like the old days—everybody sitting around eating and talking, mostly about football. The kid may have been a rising superstar and a marketing icon and a million other things, but above all, he was a Griffin. And he was home.

"That determination you see in Robert Griffin III is the same character trait that runs throughout the whole family," said Rodney Griffin. "We all have the same trait—stubborn, hard-headed. We are some very humble people from humble backgrounds. This is where we started at, and we know this is where we going to end at."

Someday historians may look back at the Redskins' second play from scrimmage in their win over the Saints and pinpoint it as the moment offensive football changed forever in the NFL. On that play, a second-and-10 from the Redskins' 32, Griffin lined up about four yards behind center—a formation known as the "pistol" (since it was shorter than a shotgun) that would become a staple of the Redskins offense—with running back Alfred Morris behind him. At the snap, he tucked the ball in Morris's midsection, while his eyes read the movements of the Saints' defensive end, and when the end crashed down to defend the handoff to Morris, Griffin pulled the ball back and ran it himself for twelve yards.

The zone-read option had already made slight inroads in the NFL—with teams like the Panthers and Broncos using it with quarterbacks Cam Newton and Tim Tebow, respectively—but never before had it been run so effectively by as fast a quarterback as Griffin. The Redskins had worked on the offense secretly all summer but had wisely kept it hidden during the preseason, trotting out a more vanilla scheme during their four exhibition games before springing it on the Saints in Week 1. By the end of the 2012 season, the Seahawks and 49ers would adopt large chunks of the zone-read offense themselves with great success, behind quarterbacks Russell Wilson and Colin Kaepernick, respectively, with the 49ers riding Kaepernick all the way to the Super Bowl.

"The zone-read—there's so many things you can do off of it," Griffin said following the Saints game. "It's kind of like, pick your poison. What do you want to stop? Do you want to stop the throws off of it? Do you want to stop the running game? Do you want to stop the running back? [The Saints] chose what they wanted to stop, and we had to make plays in other areas, and we made those plays."

That first drive in New Orleans heralded the birth of the Redskins' new offense, all built around their young quarterback. On the first drive of his NFL career—amid crowd noise so loud he would later say he felt it in his body—Griffin went 6-of-6 for 35 yards, leading the Redskins to a field goal. Most of the completions were short, quick passes to his wide receivers that may have looked like simple slant routes or bubble-screens but were far more complicated than that. In fact, they were "packaged plays" similar to some of the offensive concepts Griffin had run to perfection at Baylor—designed run plays in which some of the receivers also ran short routes, giving Griffin the option to pull the ball back and make quick throws over the middle if he felt that was what the defense was giving him. In essence, it was a triple-option, with the three options being to hand the ball off, keep it, or throw it—but dressed up and altered to suit the speed and style of the NFL. On each play, Griffin "read" the defensive end or linebacker to the side the play was designed to go, making the defender commit before he decided whether to hand off, keep, or throw.

For the Redskins to have concentrated so much decision-making power in Griffin's hands so soon showed an extraordinary level of confidence in him on the part of the coaches.

"We really don't know what's going to happen until the defense [commits]," Redskins coach Mike Shanahan said after the game. "So we had running plays called, and all of a sudden they gave us certain looks to take the running game away, and we threw a couple of [screens] early. It's pretty impressive when a young guy comes in and plays with that composure, especially in an environment like this."

By the end of the first half, Griffin was 11-of-13 for 182 yards and two touchdowns, giving him a "perfect" passer rating of 158.3. Later in the game, as the Saints' defense grew more disciplined and held its ground, Griffin simply kept handing off to Morris, his fellow rookie, who gained 96 yards on 28 carries. And later still, they all but abandoned the zone-read for large chunks of time, switching to a more conventional pro-style offense, while mixing in ample helpings of play-action and a handful of bootlegs. By the end, the shell-shocked Saints defenders simply had no idea what was coming next.

But there would still be one last dicey situation for Griffin to navigate before the win was sealed. With 2:22 left in the game, the Redskins faced a second-and-13 from their own 17-yard line. The safe call would have been to run the ball, since a couple of incompletions here would give the ball back to Brees, who, in need of a touchdown and with about two minutes left, could tie the game with a two-point conversion. But that was not a scenario the Redskins wanted to face. On their sideline during a time-out, offensive coordinator Kyle Shanahan said he wanted to go for the kill—to pass for the first down and run out the clock—and he asked Griffin if he could hit a tight seam-route pass to the tight end.

"I'm confident I can hit that," Griffin replied, and moments later he uncorked a perfect throw to tight end Logan Paulsen for a twenty-two-yard gain that locked down the victory.

In the waning moments of the game, the Superdome started to clear out of Saints fans and a large contingent of burgundy-and-gold-clad Redskins fans crept down toward the lower railing, singing "Hail to the Redskins" and chanting "R-G-3! R-G-3!" Before leaving the field, Griffin made his way to the railing and high-fived the fans, blowing kisses to them as he jogged away.

"This," analyst Steve Mariucci gushed on the NFL Network as Griffin's highlights played, "is the most athletic quarterback this league has ever seen."

In the immediacy of the moment, it was difficult to know what, exactly, we had just witnessed: The start of an offensive revolution? The first step on a march to the playoffs for the Redskins? The best debut by a young phenom since an eighteen-year-old LeBron James put up 25 points and nine assists in Sacramento on October 29, 2003? Or possibly all three? Rookie quarterbacks simply don't walk into a hostile building such as the Superdome and beat a team such as the Saints in their debut. In fact, the last rookie quarterback who had won his NFL debut on the road against a team that had been unbeaten at home the year before was John Elway,

Mike Shanahan's old protégé and Robert Griffin III's boyhood idol—but Elway had needed help to do it, getting yanked after completing just one of his first eight passes and watching as veteran Steve DeBerg steered the Broncos to a win.

"Unbelievable," said Mike Shanahan. The 40 points the Redskins put up were their most in a single game since Shanahan's arrival in 2010. In 2011, in fact, the Redskins never even cracked the 30-point barrier. Shanahan seemed to take great pride in the sleight-of-hand offense that he had unveiled that day, well aware that it would be the talk of NFL film rooms the next day.

"There are a lot of different directions we could go," he said slyly. "And we'll experiment as the year goes on."

Shanahan and Griffin had put something in the heads of the entire NFL that day, something dark and sinister and certain to cause sleepless nights for the unlucky souls—the opposing head coaches and defensive coordinators—who had to face it next.

EIGHT

THE HEISMAN

In those few anxious moments that followed the standard, scripted, faux-crescendoed, just-get-it-over-with-please lead-in (". . . and the 2011 winner of the Heisman Trophy is . . . "), his mind shut down, going pitch-black, and there was only the nothingness. Robert Griffin III's eyes stared straight ahead, but it was his ears that were honed in, shutting down the other senses, listening intently for the next consonant out of the speaker's mouth, hoping it would be an *R*. He sat completely still, hands folded in his lap, knees apart. Below the cuffs of his navy blue suit-pants peeked out a pair of garish, sky-blue Superman socks, complete with little red capes.

It was December 10, 2011, and Griffin, two months and two days shy of his twenty-second birthday, had been thinking plenty about the Heisman Trophy in the days leading up to this made-for-TV moment. He now sat in the front row of the Best Buy Theater in New York City's Times Square, next to four other stars of college football—his fellow Heisman finalists—with millions of people watching at home. He had been thinking about the journey to get here, about his parents, his coaches, his teammates, about the pride he felt in being a Baylor Bear and in having helped resurrect the school's football program. Everyone always says this, but if he won, he would truly mean it: the award was for all of them, not just him.

He had tried not to pay attention to any of the preceremony media hype. There was no need to build up his hopes any more than they already were, but with everyone calling him the favorite to win, out of necessity he had been thinking about what he might say in a victory speech. He wanted to be prepared. A few days before the ceremony, he was sitting in a dress shop in Waco, waiting on Rebecca Liddicoat, his fiancée, to pick out something to wear to New York, when a phrase popped into his head: "Unbelievably believable." Yes, that about summed it up. Unbelievable, because no one could ever imagine that a former Army brat, a skinny kid known as Ponytail, a Michael-Jordan-wannabe-turned-track-phenom who didn't play football until junior high—or for that matter, a quarterback at Baylor, of all places—could actually win the Heisman Trophy someday. But believable because—well, why else did he run all those hills with the tire, sacrifice much of his youth, grind in the weight room and the film room, except to be the best?

For Griffin even to have been in this theater on this day—alongside Stanford's Andrew Luck, Wisconsin's Montee Ball, Alabama's Trent Richardson, and LSU's Tyrann Mathieu—would have been considered a colossal upset back at the start of the 2011 football season. Luck had been the runner-up for the Heisman to Auburn's Cam Newton in 2010, and so at season's start he was the overwhelming favorite to win this time. In the season previews of countless newspapers and magazines, 2011 was being billed as "The Year of Luck," and when Las Vegas betting sites put out their Heisman odds before the season, Griffin wasn't even on the board.

Part of that, undoubtedly, owed to Baylor's almost nonexistent national profile. While Griffin had led the Bears to a berth in the Texas Bowl in 2010—Baylor's first bowl appearance in sixteen years—the school had precious little national cachet, and it hadn't produced so much as a top 10 finisher in Heisman voting since Don Trull finished fourth in 1963, the year Navy's Roger Staubach won. Pedigree matters in Heisman voting—for proof, look no further than the list of the schools that had produced the previous fifteen winners (in reverse chronological order): Auburn, Alabama, Oklahoma, Florida, Ohio State, USC, Oklahoma, USC, Nebraska, Florida State, Wisconsin, Texas, Michigan, Florida, and Ohio State. All of them college football blue-bloods.

At the moment of truth, Griffin was so locked in that he didn't even react when the announcer called out: ". . . Robert Griffin. . . ." He sat transfixed, frozen, while the rest of the room immediately burst into applause. Only when the announcer got to ". . . the third" did he break into a smile, bow his head briefly, and rise to his feet—the tension and anticipation draining out of him— to accept the congratulations of his fellow finalists, who, per the unwritten rules of televised-awards etiquette, were feigning happiness for him. After bro-hugging each fellow finalist—right-handed soul shake, right shoulder lean-in, left-handed slap on the back— he made his way back, row by row, thanking everyone who had come with him to New York: his Baylor coaches, his parents, his fiancée, and his sisters. Finally, as he ascended the steps to the lectern, he cast a quick glance at the trophy itself, displayed on a stand at stage right, and reached into his front left pocket for his speech.

"This moment right here," he said, gripping the lectern with both hands and looking up from his notes and out toward the audience, "is unbelievably believable. It's unbelievable because, in the moment, we're all amazed when great things happen. It's believable because great things only happen with hard work."

Though he had tried to remind himself to take it slow, he blew through the entire speech in less than two minutes—but still managed to drop no fewer than seven "Baylors" (compared to only three "Heismans" and two "Gods"), leaving no doubt where his heart was at that moment. "We are Baylor," he told the crowd at one point. "Baylor we are. Baylor we'll always be."

When the ceremony was over, he returned to his family for more hugs. As he approached his father he pulled him close and whispered in his ear, "Hard work pays off." It was an amazing night, and a draining one, between the ceremony and the dinner and the small talk and the handshakes and the picture-posing, but even by the end, there was still no way Griffin could sleep. He was still too fired up, too full of emotion.

It was going on 2 A.M., but back at the New York Marriott Marquis hotel, Griffin and Liddicoat changed into workout clothes and headed down to the hotel gym—there evidently being no SUV tires or ropes available to him at that moment—for a long, brisk workout.

It is difficult to pinpoint exactly when the Heisman Trophy shifted from being a pipe dream to a legitimate possibility for Baylor's

Robert Griffin III. After the fact, of course, everybody wanted to take credit for having first raised the notion. Art Briles may or may not have invoked the Heisman as a possibility when he was recruiting Griffin out of high school. Other staff members may or may not have predicted he would win the Heisman back when he was a freshman. Griffin himself may or may not have thought it possible.

"It wasn't on any checklist," he said later, "but it wasn't something I thought I couldn't do."

As the 2011 season approached, the Sports Information Department staff, which handles public relations for the Athletic Department, was building Griffin's brand, pumping the RG3 nickname, inviting regional and national media outlets to interview him, launching his website—but the overarching strategy was to get him established as a national figure in 2011, and maybe even get him to New York as a Heisman finalist, and then launch an aggressive Griffin-for-Heisman campaign in 2012, his senior year of eligibility.

Certainly, by the middle of the 2011 season, nobody at Baylor was clearing out any space in the trophy case for a Heisman Trophy. The team had started out well enough, upsetting 14th-ranked TCU in the season opener and sprinting to a 4-1 record, but in back-to-back games in October the Bears were destroyed by Oklahoma State and Texas A&M by a combined 62 points, leaving their season record at 4-3, with one of the toughest stretches of their schedule still to come.

And while Griffin was putting up huge numbers, there were whispers around the Big 12, and across the nation, that he couldn't win the big game. In the terminology of Heisman voting, he didn't have a "signature" win—a difficult-to-define concept, but you would know one if you saw it—which was something voters would surely recognize.

But then in November, Griffin and the Bears caught fire. He threw for 406 yards and three touchdowns—his third straight game passing for more than four hundred yards—in a 42–39 win over Missouri, then the following week threw three fourth-quarter touchdown passes to help the Bears overcome a 21-point deficit at Kansas and escape with a 31–30 overtime win. (That same day Andrew Luck, still the Heisman front-runner, had his worst game of the year at an inopportune time, throwing two interceptions in Stanford's nationally televised 53–30 loss to Oregon.)

November 19, 2011, was the day everything changed. On that day, the Bears hosted Oklahoma, the fifth-ranked team in the nation and the opponent that more than any other had come to define Baylor's futility in the Big 12: the Bears had played the Sooners twenty times, and twenty times they had lost. It was a perfect night in Waco, 76 degrees at kickoff with a nice breeze from the south, and the game was an epic battle, full of lead changes and long scoring plays. At the end, it came down to one play: with the score tied at 38, the ball on Oklahoma's 34, and the clock ticking down inside 20 seconds to play, Griffin dropped back to pass, felt the pocket collapsing, and slipped out to the left. Suddenly spotting receiver Terrance Williams in one-on-one coverage to the right, Griffin fired across his body—just as he was about to get pancaked by a charging Sooner defender—and hit Williams in the back corner of the end zone. Touchdown. Ball game. Bedlam.

"You just won us the game," one of Griffin's offensive linemen told him as he picked him up off the turf.

Griffin had thrown for 479 yards, a school record, and four

touchdowns. At long last, he had his signature win. ABC-TV, which was showing the game to a national audience, stayed with the shot of the student section swarming the field. "They said we needed a signature win," Griffin said later. "We got it." Suddenly, the Bears were the 18th-ranked team in the nation and Griffin's name was starting to appear on all those "Heisman Watch" lists.

"After the Oklahoma win," Griffin recalled, "when we shot up the charts, my teammates said, 'We're going to go win this Heisman for you.'" Such a thing no longer seemed so far-fetched.

But one week after the Oklahoma win, the whole thing threatened to unravel. Playing against Texas Tech at Cowboys Stadium— the billion-dollar palace in Arlington built by Dallas Cowboys owner Jerry Jones—Griffin took a hard elbow to the helmet at the end of a second-quarter scramble. Dazed, he lay on the turf for a minute or so as trainers attended to him, then walked off the field. But after just one play on the sideline, he insisted on returning, and on the next play he scored on a three-yard touchdown run. At halftime, though, Griffin couldn't remember the touchdown he had just scored, and team doctors diagnosed him with a concussion. When Griffin said he was fine and tried to lobby to be allowed to play the second half, head trainer Mike Sims took and hid his helmet—leaving him little choice but to watch from the sideline as backup Nick Florence led the Bears to a 66–42 win, their fourth straight. At one point, when the Red Raiders had closed to within 10 points, Griffin found Sims on the sideline and said, "If this game gets any closer, you're going to have to fight me for my helmet."

In the days that followed, there seemed to be little debate as to whether Griffin would play the following Saturday. When Baylor officials spoke of Griffin's condition during that week, they were careful to describe his issue as "concussion-like symptoms," rather than what it was: a concussion. ("We're in a war," Briles told CBSSports.com three days after the Texas Tech game. "Sometimes in a war you get casualties.") December 3 would mark the Bears' regular-season finale—and if Griffin chose to forgo his final season of eligibility and declare himself for the NFL draft, as many were now speculating he would do, it would also be his final home game in a Baylor uniform. The Heisman Trophy might very well be on the line. And on top of everything else, it was the Texas Longhorns who were visiting—and Griffin would enjoy nothing more than a second straight victory over the school that had condescendingly offered him a scholarship as an "athlete," not as a quarterback, back in 2007. With all that intrigue swirling around, it's no wonder ABC gave the game the coveted 3:30 P.M. EST time slot.

Griffin played, and he was brilliant—passing for 320 yards and two touchdowns and rushing for two more scores as the Bears trounced the Longhorns, 48–24. "I could be wrong," he told a television reporter on the field after the game, "but I think Baylor won its first Heisman tonight."

From their 4-3 nadir in October, the Bears had reeled off five consecutive wins, with Griffin throwing thirteen touchdown passes against only two interceptions in that span. In the days that followed, Baylor would ascend to the 12th spot in the national rankings and accept an invitation to the Alamo Bowl, and the accolades would start to roll in for its quarterback. "He's as good a quarterback as there is in the United States, at any level," said Kansas State coach Bill Snyder. "He's Jim Thorpe all over again—but with a heck of a lot more speed."

Heisman voters had to turn in their ballots two days after the Texas game, and the ceremony was a week later. As Bruce Feldman, CBSSports.com's college football columnist, put it, "A few hours from now I will submit my official Heisman ballot. A player from Baylor is going to be listed in the number one spot. I still can't quite get over that. Before last season, the Bears hadn't been to a bowl game in sixteen years. The program has only produced one guy who won any of the national individual awards in the past twenty-five years, and he was a punter. Yet here we are. In the first week of December, there is no player in the country who seems more deserving of the title Most Outstanding Player than a Baylor Bear, Robert Griffin III."

Griffin had little time to digest the enormity of what he and his teammates had accomplished, but a strange emotion filled him, somewhere between awe and satisfaction. It would be a couple more days before he found a way to define it: unbelievably believable.

Heath Nielsen had been in the collegiate PR game for the better part of twenty years, with a dozen of those years at Baylor, and so he thought he knew where the ceiling was for a publicity-magnet student-athlete. Every few years in this gig you might be lucky enough to have a player who possessed the requisite combination of athletic ability and interviewing skills, and you might be able to land him a couple of big feature stories in the Dallas papers or on one of the national websites, or turn him into a semi-fixture on the local Waco TV sports report.

And then he encountered Robert Griffin III.

"There's this air about him that's just different," said Nielsen,

Baylor's associate athletic director for communications. "I've used the phrase—and it's probably not fair—but he's almost presidential. He comports himself in a way that no one else does. He can still be silly and childlike sometimes, but he knows exactly when to flip the switch."

As far back as Griffin's freshman year, Nielsen understood what he had on his hands here: pure, unadulterated PR gold. The kid was smart, handsome, personable, telegenic, and grounded—not to mention one heck of a football player. Nielsen knew he could ride the kid to uncharted heights, if only Coach Briles would let him.

"It was really hard for me as the PR guy, because I had this stud who we could really saddle up and take far—and a coach who was saying, 'We don't want to push this guy. Make it a team thing,'" Nielsen recalled. "It wasn't until [2011] that I finally convinced Coach to just ride him—go for broke, publicity-wise. We told [Griffin] in the off-season, 'Look, we're going to push you hard. We're going to go as far as we can, media-wise.' He became not only the face of this program and this [athletic] department, but the entire campus. I'm not kidding you."

Griffin's media availability in 2011 started out as an hour every Monday, which quickly turned into ninety minutes, which quickly turned into an additional hour on Tuesdays, and then some more time set aside on Wednesdays. By November, when the Bears got hot and Griffin's Heisman chances started to rise, he was doing thirty to thirty-five interviews a week—many of them with national media outlets that had rarely if ever been to Waco for a football story. (It was a strategy that ran in stark contrast to the way the Redskins cut off almost all media access to Griffin during his rookie season in Washington. The notion that Griffin needed protection from the media was comical to those who had seen him in action in Waco.)

One of the first glimpses the greater American sporting public got of Griffin came on September 3, 2011—the first Saturday of the college football season. The Bears had played the night before, in the nationally televised ESPN Friday night opener against TCU—scoring a 50–48 upset over the 14th-ranked Frogs behind five touchdown passes from Griffin—and early Saturday morning, Nielsen drove Griffin to Arlington, Texas, an hour and a half away, where ESPN's *College Gameday* was set up for that afternoon's highly anticipated LSU–Oregon matchup. Working on just two hours' sleep, Griffin charmed the *Gameday* crew during a four-minute interview, to the point where host Chris Fowler finally gushed, "Great ambassador for the Baylor Bears football program!"

"It was the first time America got to see him—how engaging he is, how charming," Nielsen recalled. "He knocked the socks off those guys."

As the season wore on, and Griffin's profile grew, Nielsen and his staff ramped up their marketing efforts. They started a grassroots campaign on Facebook called "Join the Third," in which Baylor fans were encouraged to alter their own user names by adding a roman numeral "III" to them. They plastered Baylor's football website with videos of Griffin, including a lighthearted series of interviews called "30 with the Third," in which teammates peppered him with a series of short, silly questions.

There was one facet of Griffin's game, however, that Baylor

went out of its way to play down—his running skills. Although the dual-threat ability was central to Griffin's success—defenses couldn't focus too closely on stopping the pass because he could also beat you with his legs, and vice versa—Nielsen was cognizant of the role that race played in football and was wary of Griffin's being stereotyped as just another African American quarterback for whom passing was a secondary concern.

"In every photo, every logo, we showed him throwing the ball. We never showed him running the ball—because we were fighting that perception," Nielsen said. "We had great pictures of him running the ball—in one of them he looked almost like the Heisman pose. But we didn't use it."

In those few anxious, interminable moments before the big announcement, the Baylor campus and all of Waco, Texas, came to a standstill. And when the first syllable finally came out of every television set in the region—"Rob-"—it was as if a bomb exploded. The deafening roar. The chaos. The screams. Nobody even heard the rest of the announcement—"-ert Griffin the third!" There were hugs, tears, hands clapping, spontaneous "R-G-3!" chants, and (at least off-campus) beer bottles clicking together. People had packed into their favorite local hangouts to share this moment, crowding around the wall-mounted televisions in Shorty's Pizza Shack on 12th Street, at George's over on Speight Avenue, and at Scruffy Murphy's just down the street. In the Student Union Building on campus, every available television set had an audience of hundreds of students—in the game room, the food court, the student lounge, and the historic Barfield Drawing Room. Within minutes, the celebration spilled out onto the lawns of the campus and the streets of Waco.

It would be a few more days before Griffin could bring the Heisman Trophy back to Waco. The day after the ceremony, Sunday, December 11, was another full one, with a round of interviews in the afternoon and a private dinner with past Heisman winners and their families at Battery Gardens in lower Manhattan. On Monday, Griffin read the "Top 10 List" on *Late Night with David Letterman,* then attended the black-tie Heisman Memorial Trophy Dinner. The Heisman committee had provided Griffin with a limousine, and he invited all his fellow finalists to join him inside.

"It's amazing," he told reporters. "You feel like you're in a movie or a dream. I'm going to wake up and I'll be back in Waco and getting ready for practice, and I'll say, 'Was I asleep for five days?' "

Finally, on Tuesday he boarded a flight home—along with the twenty-five-pound Heisman Trophy, encased in a specially designed gray carrying case. He landed in Waco at 5:20 P.M. and hustled straight to campus for the Bears' 6:00 P.M. practice. He also needed to prepare for a final exam the following day. Throughout the practice, Griffin kept the focus on the field—the Bears were getting ready for their Alamo Bowl matchup against Washington in less than three weeks—but afterward, he stood in the middle of his teammates in his red no-contact practice jersey and thanked them for helping him win the sport's highest individual honor. "We're going to bring the trophy out here," he said, "so everybody can touch it—because it's all of ours."

On December 29, in San Antonio's Alamodome, Griffin led the

Bears to a 67–56 victory over Washington in what was the highest-scoring bowl game in NCAA history. The win gave Baylor just the second 10-win season in the program's 110-year history, and afterward the ubiquitous chant of "R-G-3!" soon morphed into a new one: "One more year! One more year!"

Griffin had been trying to block out the decision he would soon be facing—whether to return to Baylor for his senior year of eligibility or declare for the NFL, where he was projected as a low first-round pick in the upcoming draft—until he got past the Alamo Bowl. But in the locker room after the game, Griffin suddenly broke down in tears, and everyone knew, without his having to say a word, that he had just played his final game in a Baylor uniform.

"I kind of knew after the bowl game," he recalled. "Not that I had done everything I could in college—because you can always do more, unless you win four national titles and four Heisman Trophies and everyone on the team wins trophies as well. But I just felt it was time."

Had one athlete ever done more to lift the fortunes of an entire university? It is difficult to think of one. Before he arrived, the Baylor Bears hadn't had a winning season in thirteen years, hadn't been to a bowl game in fourteen years, hadn't finished a season ranked in the top 25 in twenty-two years, and hadn't had one of their players win the Heisman Trophy since forever. With Griffin at quarterback, they accomplished all four.

And that was just the football program. A few months after Griffin won the Heisman, Baylor athletic director Ian McCaw and some staff members sat at a conference table and tried to do some simple accounting: what impact did Griffin's amazing run to the Heisman have on the university's bottom line?

"We didn't get an exact amount, but we all agreed it's in the hundreds of millions," McCaw said. "The national and international exposure has just been amazing." That gibes with a report in the *Sports Business Journal* that said Baylor had earned an extra $250 million in "extra donations, increased ticket sales, licensing fees, sponsorship deals [and] an expected deal with Fox Sports Southwest," all stemming from the 2011 football season.

On September 15, 2012, the day before Griffin would play his second professional game for the Washington Redskins, groundbreaking ceremonies were held in Waco, near the banks of the Brazos River, for Baylor's new waterfront football stadium, set to open in the fall of 2014—with a pedestrian bridge over the river connecting the stadium to the Baylor campus. The building will be known formally as Baylor Stadium, but around Waco it is more often referred to as "The House That RG3 Built."

Some of the early artist's renderings showed a bronze statue out front. It appeared to be a quarterback who looked a lot like Robert Griffin III, cocking his arm to throw.

NINE

THE PRICE YOU PAY

Thereis such a thing, some psychologists and neuroscientists believe, as athletic intelligence—an ability to see and antici- pate the ever-shifting geometry of the playing field and the defense and to react decisively—that is separate from but no less noble than other forms of intelligence. To watch the great ones play is to know it is true. "Every time a basketball player takes a step," author John McPhee wrote in a 1965 profile of Bill Bradley, "an entire new geometry of action is created around him. In ten seconds, with or without the ball, a good player may see perhaps a hundred alternatives and, from them, make half a dozen choices as he goes along. A great player will see even more alternatives and will make more choices." An NFL quarterback, particularly a mo- bile one, faces perhaps the most complex and dangerous geometry in sports, the possibilities multiplied exponentially by his responsi- bility for the movements of ten teammates and by the permuta- tions stemming from the basic options of handing off, running, or passing. To watch Griffin commanding the position is to under- stand that he is, at least in the athletic sense, some sort of genius.

The first half of Griffin's rookie season in the NFL was defined to a large degree by two running attempts, two moves to the out- side, two instances in which he read the shifting geometry before him and made split-second decisions. This pair of gambles—one that hit big, one that missed badly—would resonate for weeks. In the first instance, against the Atlanta Falcons in Week 5, he smelled the end zone and tried to turn the corner, but the angles closed off on him, until all he could do was duck his head and absorb a skull-rattling hit to the helmet. The result was a concussion that raised anew the old questions of whether Griffin could survive in the NFL with his style of play. ("At this rate," screamed one such USA Today headline after a brutally physical loss to Cincinnati in Week 3, "can Robert Griffin III last the season?") But in the second instance, against the Minnesota Vikings the week after the concussion, he recognized the new geometry, an unexpected radius of green space, created by an overaggressive blitz, and took off on a dazzling, unforgettable sprint down the sideline for a seventy-six-yard touchdown that had even old, grizzled observers of the NFL picking their jaws up off the floor.

The risk and the reward. The pain and the payoff. This was the new normal for the Redskins and their fans. Every time number 10 had the ball in his hands, there was the potential for either extreme. The only thing you knew for certain was that you could not afford to miss a single play.

In these weeks, too, we saw this central paradox play out in Griffin himself. The scary hits humbled him, but the touchdowns emboldened him. Especially after the concussion, he said all the right things about protecting himself from danger, but then his competitiveness would get the best of him and he would launch himself recklessly into a defender or two in the name of gaining a critical first down. Sliding or ducking out of bounds was fine on first-and-10, but on third-and-2, he was hell-bent on getting to that first-down marker. At Baylor, Coach Art Briles sometimes called Griffin the "Rubberband Man" because, when contact was inevitable, he could contort his body in such a way as to avoid the brunt of the hit. And now, in the NFL, Griffin seemed to assume that this ability would always protect him, even though the defenders were bigger and faster.

"In high school, I just ran," he said in September. "Guys were a lot smaller. In college, [the coaches] tried to temper that down. Coach [Briles] taught me to get what I can, but protect myself when I get down. That's how I've become pretty good at avoiding hits, or avoiding the bigger hits. There were a couple times [the Redskins' opponents] were leading with their helmets and I had to dodge them. That's just something I've become accustomed to—being able to move my body that way."

It was curious the way Griffin often seemed to go out of his way to paint himself as a tough guy. "In college we said all the time, 'Tough guys have to be tough guys,'" he said at one point. "You can't just talk tough and play soft." He reveled in the praise heaped on him by opponents, such as when Bengals defensive end Michael Johnson—having sacked Griffin three times and hit him hard several other times—marveled, "I tip my hat to Robert Griffin. That guy is tough. He kept fighting and battling. He's a true competitor." Even Griffin's commercials played into the myth-making: "Greatness is not given," he said in one Gatorade spot. "Greatness is taken, when the weak and distracted are resting on their reputations." In a promotional video for Evoshield, maker of the rib-protector pads he has worn since his Baylor days, Griffin at one point says, "It makes you feel fearless out there, to where you could run into any kind of hit and not be bothered. I don't suggest that, but it's still good that you're protected that way."

It all added up to a treasure trove of data points for the armchair psychologists out there—at least the ones who weren't too blinded by the sheer spectacle of Griffin to notice. What was behind Griffin's need for validation as a tough guy? Could it be a quest for acceptance from his father? An overcompensation for those years of being teased as a mama's boy? Whatever the case, something kept pushing Griffin to the brink, and even when he recognized the danger, he couldn't bring himself to pull back.

In the early part of the Redskins' season, the danger confronting Griffin quickly moved from the realm of the theoretical to that of the tangible as the hits got harder and more frequent. A feeling began to grow among fans and the media that the pattern was untenable. Something had to give, and the hope was that it wouldn't be Griffin's body. The Week 1 upset of the Saints in New Orleans, with Griffin throwing for 320 yards and a pair of touchdowns in his NFL debut, might have altered the dynamic and raised expectations for both Griffin and the Redskins, but reality soon came crashing down on them.

While Griffin was the talk of the NFL after Week 1—with a piece of hardware to go along with it as the league's Offensive Player of the Week—the St. Louis Rams, Washington's opponent in Week 2, seemed to take all the hype personally. When the teams met at the Edward Jones Dome in St. Louis on September 16 (a game billed in some media reports as a referendum on the March trade between the Rams and Redskins that allowed the latter to draft Griffin), the Rams were determined not to let the rookie carve them up the way he had the Saints. Their solution was to hit him—often and hard, and sometimes after the whistle.

"If he's going to tuck it and run it, and certainly Bob Griffin can do that, you want to make it a cumulative toll," defensive end Chris Long said. "If he's going to tuck it and run it, we're going to hit him." Added linebacker Jo-Lonn Dunbar: "If he's going to run, you want to lay hacks on him. That's what you have to do with a guy like that."

The game was intensely physical, and the NFL's "replacement" referees—subbing for the locked-out regular officials, who were embroiled in a labor dispute with the league—at times came close to losing control of the game. Griffin bore the brunt of the Rams' brutality. At one point, a Rams defender taunted Griffin after a hit, saying, "We're going to hit you every play."

"Isn't this football?" Griffin shot back.

Griffin still passed for 206 yards and a touchdown and ran for 82 yards and two more scores (with much of his rushing yardage coming on designed runs such as quarterback draws), and he very nearly pulled off a last-minute comeback—marching the Redskins from their own 37 to the St. Louis 36, needing a field goal to tie, before wide receiver Josh Morgan torpedoed the drive with an ill-timed unsportsmanlike conduct penalty for throwing the ball at an opponent. As the final seconds ticked down on the Redskins' 31–28 loss, Griffin was the only teammate to go anywhere near the despondent Morgan on the Redskins' bench and comfort him with some words of encouragement: "Keep your head up and keep going."

After the game, Redskins coach Mike Shanahan appeared to accuse the Rams of taking some cheap shots at Griffin's expense—and the replacement referees of facilitating it: "This is the NFL," Shanahan said. "Everybody is trying to get after the quarterback. But this was to a different level today. It was not your typical NFL game today. It was not something that you're very proud of."

Griffin himself would echo those comments a few days later, saying, "They were doing a lot of dirty things. It was definitely unprofessional, and it does need to be cleaned up." He even invoked the Saints' "Bountygate" scandal, saying, "I don't want to tiptoe the lines of anything that's happened with bounties or anything like that, but they were definitely going after me. Some of the shots were cheap."

Predictably, Griffin's comments didn't go over very well in St. Louis ("It's not the Big 12," scoffed Rams running back Steven Jackson) or around the league. Rookies with two games' worth of NFL experience typically don't go around criticizing the referees or accusing opponents of dirty play. It was a rare PR misstep for a player who almost always seemed to say the right thing.

At the very least, the Redskins by that point were painfully aware of the target on the back of their young quarterback. But if anything, they exposed him to an even greater degree of risk the following week against Cincinnati, in the Redskins' home opener. It was a brutally physical game, with the Bengals' defense knocking Griffin to the ground a total of twenty-eight times in the Redskins' 38–31 loss—including hits on pass plays, run plays, and even after he handed the ball off. After one sack of Griffin, Johnson, the Bengals' defensive end, reached down and picked him up off the turf, saying, "Get up." Griffin didn't say a word in response.

"A lot of teams think if they hit the quarterback enough, eventually he'll stop coming after you," Griffin said. "I just want everyone to know that's never going to happen. One thing I won't do personally is quit or play scared. I've never played scared in my life."

At one point in the third quarter, when Griffin tried to score on a keeper by extending the ball out toward the pylon, he was knocked dizzy by a vicious hit and was slow to get up. Though he stayed in the game, with the Redskins scoring on the next play on an Alfred Morris run, when he got to the sideline he was tested for concussion symptoms. (The Redskins said later that he passed.)

"I thought it was a touchdown [on the keeper], and I got up to celebrate, [but] everything on the left was on the right and everything on the right was on the left, so I just fell back down and took a second," Griffin said. "I stood up and I was fine. They tried to check me and see if I had a concussion, but I didn't have a concussion. I was just a little bit dizzy—nothing to worry about."

Still, the Bengals game exposed something of a rift between the Griffin camp and the Shanahans over the Redskins' play-calling. There was little question Griffin was being exposed to an alarming number of hits. "Ridiculous," one person close to him put it when the subject was raised after the Bengals game. A microphone from NFL Films also picked up Griffin on the Redskins' sideline, imploring his teammates to keep fighting, "no matter what Coach calls"—implying some dissent. But in public, Griffin, the good soldier, was always careful with his words.

"It's football," he shrugged after the Bengals game. "There's not a person in the league that says, 'Hey, sign me up for a car accident every play.' But we know what we signed up for. There's going to be hitting going on."

However, plenty of people outside the organization were taking issue with Griffin's exposure to risk in the Redskins' new offense. Through three games, Griffin had already amassed thirty-two rushing attempts—by far the most of any quarterback in the league at that point, and more than three times as many as Michael Vick had after the first three games of his own NFL career.

"Just because a guy's athletic doesn't mean he has to run all the time," former Redskins kick returner Brian Mitchell said on the team's official postgame radio show the night of the Bengals loss. "I think when you look at it like that, it comes down to the laziness of the coach. [Griffin] is a better passer than a runner, okay? And I know Robert is going to do everything you ask him to do to help the team win. But you have to eliminate the risk of him getting hurt. And yes, he's going to run the ball sometimes. But if he's going to run the ball when he needs to, and you're going to add another ten to fifteen planned runs, you're asking for something to go wrong. He cannot take that many hits."

Steve Czaban, a sports-talk host on WTEM (ESPN 980)—the Redskins' flagship station, owned by Daniel Snyder's Red Zebra Broadcasting—went even further, opining on his blog, "Mike Shanahan clearly doesn't give two shits about possibly totaling his brand new Ferrari of a QB in Robert Griffin III. [This offense] is going to kill our star QB, a guy the same geniuses surrendered four draft picks to get."

Still, in the one place where Griffin looked for validation, the place where folks' opinions actually mattered to him—the Redskins' locker room—his valiant play had the desired effect. There was a growing sense of awe among Griffin's teammates at both his ability and his fortitude.

"Every Monday we come in here, and I'm just kind of looking at him out of the corner of my eye, making sure he's okay," left guard Kory Lichtensteiger told the Associated Press. "He's a tough guy, and he's not going to complain about it. But you don't like seeing your quarterbacks, especially a guy that's carrying the load like he is, take those kind of hits."

"You've got so many people talking about the quarterback getting hit, and I've known quarterbacks in the past who would say, 'Yeah, I'm getting hit too much,'" said backup lineman Jordan Black. "But this dude, he's not talking about getting hit—he's talking about getting up after he's hit. I know he did take a lot of hits [in the Cincinnati game], but we came back on Monday, and when we were running one-hundred-yard sprints or whatever, he was leading the pack the entire way. You expect a guy who's taken some shots maybe to have some soreness, but that guy was out there running better than everybody."

The lingering impression from the first three games of the Redskins' season was of a brilliant quarterback who was more or less on his own out there. Griffin was naked, with precious little in the way of protection. He was without his best receiver—Pierre Garcon missed both the Rams and Bengals games with a foot injury—and his left tackle, Trent Williams, was compromised by a knee injury and missed big chunks of the Bengals game. Meanwhile, his defense was basically nonexistent, having allowed 30-plus points in each of the Redskins' first three games.

In a sense, you couldn't blame Mike and Kyle Shanahan for

putting the team's fortunes in Griffin's hands. He was by far their best shot—if not their only shot—at winning.

Griffin learned—the hard way—one valuable bit of information during the Bengals game: if he faked keeping the ball, he could still be hit after he handed off to his running back. Of course, the fact that it took him that long to understand something so important brings up an even bigger, more alarming question: how was it that the starting quarterback of the Washington Redskins was allowed to play two full games (and three in the preseason) without being informed of a rule that might have helped keep him safe?

"I thought they were not legal hits, but Coach informed me that technically [defenders] can hit me," Griffin said a few days after the Bengals game. "Now, they're not supposed to hit me in the head, but they can hit me if I'm carrying out the fake. I didn't know that, so I guess I'll just be running with my arms up a lot more, letting [the defense] know, 'Hey, I don't have the ball. Please hit me if you want to get a fifteen-yard [penalty]."

In any case, before the Redskins' game at Tampa Bay on September 30 at Raymond James Stadium, Griffin made a point of clarifying the rule with the referee—that weekend marking the return of the NFL's regular officials, who earlier in the week had struck a labor deal that ended the contentious lockout—and then followed through by raising his arms in a "not me" gesture after he handed the ball off. At one point, when he forgot to do so, the referee reminded him, and Griffin said, "Yes, sir. I'll do it next time." Griffin noticed a difference with the regular refs on the field, a higher degree of control over the physicality of the game, and he was knocked to the ground only ten times the entire game, or eighteen fewer than in the Cincinnati game the week before.

The Tampa Bay game was most notable for producing the first fourth-quarter, game-winning drive of Griffin's career—one that came with an unusually high degree of difficulty after Griffin's headset went out during the drive (a curious bit of timing that the Redskins were convinced was the result of sabotage on the part of the home team). Here, an important bit of crisis management planning came in handy. Once a week in practice, during their two-minute drill, the Redskins simulate a headset malfunction: when this happens, either plays have to come from the sideline via hand signals or Griffin has to call them himself.

Suitably prepared, Griffin handled the difficult situation with remarkable poise. Down a point, with 1:42 left on the clock, the ball on the Redskins' 20, and only one time-out remaining, he marched the Redskins 56 yards on 7 plays—running the no-huddle offense to near-perfection, completing all four of his passes on the drive (not counting an intentional spike to stop the clock), and also scrambling 15 yards for another critical first down—to put the Redskins in field goal range for Billy Cundiff's 41-yard game-winner. Watching from one knee on the Redskins' sideline, Griffin sprang to his feet as the kick sailed through the goalposts, then sprinted onto the field with his teammates.

And so Griffin came out of Week 4 with a 2-2 record and the fourth-best passer rating in the NFL (ahead of Tom Brady and Aaron Rodgers, among others) as the Redskins approached their toughest test of the young season—a Falcons team that was 47-21 during the Matt Ryan era, including a perfect 4-0 to that point in

2012. It was the start of a dangerous stretch of schedule: three of the Redskins' four October opponents had made the playoffs in 2011, including the Super Bowl champion New York Giants.

(More to Griffin's liking was the relaxation in October of the league's draconian uniform policies: during Breast Cancer Awareness Month, players were allowed to wear hot-pink shoes and accessories. Never one to shy away from a fashion statement, Griffin dialed up the pinkaliciousness. His game-day getup for the Falcons game on October 7 included pink cleats, a pink hand towel, a pink sleeve and glove on his left arm, and a pink skullcap holding his braids in place. It was in keeping with Griffin's penchant for individual expressions of in-game fashion. Once, when he was asked why he wore the sleeve on his left arm, he quoted an old Deion Sanders line: "When you look good, you feel good, and when you feel good, you play good.")

Everything was going fine—which is to say, Griffin and the Redskins were holding their own against the Falcons' excellent defense—until the Redskins' second drive of the third quarter. The Redskins had moved deep into Falcons territory, in a 7–7 game, and were facing a third-and-goal from Atlanta's 3, when Griffin dropped back to pass. Feeling the pocket collapsing, he sprinted out to the right, trying to buy some more time, but with Falcons defensive tackle Jonathan Babineaux in pursuit, he suddenly tucked the ball and tried to run to the corner of the end zone, a blur of burgundy and gold with neon-pink streaks.

He never got there. From Griffin's left came Falcons linebacker Sean Weatherspoon, at a full sprint, closing in at a sharp angle. Griffin saw him the entire way and could have ducked out of bounds and avoided a hit altogether—but to do so would have meant settling for a field goal, and so Griffin tried to beat Weatherspoon to the right pylon. Finally, as Griffin saw he couldn't make it, he tried to slide to avoid the hit. But it was too late. Weatherspoon lowered his shoulder, with 244 pounds of hurtling mass colliding directly into Griffin's helmet—a clean, legal hit, but one that left Griffin sprawled out, facedown on the turf near the 5-yard line.

"If I had slid a half-second earlier," Griffin later lamented, "I would have been safe. In the future, looking back on it—hindsight is twenty-twenty—I would have either thrown it away or gotten out of bounds."

Team trainers got Griffin to his feet and got him off the field, but it was clear he was not right. After stitching up a gash on Griffin's chin, the medical staff took him to a small shed behind the bench that served as an observation room for injured players and peppered him with questions from the NFL's Standardized Concussion Assessment Tool (SCAT) that he suddenly couldn't answer: Where are we? What quarter are we in? Who scored last in the game?

When Mike Shanahan was informed that Griffin had failed the concussion test, he came over to check on him, and Griffin said, "I'm fine, Coach."

"No," Shanahan told him, taking note of the glassy look in his eyes, "you're not."

Within minutes, Griffin was walking to the locker room, accompanied by a team doctor, raising his hand dutifully to high-five the fans leaning over the railing above the tunnel. His helmet was nowhere to be seen. His parents hustled down to see him in the locker room. It was some fifteen minutes after the concussion, and Griffin was telling everyone—his parents, the doctors, the trainers—that he was fine, going into great detail as he described the play and the game situation, in a futile attempt to convince the medical staff that he had all his faculties and should be allowed to go back in the game.

"It's too late," they told him. "Shower up and watch the rest of the game."

"You want to play," Griffin explained later, "and your survival instincts take over. It just shows that I care about this team and I didn't want to leave them hanging."

The Redskins wound up losing, 24–17—the team's eighth straight home loss, dating to October 2011—with backup quarterback Kirk Cousins throwing one touchdown pass but also a pair of late, ugly interceptions. In the locker room afterward, teammates came up to offer encouragement to Griffin. And to each one, he replied with an apology:

"I'm sorry, man," he told them. "I feel like I let you all down."

For obvious reasons, the NFL had a particular interest in how its concussion protocols were followed—or, a cynic might say, how its concussion protocols were *perceived* to be followed—during the 2012 season. Under fire for turning a blind eye to the concussion problem for years (as recently as 2009 it denied the existence of a link between football and brain injuries), the league had issued new guidelines on how to diagnose, treat, and monitor concussed players, and it went to great lengths to enforce the guidelines.

The Redskins' handling of Griffin's concussion drew at least one red flag from the league, which fined the team $20,000 for hiding the concussion announcement from the media. (Team officials had announced in the press box that Griffin had been "shaken up" and that his return was "questionable." The NFL's concern was that, by falsely reporting the injury, the Redskins theoretically could have tried to circumvent the rule forbidding a concussed player to return to the game.) Some in the medical community also took issue with Shanahan's using the term "mild concussion" to describe Griffin's condition to the media immediately after the game—there being no such thing, most experts agree, as a "mild" concussion. The Redskins largely shrugged off the criticism.

The more pressing concern around Redskins Park, of course, was whether Griffin would be able to play the following Sunday against the Minnesota Vikings. Per NFL rules, he wasn't allowed to practice or speak to the media until being cleared by both a team doctor and an independent neurologist. That clearance came on Wednesday, a day that began with Griffin standing before the entire team prior to practice and repeating his apology for letting his teammates down in the Atlanta game.

"I promise I won't let it happen again," he said. "I'm not going to leave you hanging."

At one point during the practice that followed, Griffin ducked out of bounds on a keeper, and immediately the rest of the team broke into sarcastic applause, drawing a sheepish grin from the rookie quarterback. When he met with the media afterward, he acknowledged that he was still learning where to draw the line between staying safe and staying aggressive.

The concussion "doesn't make you less aggressive, but it is a learning lesson," he said. "The one thing I learned was, I can't do that to my team, to the fans, or to my family, because life is more important than the game of football. I have to make sure I keep myself safe while still being the same player that I am. . . . It's not about being soft. I don't have anything to prove to anybody. The team has let me know that. Everyone knows I'm a tough guy. I promised I'd get up from hits like that, and I did get up. I kept that promise."

Later, however, Griffin seemed to show a total disregard for the seriousness of the situation, saying, "I still refuse to say I had a concussion. I had temporary memory loss." He joked that his only symptom was "irritability"—because the doctors kept "asking me the same questions."

And so the Redskins' tough-guy quarterback, evidently recovered from his non-concussion-related bout of temporary memory loss, was cleared to play against the Vikings—over the objections of some in the media who argued that Griffin should have been held out a week for his own protection. As late as the Fox-TV pregame show just prior to the kickoff of the Vikings game, analyst Howie Long was arguing in favor of benching Griffin.

Perhaps because everyone was watching so carefully now, it appeared that Griffin was playing smarter against the Vikings. He slid to avoid one hit. He ducked out of bounds to avoid another. He threw one ball away—drawing a roughing-the-quarterback penalty when the defender hit him after he let go of the ball. It was a clinic in how a mobile quarterback could survive in the NFL. (Of course, it should be pointed out that none of those acts of self-preservation came at a point, such as the one against Atlanta, where a few extra yards were crucial to the Redskins' fortunes. At one point early in the fourth quarter, the Redskins led by 19 points.)

And then it happened.

Less than three minutes remained in the game, and the Red-skins had the ball following a Vikings touchdown that had trimmed Washington's once-commanding lead to 31–26. The teams were coming out of a time-out called by the Vikings moments before. It was third-and-6, the ball resting on the Redskins' 24—a danger-ous situation, since the Vikings would have plenty of time left for a game-winning drive if the Redskins were forced to punt. "Some-body's got to make a play," veteran receiver Santana Moss said in the Redskins' huddle.

The play-call was a pass designed to pick up the first down, with both outside receivers running "out" routes toward the side-lines. But Griffin, from the pistol formation, could also see two Vikings linebackers cheating up, showing blitz. With a six-man rush, he knew he might be able to get into the secondary and pick up the first down with his legs. And when he saw both blitzers come through the same hole—the "A" gap between the center and right guard—he took off. One blitzing linebacker dove at his an-kles and missed as Griffin went past, and the other was picked off nicely on a block by running back Evan Royster.

Now Griffin headed toward the Redskins' sideline, where re-ceiver Josh Morgan had sealed the corner with a nice block and a jumble of shouts from his teammates was merging into a delirious cacophony. Some were shouting at him to get out of bounds—to protect himself. ("I thought about getting out of bounds," he joked later, "because everyone has been telling me that lately.") Others were yelling for him to get down—in order to keep the clock run-ning. But as Griffin high-stepped to avoid a diving tackle by safety

Harrison Smith, the last defender to have a good shot at him, those shouts suddenly coalesced into one chorus: "Go! Go! Go!"

All that was left was a footrace—Griffin, with a five-yard lead, chased by Vikings safety Jamarca Sanford. And it was no contest. The 2008 Big 12 conference champion in the 400-meter hurdles toyed with his pursuer, casting a couple of long, playful glances behind him at Sanford. Put a stopwatch on Griffin and it would show he ran those final 40 yards in 4.08 seconds.

He crossed the goal line and kept going, across the back of the end zone and toward the retaining wall of the stands—whereupon he leaped headlong into the arms of a group of fans, who tugged on Griffin's jersey to pull him up to a seated position. If it seemed as if he stayed there a few moments too long, it was because the fans wouldn't let go of him. Every newspaper in the region the next morning had a picture on its front page of Griffin engulfed by shrieking, delirious Redskins fans in the front row—at least the second iconic image of him so far that season, joining the "Griffin-ing" pose on the floor of the Superdome in the New Orleans game.

When the Redskins' 38–26 win was complete—snapping that ugly eight-game losing streak at FedEx Field—Griffin had rushed for 138 yards, a total surpassed in NFL history by only two other quarterbacks. Six games into his NFL career, he already owned a touchdown pass of 88 yards and a touchdown run of 76 yards—no other player in history had two such scores of 75 yards or longer in the same season.

After the game, one Vikings player was frantically searching for Griffin amid the chaos. It was Adrian Peterson, the great running back—who was back this season after a warp-speed rehab from knee surgery the previous December and who would wind up being voted the league's MVP at the end of the year. On this day, he had been outrushed by the Redskins' rookie quarterback by nearly 60 yards. Finding Griffin near midfield, Peterson grabbed him around the neck and said, "You have the heart of a champion."

In a raucous Redskins locker room, there were shouts of "Black Jesus!"—a new nickname his teammates had coined for Griffin—and then Mike Shanahan stepped to the center of the room to hand out game balls. "Robert," he said, tossing a ball at Griffin, "that was one heck of a job."

Over the course of seven days, the Redskins and their fans had experienced the worst and the best of life with RG3 as their quarterback—the sobering image of his crumpled, brain-rattled body on the turf, and the sight of him exploding across that same turf a week later. One was an image you tried to push out of your mind. The other was one you wanted to keep forever. It was a moment, and Griffin was a quarterback, you wanted to wrap your arms around and never let go of.

TEN

THE LEADER OF MEN

The patch was about four inches tall, a white "C" above four stars, sewn onto Robert Griffin III's jersey in mid-November—a few days after his teammates voted him a team captain and a few days before the Washington Redskins' game on November 18 against the Philadelphia Eagles. The work was done by a tailor at Central Cleaners in Falls Church, Virginia, a mom-and-pop operation with whom the Redskins contract their uniform-tailoring. Because this was Griffin's first year as a captain, the tailor knew to make only one of the four stars a gold one. In subsequent years, more white stars would turn to gold, until by year four all four stars, as well as the "C" itself, would be gold—as they were on the jersey of linebacker London Fletcher, the Redskins' longest-serving captain in 2012.

The first time Griffin laid eyes on his new captain's patch was when he walked into the Redskins' locker room at FedEx Field the morning of the Eagles game and spotted his jersey hanging in his locker. For this son of two Army sergeants, who had been taught to understand the concepts of duty, honor, and leadership at an early age, the symbolism of that small patch resonated deeply.

"It means a lot," he said. "I'm a twenty-two-year-old kid to most of these [teammates], so for them to vote me as their captain shows that they truly believe in me as their leader. To have that 'C' on your chest means something."

In one sense, it was an extraordinary gesture on the part of Griffin's teammates. Nobody—not even Mike Shanahan, who had worked in the NFL since 1984—could recall another instance of a rookie being named a team captain. But the most amazing thing about Griffin's captaincy was how much of a slam-dunk it was. Indeed, the vote had only confirmed the obvious: just nine games into Griffin's NFL career, the Redskins were already very much his team. And it wasn't only his physical ability or the position he played that made it so: increasingly—especially on offense, but throughout the entire locker room as well—the Redskins were taking their cues from the twenty-two-year-old rookie with the preternatural presence.

"He's six or seven years ahead of what I've seen from anyone in our locker room in terms of his status in the locker room, his ability to control a football team, his leadership," veteran tight end Chris Cooley said around this time. "If you forget for a second that he's a rookie, it doesn't mean anything to you. You're like, 'Yeah, this guy is awesome. He's the leader.' But then you step back and think, he's only twenty-two [and] he's been in the NFL for six months. I mean, it blows me away."

The timing of Griffin's ascension to captain status came at a critical point in the Redskins' season. If ever there was a time when the team needed some leadership, it was at that very moment. Heading into the Eagles game, the Redskins were coming off three consecutive losses that had dropped their record to 3-6, and with a bye in Week 10, they had two full weeks in which to stew over their gruesome collapse and the attendant palace intrigue that had sprung up around it. The entire season was very much on the verge of collapse, with most of the scrutiny from fans and media focused squarely on head coach Mike Shanahan, who, following a 21–13 home loss to the Carolina Panthers in Week 9, had acknowledged in strikingly blunt terms the team's seeming hopelessness. The Redskins, Shanahan said, were now "playing to see who . . . is going to be your football team for years to come"—comments that were widely interpreted as his having given up on the rest of the season.

For Griffin, though, the captaincy was the natural continuation of the leadership roles he had assumed at Copperas Cove High and at Baylor, as well as a validation of the subtle but assertive approach to leadership he took upon joining the Redskins. He had come to Washington with a game plan, but the plan was to have no plan— or at least not one that was obvious. In the NFL, a wannabe-leader, a climber, a fraud, can be sniffed out from a mile away. Griffin knew from the beginning that he needed to make the Redskins his team—to mold it to his will, to instill his battle-tested beliefs and values—but that he had to do it the right way: slowly, organically, respectfully. There was a tradition to uphold, a protocol to follow—he was a rookie, after all, even if he had been anointed as the face of the franchise before taking his first snap—and Griffin, largely owing to his upbringing, possessed a deep and innate understanding of the right way to do things.

"My strategy was to come in and try to lead by example first," Griffin recalled. "You do it one step at a time. I tried to make sure I came in and showed them, first, the kind of player I am, the kind of person I am—my work ethic and how hard I work. The one thing you can't do as a leader is come out and say that you're a leader."

To all who knew him, Griffin possessed something difficult to define—a power of belief, relentless and infectious, that swept up everyone who had the good fortune of being on his side. Troy Vital, the Copperas Cove running back, saw it that night in the 2007 Texas high school playoff game when Griffin willed the Bulldawgs out of a hopeless fourth-quarter hole and all the way to victory by getting his teammates to believe they could do it. His Baylor teammates witnessed it over the course of his four years there as he vowed to turn the school's moribund football program into a powerhouse—and then went out and did it.

"People started to believe in him at Baylor—believing what he was saying about turning it around," his mother, Jacqueline Griffin, explained. "And that's what he knew he was going to do in Washington."

All the way back in July, when someone had asked Griffin what part of his game would translate best in the NFL—the obvious choices being his drop-back passing game, his running ability, or perhaps his familiarity with the zone-read option—he instead said, "The ability to lead." But for a twenty-two-year-old rookie to step into a locker room full of crusty veterans, some of them ten years older—and many of them set in their ways, accustomed to losing, and playing for the paycheck, having long since lost the passion of youth—and get them all to believe in him?

"It's an unbelievably hard thing to do," Cooley said. "I don't think he came in and in his mind said, 'I have to make everyone believe in me.' I think he came in and said, 'I believe in myself, and I'm going to do what I do best.' And the rest just falls into place. . . . His expectation of winning and playing great is a huge influence in here. It's been a drastic change of culture, and you could say Robert has been the biggest part of that. He's a natural leader. When he talks, people listen—and people believe."

But the Redskins' plight in November 2012 was going to test even Griffin's leadership skills and powers of belief. How did they ever get to this awful place—stuck in last place in the NFC East with a 3-6 record, and with confidence at its lowest all season—and how in the world could they get out?

Each of the three straight losses that had sunk the Redskins to 3-6 had its own narrative, its own deep underpinnings, and its own stench. But taken as a whole, these losses painted a picture of a franchise in seeming disarray, with too little talent and too little depth surrounding its brilliant rookie quarterback, too few building blocks for the future, and no obvious path toward getting better anytime soon—partly because of its lack of first-round draft picks in 2013 and 2014, courtesy of the trade that brought Griffin to Washington.

A 27–23 loss to the New York Giants in Week 7 had exposed the Redskins' deficiencies in the secondary, as the game turned on a no-way-that-just-happened 77-yard touchdown pass from Giants quarterback Eli Manning to receiver Victor Cruz in the final 30 seconds—made possible by the type of epic breakdown in the defensive backfield that was becoming all too common for the

Redskins. Just moments before, Griffin had led the Redskins on a 7-play, 77-yard touchdown drive for what should have been the winning score—highlighted by a remarkable, scrambling 19-yard completion to tight end Logan Paulsen on a fourth-and-10 and capped by a perfectly thrown 30-yard feather pillow of a touchdown pass to Santana Moss.

Had cornerback Josh Wilson and safety Madieu Williams not botched the coverage on the Manning-to-Cruz miracle, the entire league would have been talking about Griffin's game-winning drive, and how he had gone into the home of the defending Super Bowl champs in his seventh NFL start and outdueled the two-time Super Bowl MVP. As it was, even in their victory the Giants understood the implications of what they had just witnessed out of the Redskins' rookie quarterback—a guy they would be facing twice a year for the next ten years or so.

"That guy is flat-out unbelievable, man," Giants defensive end Osi Umenyiora said of Griffin, shaking his head in awe. "I'm not gonna lie. That's the best quarterback we've played this year."

Griffin "takes away from your enthusiasm for the game a little bit," said Giants defensive end Justin Tuck. "I'm really mad at the football gods for putting him in the NFC East." Later, Tuck would say of Griffin, "Until I exit stage right, it seems like he's going to be a fixture in my dreams and nightmares."

A 27–12 loss at Pittsburgh in Week 8, meantime, highlighted the limitations of the Redskins' receiving corps. Especially without Pierre Garcon, whose foot injury kept him out of his third straight game, and tight end Fred Davis, who was lost for the season after tearing his Achilles tendon the week before against the Giants,

Griffin had a critical shortage of playmakers around him, and on a day like that one at Heinz Field, when his receivers dropped no fewer than ten passes that hit them in the hands—resulting in the lowest completion percentage (47.1) he would post all season—it was downright impossible to win.

And what were we to make of the Shanahans' play-call on a third-and-4 late in the second quarter? Perhaps recalling the trick play that Griffin and Baylor buddy Kendall Wright ran at the end of their Pro Day showcase in Waco back in March (a key fact about that play: there was no defense on the field at the time), the Redskins' brain trust had Griffin hand off to receiver Josh Morgan, then drift down the left sideline as the targeted receiver for a long pass from Morgan. Bad idea. What, Griffin wasn't absorbing enough hits on his designed runs and his drop-back passes, so now you needed to send him into the Steelers' defensive backfield unprotected? Sure enough, Griffin absorbed a stinging hit from Steelers safety Ryan Clark—and also got flagged for offensive pass interference—on what was an absolute train wreck of a play, one that did not sit well with the Griffin camp.

"After looking at that play, you feel like a complete dumbshit," Mike Shanahan said the next day. "Usually, against the right defense—which is man coverage—nobody accounts for the quarterback and he's by himself out there."

The Redskins might have hoped the Steelers loss was their rock bottom—dropping them to 3-5 at the halfway point of the season—but there was still another level below that, as the Redskins discovered in an ugly 21–13 home loss on November 4 to the Carolina Panthers, who had carried a 1-6 record into the game.

The day was billed as "Homecoming" at FedEx Field, and nearly two hundred Redskins alumni—many of them in wheelchairs, using walkers, or just lurching around on battered and surgically repaired legs—were honored before the game, while the current Redskins were decked out in snazzy 1937 throwback uniforms and helmets. The game was also notable for its much-hyped matchup of Griffin against Carolina counterpart Cam Newton—who won the Heisman Trophy the year before Griffin and who was the NFL quarterback, along with Philadelphia's Michael Vick, to whom Griffin was most frequently compared. On the Wednesday before the game, having finally grown weary of the questions about Newton, Griffin said, "I'd rather be compared to Aaron Rodgers, or a guy like that, someone who has won Super Bowls"—a comment that was taken in some corners as a slap at Newton, but that really only spoke to Griffin's preference for championships over flashy statistics.

The turning point in the game very well may have come on a fourth-and-goal for the Redskins at the Panthers' 2-yard line late in the second quarter, already trailing 7–3—and again, the play-call was one that left the Shanahans open to criticism. From the pistol formation, Griffin took the snap and sprinted to the right. There was no deception on the play, no play-action, no pass option, no pitch option. Alfred Morris, the Redskins' hard-nosed rookie running back who had already rushed for thirty yards on the drive, wasn't even on the field. It was just a straight quarterback keeper, with backup running back Evan Royster the lead blocker. But Griffin never got close to the end zone and in fact didn't even make it back to the line of scrimmage before getting stretched out and smothered by three Panthers defenders—a terrible way to end a sixteen-play drive. After Newton promptly drove the Panthers ninety-eight yards the other way for a touchdown, the Panthers had a 14–3 lead.

Afterward, it was revealed that Griffin had suffered a rib injury in the first quarter, which had been deemed bad enough to require X-rays at halftime (though they were negative). All of which, of course, led to the question: Why would the Redskins ask Griffin to try to bang it into the end zone on a fourth-and-goal from the 2-yard line, especially on a play-call straight out of some 1930s single-wing playbook, when he was dealing with serious pain in his ribs? How much more of this could he take?

The answer: more than you would think. Late in the game, with the Redskins now down 21–6 and facing another fourth down, Griffin dropped back to pass, saw an opening over the middle, and took off running—only to find his path cut off by three Panthers defenders as he approached the first-down marker. His solution was to launch himself headlong into them, initiating a brutal collision that knocked one Panthers defender's helmet loose and sent Griffin spinning sideways through the air, helicopter-style—not unlike that famous John Elway play in Super Bowl XXXII that the seven-year-old Griffin had tried to emulate in his front yard.

Asked about the helicopter launch on the fourth-and-4 run late in the game, Griffin answered matter-of-factly. "If it's fourth-and-four, it's worth anything," he explained. "That's the way I looked at it. If it was the first quarter and it was third-and-three at the third-yard marker and there was a couple guys there, I would've slid or just gotten down. [But] it was a fourth-down play, and we needed a first down. You make that decision in the heat of the moment. . . . Guys see that—they see their quarterback putting it on [the] line every single play, [and] it makes them want to put it on the line every single play. So it's more about inspiring guys, and no matter what the score is, no matter what the down and distance is, we can make it happen."

Sore ribs and all, Griffin got the first down, which was all that mattered to him. Sliding short of the first-down marker in order to protect yourself was for lesser humans—or perhaps for the first quarter.

Once again, his teammates seemed in awe of Griffin's competitiveness and fortitude. "You don't see too many quarterbacks giving themselves up like that," fullback Darrel Young said. "He competes. It's what he does every play. Even when we're down, he comes in [the huddle] and says, 'C'mon, guys, this is what we need to do. We can do this.' Eighteen seconds left on the clock, and he's like, 'We've got a chance.' He's special."

After the game, Griffin undressed at his locker slowly and gingerly. A single Band-Aid covered a gash on his midsection, right above where his left kidney resides. If this was how he looked as a twenty-two-year-old with nine NFL games under his belt, how was he going to look at season's end? How about after three years of this? How about ten years? Would he be one of those busted-up ex-Redskins staggering around FedEx Field on Homecoming Day, balancing himself on his cane with one hand and waving to the crowd with the other when his name was announced?

It was 4:26 P.M. on November 4, a few minutes after the end of the Carolina game, when Mike Shanahan stepped behind the lectern in the Redskins' interview room in the bowels of FedEx Field. His white, long-sleeved Redskins pullover set off the bright red of his face. He fidgeted with the microphone that sat before him. He touched his nose and pursed his lips when the first question came—"Where do the Redskins go from here?"—then shifted his gaze from the questioner to the back wall, letting his eyes drift aimlessly as he spoke in a voice that was hoarse and lifeless.

"When you lose a game like [this], now you're playing to see who, obviously, is going to be on your football team for years to come," said Shanahan. "Now we've got a chance to evaluate players and see where we're at. Obviously, we're not out of [the playoff race] statistically, but now we find out what type of character we've got, and how guys keep on fighting through the rest of the season."

Media members glanced at each other, then took out their smartphones and started tweeting furiously. Did Shanahan really just say that? Was he giving up on the season—just nine games in? It certainly sounded that way, and in the hours and days that followed those comments would be scrutinized, dissected, debated, criticized, defended, and backed away from. It would be two weeks until the Redskins played another game, and the bye week now had its story line—one that revolved around a head coach who was 14-27 since arriving in Washington.

In the Redskins' locker room, players were blindsided when Shanahan's comments were relayed to them. "I'm not thinking about next year," special teams captain Lorenzo Alexander told the *Washington Post*. "That's an off-season thing for me. But you know it's hard when you see yourself in that type of position and your head coach is saying those types of things. It's disappointing."

On the NFL Network, analysts Tony Dungy and Rodney Harrison were similarly incredulous.

"I would never tell my team that," said Dungy, the ex-coach.

"If you told me that," said Harrison, the former Pro Bowl safety, "I would look at you and say, 'Coach, we have seven games left. Why are you giving up on us?'"

A few minutes after Shanahan slinked away from the lectern, another figure climbed the same steps, took his place behind the same bank of microphones, and projected an entirely different stance toward a similar set of questions. Robert Griffin III, apparently unaware at that point of what Shanahan had just said, wore a black-and-gray argyle sweater and had his braids pulled back in a hairband, and he spoke in a tone of humility and determination, with an emphasis on personal responsibility. When he was done, nobody wondered where he stood on the question of where the Redskins' season went from here.

"I promise you I'll come back, and I'll be a better quarterback the second half of the season for us, for this team," Griffin said, his trademark smile absent. "And prayerfully, everybody comes back with the same mind-set. After the bye, I think you'll see a different team. . . . No one's ever going to question the fight I have inside of myself to be the greatest and to help lead this team to victory. It doesn't matter what [the situation] is—I'll make sure I continue to help this team win games, and it starts right after the bye week."

Weeks later, when the Redskins were deep into their second-half winning streak that would lead them—improbably—all the way to the NFL East title and into the playoffs, you could look back and trace the turning point, the molecular change that took place in the Redskins' collective soul, to that very moment in that very room, as Shanahan's defeatism gave way to Griffin's resolve. Griffin wasn't merely the leader of the locker room—he was the face and the voice of the franchise, better equipped than anyone, Shanahan included, to rally the troops, reassure the fans, and keep the focus on the task at hand. If anyone doubted that, they needed only to watch these two back-to-back news conferences at the lowest point of the Redskins' season.

Back in the locker room moments after his news conference, Griffin stopped to go on the air with the Redskins' radio network and promptly doubled down on the challenge he was issuing to his teammates.

"Guys just shouldn't come back [from the bye week] if they're going to feel sorry for themselves," he told radio announcers Sonny Jurgensen and Larry Michael. "I know for myself, I'm not going to stop working. I'm not going to stop putting it on the line every week, every play. . . . We're in dire straits. We've got to get wins and hopefully still make the playoffs. For me, it's an uneasy feeling because you don't know what to say or how to feel, so the only thing I know to do is to fight back."

It wasn't until the next morning, when the newspapers hit his doorstep and the airwaves and the Internet filled up with vitriol directed largely at him, that Shanahan realized the impact of his comments and the pressing need for some damage control. He was going to have to convince the fans and his own players that he wasn't giving up on the season, and the best way to do that, he figured, was to blame the usual suspects—the media. His first attempt to walk back the comments came in an interview that morning with ESPN.com blogger Dan Graziano. Rather than apologize for some inartful phrasing, Shanahan took the D.C. media to task for misinterpreting his comments. "To insinuate I was giving up on the season," he said, "is completely ridiculous."

In his usual day-after press conference that afternoon, Shanahan, wearing a blue button-down oxford and slacks, began by reading aloud his comments from the day to the assembled media and again said—with a number of Redskins players watching on television monitors around the building—that he had been misinterpreted. Tellingly, he used the word "obviously" three times in the first thirty seconds—implying his real meaning was apparent to everyone with half a brain—and added, "I think everybody that knows me since I've been here [knows] it doesn't matter what your record is—we're going to play to win every game."

Tuesday, November 6, was Election Day, and Shanahan stopped off at his local polling place early that morning on his way in to Redskins Park, where a couple of hours later he finally addressed the team as a whole. He repeated his assertion that the media had misinterpreted his comments and showed his players the remaining schedules for the four teams in the NFC East—highlighting those of the first-place New York Giants, who faced by far the toughest remaining schedule, and the Redskins themselves. Of particular note was the fact that five of the Redskins' remaining seven games were against division opponents. The door was open, in other words, for them to get back into the NFC East race.

"We control our own destiny," Shanahan said.

The blame-the-media-for-everything strategy and its close cousin, the nobody-believes-in-us-except-us rallying cry, are among the oldest tricks in the coaching playbook, but they worked to perfection for Shanahan that week.

"The media flipped what Shanahan said," Young, the Redskins' fullback, said later, "and that kind of makes you upset."

The NFL's labor agreement stipulates that players must get

four full days off during their team's bye week, and so the Red-skins coaches prepared to cut the players loose at the end of Tues-day's meetings. But there was one more item of business that day—the team picture. At the appointed time, they all took their places, arranged by jersey number, on a section of bleachers set up in the middle of the team's indoor practice bubble. On the floor up front, Griffin, wearing his familiar number 10, sat cross-legged in between number 8, Rex Grossman, and number 11, Aldrick Rob-inson. The coaching staff, in white polo shirts, stood in formation on either side.

They looked like one nice, big, happy, smiling family—sixty-odd strong—but undoubtedly, for many if not all of them, the smiles masked a darkness. The soul-searching had already begun. When they stepped down off those bleachers and changed back into their street clothes, the Redskins wouldn't be together again for five days, and as everyone got set for their mini-vacations with their families and quiet getaways, nobody knew what the immedi-ate future held.

At one point before everyone went their separate ways, Kyle Shanahan pulled Griffin aside. By then, he knew his quarterback well enough to know he would probably just stay in Virginia and work out at the Redskins' facility each day, if no one told him otherwise.

"Robert," he told him, "make sure you get away."

By early November, Griffin was growing more comfortable in his suburban digs and beginning to feel like part of a community. One Friday night in October, some kids from Broad Run High

School, a couple of miles from his house, took to Twitter to try to coax him to come to the school's football game that night in support of its breast cancer fund-raiser—and when he showed up unannounced around halftime, it produced one mini-riot and a hailstorm of photos (mostly Griffin posing in the middle of huge groups of smiling suburban teenagers) posted to Twitter and Instagram.

On Halloween night, a few days before the fateful Carolina game, he and his fiancée had started handing out candy to the neighborhood kids—but once word got out that Robert Griffin III himself was answering the door, he and Liddicoat soon had hundreds of kids knocking and quickly ran out of treats. Griffin's solution was to start giving out Adidas socks and T-shirts from the boxes of merchandise he had stashed in the garage.

He probably would have been content spending his bye week at home, watching movies from Redbox and hanging out with Rebecca and his parents. But he also knew it would be good for him to get away, and so he booked a room at a resort in Cambridge, on Maryland's quiet Eastern Shore, just a few hours from his house. The goal, he would say later, was "to get away from the familiar."

"Just clear my head," he said, "and make sure I come back even hungrier."

But before Griffin could leave, he had some obligations to fulfill—a video to film for Gatorade, and a series of interviews with local media outlets that had been previously scheduled for the bye week. These sessions, limited to five minutes each, would be the only opportunities most local reporters would have to interview Griffin on a one-on-one basis all season. Five minutes over the course of a five-month season, including training camp. It's a shame, because as great as Griffin is in press conference settings—where the lack of intimacy makes it feel more like a performance in front of an audience than an interview—he is even better in the more relaxed setting of a one-on-one. Given the timing of these interviews—with the Redskins on the verge of collapse going into the bye week—there was an increased urgency to the questions, and Griffin was typically thoughtful and insightful with his answers.

Asked in one of these interviews about the difficulty in turning around the Redskins' mind-set, Griffin said, "It's something I've experienced before," noting that he'd had a chance to do it on a smaller scale at Baylor. "But it takes more than one guy. And that's what we had [at Baylor]. We had more than one guy willing to put it on the line, willing to not make excuses, and not being satisfied with just, 'Oh, we got close,' or, 'We tried extremely hard.' We had a bunch of guys out there fighting, putting it on the line every day. And that's what we have to have here."

It almost seemed as if Griffin was implying that some of his Redskins teammates were excuse-makers who lacked the fortitude or the will to fight to the finish. But pressed on the issue, he refused to get any more specific than that.

"I'll never throw anybody under the bus," he said. "It's just a matter of—we just can't look for excuses as to why we're not successful. If I make a bad pass, it's because I made a bad pass. It's not because Kyle called a bad play. It's not because [the offensive line] didn't block. I'll never make that excuse. So we just have to find guys and have everybody buy into that. It's just a matter of owning your mistake and learning from it."

And then he said something that, to a cynic, was laughable on the surface—cute and precious, in a kids-say-the-darnedest-things sort of way. Except that he was dead serious, and he might have jumped across the table and seized you by the throat if you had laughed.

"I feel like we have the team," he said, "to come back and pull off a seven-game winning streak here."

During his retreat to Cambridge, try though he might, Griffin couldn't put the Redskins' plight out of his mind. He was formulating some thoughts and beginning to think the time might be right, once everyone returned from the break, for him to step out of his rookie's self-imposed shell and make a speech to the team. He tested out his message in a couple of tweets: "At the end of the day, do you find yourself fixing your mistakes or making excuses for them," one of them read, with the hashtag #NoExcuses.

On his way back to his Leesburg home, he stopped at his parents' house in Gaithersburg, and his mother once again braided his hair. She took note of his unflagging belief in his team and his faith in where it was headed.

"He wasn't thinking playoffs," Jacqueline Griffin recalled of that conversation. "He was thinking Super Bowl."

On Monday, November 12, when the Redskins reassembled at their headquarters in Ashburn, Griffin told his teammates he had something to say. He stood before them and told them their season was far from over. Just the day before, while the Redskins were off, the division-leading Giants were upset in Cincinnati, bringing them one step back toward the rest of the division. "We can still flip this script," Griffin told them in a stirring speech that one veteran said had the team "ready to run through a wall."

"Everybody was like, 'Uhhhhhh,'" recalled tight end Niles Paul, making an expression of deep skepticism. "But just how he believes what he's saying, it just kind of motivates everybody."

In individual conversations, he told his teammates he didn't merely want to beat the Eagles—he wanted to dominate them, to set a new tone for the rest of the season. "I thought I was hungry before the bye week," Griffin recalled. "You come back and you realize how much more energy you have just having that week off."

It was two days after that—on the Wednesday before the Eagles game—that each of the Redskins players was handed a blank sheet of paper and told to vote for a new captain, part of a Redskins tradition of electing new captains at the midway point. The electees were nose tackle Barry Cofield on defense and Stephen Bowen on special teams—both of them seven-year veterans—and Robert Griffin III, the twenty-two-year-old rookie quarterback, on offense. When Mike Shanahan announced the results to the team on the practice field prior to that afternoon's practice, Griffin barely had time to thank everyone before the first drill commenced. That day, it felt as if a change was coming.

With a hop, skip, and jump, Griffin came sprinting out of the giant inflatable Redskins helmet in a corner of the end zone and into the sunshine, waving a giant American flag and shouting, "Woooooooooooooo!!!" It was a perfect fall afternoon at FedEx Field, 52 degrees and cloudless, on "Salute to Service Day"—which Griffin marked by having his parents' names stitched into the tongues of his Adidas cleats. When it was time for the coin toss, for the first time he took his place among the Redskins' other captains and marched out to midfield.

It took exactly two offensive plays for Griffin and the Redskins to strike a new tone for the rest of their season. Following a DeAngelo Hall interception, the Redskins started their first offensive series on the Eagles' 9-yard line, and on their second play Griffin made what could have been a critical mistake—calling for a pass play out of the wrong formation. However, at the snap of the ball, he improvised, hitting Young, the fullback, for a touchdown pass. Rather than celebrate with a kneel-down and a quick prayer of thanks, as was his routine, Griffin instead sprinted straight to the Redskins' sideline to apologize to Kyle Shanahan for getting the play-call wrong.

"It doesn't matter when you score a touchdown," Shanahan said incredulously. "So don't worry about it."

Griffin had resolved to dominate the Eagles, and that is precisely what he did. In what was arguably his finest game of the season, he threw four touchdown passes and no interceptions, completed fourteen of his fifteen attempts, and recorded a perfect passer rating of 158.3 as the Redskins romped, 31–6. Two of his touchdown passes were long balls—one of forty-nine yards to Aldrick Robinson, the other sixty yards to Santana Moss—and in all he had four completions of twenty or more yards, plus three runs of at least that length, becoming the third quarterback in history (after Randall Cunningham and Michael Vick) to throw at least four touchdown passes and rush for at least eighty yards in the same game. It was no exaggeration to say that, at that point, Griffin was probably the most dangerous big-play threat in the NFL.

"He's got an aura about him. He just exudes confidence," veteran long snapper Nick Sundberg said of Griffin. "Without even saying a word, we know he's going to go get the job done. It spreads to all of us. It's something that's vastly different from a year ago. His attitude, his want-to, above all else, is what's leading us."

More important than the final score, Griffin had noticed a more aggressive, more sustained effort from his teammates. "We all knew it [wasn't] time to panic," he said afterward. "But it was time to bunker down, and the way we played physically, offense and defense, it was extremely impressive."

As good as Griffin was that day, and as good as he was all season, it can be argued that his greatest achievement in 2012 was changing the culture of the Redskins' locker room. It had taken ten games, but the Redskins were finally coming around to the worldview of their new offensive captain: there are no excuses, believing in yourself is half the battle, and losing is not tolerated.

"Everybody gets in line behind him," said Moss, "and says, 'Take us to the promised land.'"

ELEVEN

THE SUPERSTAR ASCENDANT

You never missed Thanksgiving dinner at Jacqueline Griffin's house if you knew what was good for you. She always had a houseful of people, and they all knew what to expect: turkey and dressing, a huge pot of gumbo, mashed potatoes, greens, and—no lie—about twenty sweet potato pies. She had to make that many because the Griffin men, Robert Jr. and Robert III, would claim them and hoard them and hide them. The latter may have been young, but he was crafty—his favorite trick was to eat half of a pie on the spot, hide the other half deep in the fridge, then dig it out a couple of hours later, maybe after the last football game of the day, and eat the other half. If he found out you had helped yourself to even a tiny sliver of it, you were going to have a problem.

If any American family had something to be thankful for as they sat down for dinner on Thanksgiving Day 2012, it was the Griffins. They were healthy, happy, and prospering—and one of them, Robert III, that pie-hoarding son of Jacqueline and Robert Jr., was one of the most famous and most popular athletes on the planet, never more so than on that very day. Earlier in the afternoon, in fact, he had been the guest of honor at virtually every Thanksgiving dinner in the country, his talents exploding out of

living room TV sets everywhere as he led the Washington Redskins to a nationally televised 38–31 victory over the Dallas Cowboys at palatial Cowboys Stadium in Arlington, Texas.

The only downside was that Griffin wasn't going to get to tear
into one of his mother's famous home-cooked Thanksgiving dinners that night. But this was the next-best thing. Late on Thanksgiving night, November 22, Griffin found himself at a large table
in the restaurant of the Four Seasons Resort in Dallas, alongside
his parents, his sisters, his fiancée, his fiancée's parents, and Daniel and Tanya Snyder—the Redskins' owner and his wife.

This was the weekend it all came together for Griffin—his
past, his present, and his future. It was the weekend his superstardom reached another, mind-blowing level—by the following Monday ("Cyber Monday," in marketing-speak), his Redskins jersey
would be the top seller in the NFL. It was a weekend for recon-
necting with his roots—first on Thanksgiving Day at Cowboys
Stadium, about 170 miles from his hometown of Copperas Cove,
for his first professional game in Texas, then back in the same
building two days later to watch his alma mater, the Baylor Bears,
battle Texas Tech. It was a weekend for marveling at the joys of life
and for giving thanks for God's generous gifts.

It was all made possible by one fortuitous scheduling quirk: the
Redskins and Bears would be playing games in the same building
some forty-eight hours apart. Ever since he realized the overlap,
Griffin had been pestering Redskins coach Mike Shanahan for
permission to stay back in Texas after the Thanksgiving Day game
instead of flying back to Virginia with the team, and Shanahan
finally relented on the Tuesday before the game, deciding to give

the entire team the rest of the weekend off. And so, while most of his Redskins teammates left, Griffin kept his room at the Four Seasons, had Thanksgiving dinner after the game with his and Rebecca's families and the Snyders (who graciously picked up the tab), and hung around the hotel until Saturday, when he dressed in Baylor gear and joined the throngs headed to the stadium for the big game and the Bears' attempt to become bowl-eligible for the third straight year. And if every one of those people wanted their picture made with him that day (and it certainly seemed as if they did), he was happy to do that.

It was like Homecoming, and Robert Griffin III was the Homecoming King.

At noon on Thursday, he had stood on the iconic blue star at the 50-yard line of Cowboys Stadium—straight off the Redskins' bus, still wearing street clothes and headphones, looking around in all directions, mouthing the words to a song, lost in thought—and barely forty-eight hours later he was rushing out to almost the exact same spot, joining the celebration of his former Baylor teammates in the aftermath of their overtime, bowl-berth-clinching win. It was a weekend when the wins came in pairs, the touchdowns came in bunches, and the love came by the bushel.

Oh, and the best part? He still had a full Thanksgiving dinner waiting for him in his freezer at home, cooked for him the week before by his mother, who wanted to be prepared for the possibility her son would have to go back to Virginia with the Redskins after their game.

She had made it all: turkey, dressing, gumbo, potatoes, greens. And yes, plenty of sweet potato pies.

. . .

As an eerie silence descended upon Cowboys Stadium late in the second quarter—the sort of silence that any hard-core sports fan knows can only be the result of a butt-whupping put on the home team by the visitors—the first faint strains of a new chant could be heard from somewhere down in the lower bowl:

"R-G-3! R-G-3!"

Griffin and his Washington Redskins were having their way with the Dallas Cowboys on their way to a shocking 28–3 halftime lead, but this—well, this just didn't happen. No visiting player walks into Jerry Jones's billion-dollar football palace and makes the crowd chant his name. In their seats up in the stands, Jacqueline and Robert Griffin Jr. looked at each other in amazement as the chant picked up steam. True, there was deep love for their son in these parts. The Griffins figured they personally knew about a thousand people in attendance that day. So popular was RG3 in Waco, about a hundred miles from Cowboys Stadium, that the local Cowboys radio network affiliate had begun airing Redskins games too, as long as they didn't conflict with the Cowboys' games. But even so, the Griffins never expected to hear an "R-G-3!" chant in this building.

The chant came back again, louder and mixed with some boos directed at the home team, as the teams jogged off the field at halftime. In the second half the Cowboys mounted a furious comeback, pulling to within a touchdown with 8:24 left in the game. Now the partisan Cowboys crowd was coming to life—until Griffin coolly led the Redskins on an eleven-play drive that bled five minutes off the clock and resulted in a forty-eight-yard field goal by kicker Kai Forbath to ice the game away.

Griffin not only broke the hearts of Cowboys fans that day but, to judge from the chants, also stole more than a few. At the very least, how could they not come away impressed by the young man? This was the biggest stage he had ever played on—his first game back in his home state, his first taste of the bitter Redskins–Cowboys rivalry, his first pro game on national TV—and he had been brilliant. He threw for 304 yards, a 131.8 passer rating, and four touchdown passes—giving him eight over a five-day period, going back to the win over the Eagles the Sunday before. One had been a beautiful sixty-eight-yard bomb to Aldrick Robinson.

"I couldn't have asked for a better homecoming," Griffin said. "Or as my dad calls it, a business trip."

In the middle of a somber Cowboys locker room, Jones, the owner, seemed to be speaking for all his team's fans when he gushed, "Really, I was in awe. I was disappointed in our play, but I was in awe of RG3."

On Fox's postgame show, analyst Jimmy Johnson, himself an ex–Cowboys coach, seemed just as incredulous. "I think he's the most valuable player in the National Football League," Johnson said of Griffin. "He is that good. For a rookie, it's amazing. I haven't seen anything like this."

Shanahan, meantime, reached into 1970s-era Hollywood for a comparison to Griffin: "He's like Cool Hand Luke," he said. "He focuses on his job and doesn't let anything seem to bother him." When someone brought up that quote to Griffin, he grinned and admitted he had no idea who Cool Hand Luke was.

Since he didn't have to hurry to get dressed and catch the team bus to the airport, Griffin soaked in the postgame atmosphere in the Redskins' locker room and beyond. "The mission was accomplished," he said, "and now I can just enjoy the trip." At one point, he emerged and made his way down a corridor toward a huge group of fans waiting to get players' autographs, and for the next twenty minutes or so he patiently signed for the fans, working with astonishing efficiency and brushing off attempts at small talk so that he could sign the maximum number of items. But then one Cowboys fan made his way to the front and pointed at his chest, and Griffin stopped and said, "You want me to sign it right here?"

And when the answer was yes, Griffin smiled and signed the man's Cowboys number 82 Jason Witten jersey, right across the chest, in big, looping letters: "Robert Griffin III #10."

Griffin makes a point during the season of avoiding media hype and hysteria aimed in his direction, but had he turned on *First Take* on ESPN2 the next morning in his Four Seasons hotel room, he would have heard the panelists discussing whether he was now a legitimate MVP candidate. Had he switched over to the NFL Network, he would have heard a debate over whether his rookie season was a contender for the best in NFL history. Had he picked up a copy of the *Dallas Morning News,* he would have seen a photo of himself dominating the front of the sports section, showing him with both index fingers pointing to the sky following another touchdown, under a headline that read, "The Power of III."

This would be the weekend when ESPN, and by extension the greater American sporting public, discovered Robert Griffin III as a cultural phenomenon. The "Worldwide Leader" would be carrying the Redskins' next game, a *Monday Night Football* showdown against the division-leading Giants on December 3, and over the next ten days would go into hyperdrive to pump up the NFL's hottest new star. He would do a lengthy sit-down interview with ESPN analyst Jon Gruden, and there would be an *Outside the Lines* show devoted to the RG3 phenomenon. Everywhere you looked—*SportsCenter, Pardon the Interruption, First Take*—there he was.

Griffin had done the impossible: he had made ESPN forget about Tim Tebow. He was, in fact, Tebow with talent.

But on the day after the Thanksgiving Day win over Dallas, Griffin's primary mission was to lay low, out of sight, and relax. His biggest outing all day was to the hotel spa downstairs, where he and Liddicoat enjoyed massages and mani-pedis. His parents, meantime, went back to Copperas Cove to check on the house and see some friends, and Robert Griffin Jr., who was still the head coach of the Five Hills Track and Field Club, managed to oversee three practices between Friday and Saturday. (His grand plan for the weekend—Cowboys–Redskins on Thursday, Copperas Cove High playoff game on Friday, Baylor–Texas Tech on Saturday—fell through, however, when the Bulldawgs were eliminated with a loss the week before.)

On Friday evening, Robert Griffin III had an appointment to keep. The Baylor football team had arrived in Dallas on Friday for their game the next day at Cowboys Stadium, and Bears coach Art Briles—who visited with Griffin on the sidelines before the Redskins–Cowboys game—had asked him to speak to the team. Griffin agreed, of course, and in the early evening he took a hotel courtesy car to the Baylor team hotel.

His speech, which he pulled off without notes, was suitably inspirational and full of Baylor pride. Some of the players had been in his same recruiting class of 2008, while a handful of true freshmen had known him only in passing, but he spoke to all of them.

"I love you guys," he said, "and I miss you, and I'm going to be there for you, no matter what." To that end, he gave out his cell phone number—for those few who didn't already have it—and told them they could call or text him anytime.

But there was also a streak of melancholy and nostalgia that ran through Griffin's short speech, as if being around his old teammates had reminded him of all the things he missed about college football and college life. Not that he wasn't enjoying the NFL—but life gets a lot more complicated, and the locker-room relationships more impersonal, after you pass through the iron gates and leave campus life behind.

"Cherish where you are," he told them, "because the NFL is a different monster. It's not four or five years with the same group of guys, getting to build and grow and know each other—not just who you are and what you represent, but everything about a person. Make the most of this, and then for those of you who get a chance to go to the next level, do it."

The next morning, as Griffin was getting ready to head to Cowboys Stadium for the Baylor–Texas Tech game, the phone in the hotel room rang. It was the front desk calling to say a package had arrived for him at the front desk. Would it be okay if someone brought it up to him?

A few minutes later, a bellman showed up at the door and handed Griffin a large envelope, with a Redskins logo and a return address for Redskins Park in Ashburn. He opened it, and inside was a note from Mike Shanahan and a DVD copy of *Cool Hand Luke*. Griffin laughed and immediately tweeted out a picture of himself posing with the DVD to his five-hundred-thousand-plus followers.

"He must be pretty cool," Griffin wrote. "Thanks for the DVD, Coach."

There was a football game that Saturday, November 24, at Cowboys Stadium, Baylor against Texas Tech. There were old friends to see. There were hugs and handshakes. There were a handful of interviews. But mostly, for Robert Griffin III, there were pictures—literally thousands of them. Candid snapshots of his back or the top of his head as he made his way around the stadium and down on the sideline. And posed photos with an assortment of characters—Baylor fans, Texas Tech fans, babies, cheerleaders, dancers, coaches, trainers, Texas Highway Patrolmen, referees. At one point, a group of Saddle Tramps—the traditional, males-only spirit squad from Texas Tech—approached Griffin with their matching red uniforms and cowbells and asked for a picture with him. He happily obliged.

It had to be exhausting—all those fake smiles, all those arms draped across strange shoulders, all that "Cheese!" Griffin walking around Cowboys Stadium during a Baylor game in 2012 was what it must have been like for Elvis to walk around Memphis in 1970—except everyone here had a camera-phone. If you got near Griffin that day and didn't get your picture taken with him, it was only because you didn't ask. At one point, he needed a breather—and something to eat—so he made his way up to the suite where his parents were watching the game. But it was hardly an escape. The people in the elevator wanted a picture, and so did the other guests in the suite. He obliged them all.

When it came to the Baylor players, Griffin knew his place. He visited with them in the locker room some ninety minutes before kickoff, but he made sure to head back outside as game time approached and Coach Briles got ready to deliver his pregame pep talk. He understood that this is a sacred time between a coach and his players, and he gave them the proper distance. When the players emerged to head out onto the field, Griffin met them at the door, delivering high fives and back slaps and words of encouragement: "C'mon!" "Time to go to work!" "I love you guys!"

He watched most of the game seated atop a giant equipment trunk on the Baylor sidelines, with Liddicoat—herself a Baylor alum—by his side. It was a typical Baylor shoot-out of a game—the kind Griffin had trademarked the year before—and as the final minutes ticked down he stood up on the trunk and waved with both arms for the crowd to make some noise.

In overtime, when Texas Tech's last-ditch pass on fourth-and-4 fell incomplete, Griffin joined the stampede of players converging on midfield in celebration. There would be some more hugs, and a lot more pictures, but then he and Liddicoat made their way to the car waiting for them in the bowels of the stadium, leaving behind a celebration that was still raging. The plan was to work out together at the hotel, get to bed early, and catch the first flight to Dulles on Sunday morning. On Monday, Griffin would be starting another workweek with the Redskins, as their *Monday Night Football* battle with the Giants approached.

"To play the way we played on Thursday," Griffin said as

he climbed into the car, "and then to get to come to this game and watch the Bears become bowl-eligible for the third straight year—it's just been an amazing few days."

The car pulled away and disappeared around the bend. The Homecoming King was gone, and it was as if someone had unplugged a vacuum cleaner. Suddenly, you were aware of the silence.

T he two electrifying rookies exploded onto the scene with killer smiles, undeniable gifts, an affinity for superheroes, poise beyond their years, and the ability to play at top form when it's all on the line," began op-ed columnist Maureen Dowd's piece in the *Sunday New York Times* on November 25. "Both stay so calm under pressure that they have evoked comparisons to Cool Hand Luke. The capital of winning and losing now revolves around two natural-born world shakers: the president of the United States and the quarterback of the Washington Redskins."

It was no longer enough for the media to compare Griffin to Michael Vick or Cam Newton or Randall Cunningham or Roger Staubach. Now we were comparing him to President Barack Obama. Not only that, but Dowd, in her column, concluded that Griffin was a better leader than the commander in chief: "While Obama prefers to preen as the man alone in the arena," she wrote, "[Griffin] never passes up a chance to share credit."

Griffin, in fact, was becoming a favorite subject of Washington's political press corps, as stories began appearing before the election—mostly tongue-in-cheek—about how he was the only man who could truly unify this bitterly divided city.

"It's tough to unite this city around anything," Obama said into the camera in a Fox-TV feature that aired during its pregame show some two weeks before the election. "Believe me, I know. But RG3 makes it look easy."

"RG3 has really struck a chord with sports fans, uniting Democrats and Republicans," Republican nominee Mitt Romney said in the same piece.

(How was Fox able to line up both presidential candidates so close to the election? Perhaps it had something to do with the fact that Virginia, where both Griffin and the Redskins were based, was a critical swing state.)

Around the same time, the NFL Network aired a piece called "RG3 for President" that opened with a shot of the Washington Monument, interspersed clips of Griffin carving up defenses with clips of a famous political commentators extolling his virtues, and finally ended with Griffin himself reciting the obligatory kicker: "I'm Robert Griffin the Third, and I approve this message."

(While candidates from both parties wanted nothing more than to align themselves with him, Griffin's own political leanings were something of a mystery. He wouldn't reveal which candidate got his vote in the presidential election, and he considered politics, along with race and religion, to be a subject it was best not to discuss publicly. However, on his old Myspace.com homepage [ca. 2009], which was still available as of this writing, he featured a picture of Obama under the words "The history maker." When I asked Troy Vital, the former high school teammate and best friend, whether Griffin was politically inclined, he said that, on the contrary, he was famously apolitical. Once, according to Vital, when they talked about the 2012 presidential election, Griffin—

who happens to share a birthday with Abraham Lincoln—had said, "If Obama wins, that's great. And if Romney wins, that's good too, because it'll mean lower taxes.")

Between ESPN's wall-to-wall Griffin coverage and the larger pop-culture status he was beginning to attain, it was no exaggeration to say that—at that very moment, at least—he was the future face of the NFL. Peyton Manning and Tom Brady, after all, were by then thirty-six and thirty-five years old, respectively—ancient by NFL standards—and among the younger generation, nobody else had Griffin's combination of breathtaking ability, public-speaking skills, camera-ready looks, outsized personality, and impeccable image. He also played the right position (quarterback) in the right sort of large media market (Washington, D.C.) and had enormous appeal with both white and African American fans. In December, ESPN.com reported that Griffin's Redskins jersey not only was the top seller in the NFL for 2012 but had also set a single-season record for jersey sales, surpassing Brett Favre's 2009 Minnesota Vikings jersey.

How long would it be before Griffin was hosting *Saturday Night Live*?

This explosion of Griffin's fame—beyond the confines of sports and into the nation's cultural zeitgeist—was the backdrop for his *Monday Night Football* debut, against the Giants on December 3. It was the first meaningful December game at FedEx Field in half a decade, and the sellout crowd was the loudest anyone could recall in that building's history. Griffin didn't take a single step during the pregame—or throw a single warm-up pass or blow a single kiss to his family—that wasn't recorded by a handful of television cameras.

It would not go down as Griffin's finest game—he threw for only 163 yards, his lowest total since the Atlanta game in which he suffered the concussion. But he ran for another seventy-two yards—including a forty-six-yard burst on an option keeper—to break Cam Newton's single-season NFL record for rushing yards by a rookie quarterback. And he had a part in two touchdowns. On the first, he fumbled at the end of a twelve-yard run, but the ball wound up in the arms of receiver Josh Morgan, who caught it perfectly in stride and took it into the end zone to complete a twenty-eight-yard touchdown. And on the second, with less than twelve minutes left in the game, he hit Pierre Garcon for an eight-yard touchdown pass, giving the Redskins the decisive points in a 17–16 win.

"Griffin," wrote the esteemed *Washington Post* columnist Thomas Boswell, "has the aura of victory. That inspires. That elevates."

In one remarkable three-game stretch, with the last two coming on national television, Griffin had led the Redskins to a sweep of their NFC East rivals—Philadelphia, Dallas, and New York—while throwing nine touchdown passes against only one interception in the process. Remember when he had stood in front of the team, when things were at their lowest coming out of the bye week, and implored them to keep fighting, saying, "We can still flip this script"? This was what he meant by flipping the script. From the 3-6 hole they had occupied just a few weeks earlier, the Redskins had now climbed back to sea level. At 6-6, they already owned more wins than the previous year's squad, and they suddenly trailed the first-place Giants (7-5) by just one game in the standings.

Four games remained in their season, and all of a sudden the notion of a playoff run no longer seemed so preposterous.

One night after the win over the Giants, Griffin made a rare venture into D.C. proper in order to attend the Washington Wizards–Miami Heat game at the downtown Verizon Center. He sat, along with Liddicoat, in the courtside seats belonging to Wizards owner Ted Leonsis, and when fans began to spot him, a spontaneous chant of "R-G-3! R-G-3!" rose to the rafters, reappearing at various points in the game. When the Wizards' upset victory was complete, most of the Heat's players slinked off the court, but one of them made his way to Griffin. It was LeBron James, coming over for a quick hug and a handshake.

On this night, King James was just another guy in Washington with a man-crush on the quarterback of the Redskins—just another commoner paying his respects to the man of the hour, the man who owned the town, the King of D.C.

TWELVE

THE RACE QUESTION

The late, blind-side hit, metaphorically speaking, came out of nowhere. Robert Griffin III was trying to do the safe thing, the news-conference equivalent of ducking out of bounds to avoid a direct collision—but he didn't see the sniper, the unhelmeted strong safety, bearing down on him, hell-bent on hurting him. Griffin, unable to protect himself in time, didn't stand a chance.

It was a cool morning, deep in the season, and Griffin was going about another workday at Redskins Park, on his mission to keep the Redskins' season alive. Later that day, he stopped at his locker and picked up his phone to check for messages, expecting to see the usual assortment of loving texts from his family and wisecracks from some buddies back in Texas, and maybe a missed call or two. Instead, his in-box was blowing up. Did you hear, everybody was asking, what some guy said about you on ESPN? Can you believe that idiot went there? It didn't require much investigating on Griffin's part to figure out what everyone was talking about: that morning, on ESPN's *First Take* show, cohost Rob Parker had used his platform to essentially question Griffin's credentials as an African American—a figurative cheap shot at a defenseless player. Parker, himself an African American, had said, "My question, which is just a straight, honest question, [is]: is he a brother, or is he a cornball brother?"

When another host asked him what he meant by that, Parker replied, "Well, [that] he's black—he kind of does his thing—but he's not really down with the cause. He's not one of us." Noting Griffin's white fiancée and political ambiguity, Parker concluded, "I'm just trying to dig deeper as to why he has an issue."

An issue? The way Griffin figured, it was everybody else, not him, who had an issue—an obsession even—with race. But the implication was clear: right there, on national television, somebody who had never met Griffin was calling him, in so many words, an Uncle Tom—all because Griffin, the day before, had answered a reporter's question about race honestly and thoughtfully.

The original question had been posed, as it happened, by another ESPN reporter working in advance on a piece for Martin Luther King Day. "The fact you have not allowed yourself to be defined by your race—how has that shaped your identity?" the reporter, Mark Schwarz, asked.

"For me, you don't ever want to be defined by the color of your skin," Griffin replied to Schwarz. "You want to be defined by your work ethic, the person that you are, your character, your personality—and that's what I strive to go out and do. I am an African American, in America, and that will never change. But I don't have to be defined by that." When Schwarz followed up by asking about African American fans in D.C. for whom his race did matter, Griffin showed an understanding of the bigger picture: "I am [aware] of how race is relevant to them. I don't ignore it. I try not to be defined by it, but I understand different perspectives and how people view different things. So I understand they're excited their quarterback is an African American. I play with a lot of pride, a lot of character, a lot of heart. So I understand that, and I appreciate them for being fans."

It was nothing Griffin hadn't said before. Over the course of his rookie season, he had been asked repeatedly about race and, against his better judgment, had always not only answered the question but done so with typical grace and candor. His parents had raised him to not focus on skin color—his own or anyone else's—and that was the way he lived his life. But this time the *Washington Post* and *USA Today* ran Griffin's comments, and the quotes evidently made their way into Rob Parker's consciousness, and before you knew it Griffin was getting thrown into a decidedly ugly discussion about his own "blackness." You knew Parker had gone too far when ESPN's resident gas-on-fire artist, "Screamin'" Stephen A. Smith, had to serve as the voice of reason, chiming in after Parker to say, "I'm uncomfortable with where we just went. RG3, the ethnicity, the color of his fiancée, is none of our business."

ESPN would fire Parker four weeks after his comments about Griffin.

The unprovoked attack on Griffin's self-identity shook the young quarterback and his inner circle and was an unfortunate development for anyone with a stake in the race debate—because what lesson was Griffin supposed to take from this, other than to never answer another race question as long as he lived?

At a certain level, it was unfair in the first place for Griffin to be confronted with these questions. He was twenty-two years old, just out of college, so his worldview could hardly be considered fully formed. He wasn't asking to be a spokesman for his race.

Besides, what other prominent African American athlete was getting asked over and over to articulate his views on race? LeBron James? Ray Lewis? Russell Wilson? No, no, and no.

But as Griffin was beginning to realize, he had arrived that year, through no fault of his own, at the intersection of three different histories that had race as a central theme: the history of a position, quarterback in the NFL, that for years had remained a largely whites-only job; the history of a city, Washington, D.C., where race was still a highly divisive issue; and the history of a franchise, the Redskins, with its own checkered past when it came to race relations (not to mention a name that many Native Americans considered to be offensive).

If LeBron James wasn't getting grilled constantly about race, it was because he played in the NBA, not the NFL. If Ray Lewis didn't face these questions over and over, it was because he played linebacker, not quarterback. If Russell Wilson rarely had to define his racial outlook, it was because he played in Washington State, not Washington, D.C.

And as Griffin may have also suspected, he was getting the race questions because he mattered—in a way that few who had come before him ever did. Washington had had African American superstars in the past, and the NFL had boasted great African American quarterbacks before, but none of them had ever seemed like The One—the sort of transcendent figure, so brilliant on the field, so likable and marketable off it, who could become a global icon, unite people, and use his influence to work for good. It was no wonder people were quick to compare Griffin to President Obama—their arrivals in Washington, four years apart, engendered many of the same emotions. "Hope and change" might as well have been the Redskins' slogan in 2012. Sometimes Griffin, unconsciously, even sounded like Obama.

"My job," he said during an interview on ESPN's *SportsCenter* in October, "is to unite people. I try to unite this team, try to unite this city. That's my job."

All those commercials before his first NFL snap, his distinctive style and appearance, his universal magnetism, his color-blind views on race—it all seemed to be setting Griffin up to be a post-racial icon for America. But as he was finding out, never more so than during the Rob Parker episode, the concept of a "postracial" America was fraught with danger.

Way back in the beginning, when Griffin and his father decided to hold firm in their insistence that he would be a quarterback, period, it ensured that race would always be part of the discussion—whether outwardly or, more typically, just below the surface. It meant folks in Copperas Cove would whisper to each other about whether the town was ready for an African American quarterbacking the Bulldawgs. It meant Coach Jack Welch would have to show the door to college recruiters who wanted Griffin to switch positions. It meant Baylor's PR material for the Heisman campaign would never depict him running the ball, because that only played into stereotypes about African American quarterbacks. It meant pointed questions in the media before the draft, almost always credited to anonymous "sources," about Griffin's makeup: Could he run an NFL offense? Did his athleticism make him an injury risk? Was he "selfish"—as that *Milwaukee Journal-Sentinel* story had claimed the week before the draft?

And it meant, once Griffin got to the NFL, he would constantly be compared to the same handful of quarterbacks, all of them African American—Randall Cunningham, Michael Vick, Cam Newton, etc.—even though Griffin's father had used mostly white quarterbacks, such as Roger Staubach, Kenny Stabler, and Fran Tarkenton, as templates when he was molding his son's talents. Still, Griffin could handle all of that. He understood human nature, and he understood the media. He got it.

"We always try to find similarities in life, no matter what it is," Griffin said in December, "so they're always going to try to put you in a box with other African American quarterbacks—Vick, Newton, Randall Cunningham, Warren Moon. [But] Warren Moon and Doug Williams really didn't run that much. That's the negative stereotype when it comes to African American quarterbacks—that most of us just run. Those guys threw it around. I like to think I can throw it around a little bit. That's the goal—just to go out and not try to prove anybody wrong, but just let your talents speak for themselves."

When Mike and Kyle Shanahan began implementing the read-option elements of their offense over the spring and summer, Griffin kept his mouth shut and ran the offense—because he believed in his coaches and because he wanted to win more than he wanted to bust up stereotypes.

"I don't want people to think I'm just an option quarterback," Griffin said in May 2012. "It's not something you can prove, I don't think. Perception is reality, so it doesn't matter how many yards you throw for, what you do in practice, or what you do in the games—if you can run a little bit, you'll always be smacked with that stereotype."

"Just be yourself," Doug Williams had told Griffin back on the night of the NFL draft, April 26. Williams, from his home in Louisiana, had sought out Griffin in order to welcome the young man to the Redskins family and to the league's fraternity of African American quarterbacks. "If you'll just be yourself, people are going to love you."

Williams, of course, had quarterbacked the Redskins to the Super Bowl title in 1988, becoming the first African American to win a title in that role. Now the head coach at Grambling University, Williams had been watching Griffin closely for the past few years and had come away with one overwhelming thought: this kid was the perfect person to carry the torch forward.

"In the last decade or so, there've been two young athletes that I've seen handle themselves as well or better than anyone I can remember," Williams said. "The first was a young LeBron James. I saw him do an interview coming out of high school, and he was just incredibly impressive. And watching Robert at the podium is the same thing. It's a good feeling. You don't want to put the race card in [play], but as a young black man, he handles himself as professionally as anyone possibly can, no matter what race they are."

It would be nice to talk about how far the NFL has come in advancing African American quarterbacks since Williams won the Super Bowl in 1988—but twenty-five years later, he remains the only one to do so. Likewise, Tennessee's Steve McNair remains the only black quarterback to win the league's MVP Award. That came in 2003, the same year commentator Rush Limbaugh was forced to resign from ESPN's *Sunday NFL Countdown* for suggesting that Philadelphia Eagles quarterback Donovan McNabb had been undeservingly lauded by a media pack that simply wanted to see black quarterbacks succeed.

Of course, the NFL has become much more hospitable toward African American quarterbacks in the decade since then—right? Well, maybe, maybe not. In 2003 there were seven African American quarterbacks who started at least thirteen games for their teams; in 2012 the number was down to four (Griffin, Russell Wilson, Josh Freeman, and Cam Newton). Four black starting quarterbacks in a thirty-two-team league. That comes out to 12.5 percent—in a league in which 67 percent of all players are African American.

There was plenty of anecdotal evidence out there to suggest that the quarterback position in the NFL was more of a meritocracy than ever before—and that the increasing athleticism of defensive ends and linebackers, in fact, had made mobility at quarterback more essential than ever. But for whatever reason, those raw numbers suggested something else.

Chocolate City?" Jacqueline Griffin said out loud. "What does that mean?"

The Griffins were in their living room in Copperas Cove, a few days after the 2012 draft, and the television was tuned—as it pretty much always was in the Griffin home—to ESPN. One of the announcers was talking about the new marriage between Robert Griffin III and the Washington Redskins and about how folks were going to love Griffin in D.C.—because, after all, they didn't call it "Chocolate City" for nothing.

"I had no idea that Washington was called Chocolate City. I was totally oblivious to that. So was my son," Jacqueline Griffin recalled. "We love our race, don't get me wrong. We wouldn't change it for the world. [But] we just don't talk about race in here."

Jacqueline and Robert Griffin Jr., both former Army sergeants, had made a conscious decision decades earlier to raise their children to be largely color-blind. "It's not about anybody's race," Jacqueline Griffin said. "It's about humanity. God wants to love everybody, no matter their background. The only reason people become afraid is because of ignorance. I don't want them to see color. It's not about that." The Griffins didn't deny the existence of racism—they had both grown up in New Orleans, after all—but "any experience we had in dealing with racism," she said, "we always told our kids, 'You learn from that. Don't do that to others.'"

It was only as he got older that their son realized his views on race were not shared by everyone. Skin color was the last thing he may have noticed about someone, but for most other people it was the first thing they noticed about him.

"My parents raised me to not ever look at race or color," Griffin said in October 2012, "so it doesn't have a big part in my self-identity. [But] I think it has played a big part in how other people view me, just going back to when I was a kid, to even now, doing the things that I've been able to do. As an African American, I think other people view that in a different way than I do."

He found it intriguing that there could be such divergent viewpoints on race within the same ethnic group. Baylor professor Joseph Brown, who had Griffin in an upper-level class on minority and ethnic group politics, said the young man often led classroom discussions on race, which sometimes highlighted those differences. "He knows his heritage and his history," Brown said. "But he didn't view his heritage in such a way that it would restrict his perceptions of other people and his relationships with other individuals."

But even Griffin's willingness to accept and embrace viewpoints on race that differed from his own didn't quite prepare him for what awaited him in D.C.

The city of Washington, D.C.—carved out of a swath of land alongside the Potomac River that had been donated to the federal government by a pair of slaveholding states, Virginia and Maryland—has been seen as a special place for African Americans since at least April 1862, when, nine months before the Emancipation Proclamation, President Abraham Lincoln signed the Compensated Emancipation Act, effectively ending slavery in the District by paying slave owners up to $300 per freed slave. African Americans made up 30 percent of the city's population by the turn of the twentieth century, and that figure had risen to 70 percent by 1970 before beginning a steady decline. Before the Harlem Renaissance, Washington was the center of African American culture, with Duke Ellington, Langston Hughes, and Zora Neale Hurston all calling it home.

But between the civil unrest of the 1960s, the crack epidemic, the flight of the black middle class, and the encroaching gentrification—among other reasons—D.C. eventually lost its status as a majority-black city. "Chocolate City" was no more. But

Washington was still a largely segregated city, and it remains that way to this day.

One of the few institutions that unites whites and blacks in D.C., in fact, is the Redskins—especially the Redskins under Griffin. But there is one critical point of difference between white and black fans: while white fans generally speak of Griffin's race as being irrelevant, to many African American fans it is anything but. White fans may have welcomed Griffin with open arms, but black fans more or less *adopted* him—he was one of theirs. The connection was simply different, and no one understood that difference better than some of the Redskins' African American veterans.

"He's what this franchise and this community have been looking for, for over twenty years—a superstar quarterback," said London Fletcher, the veteran linebacker. "But he's more than that. He has the persona, the charisma, the talent. There's another dimension he brings. He's someone who can relate to anyone. You see everyone's falling in love with him. But for African Americans, it's an even different connection. In a lot of cities, it might not mean as much. But this is Washington, D.C. It means a lot."

Griffin's race "does matter," echoed Lorenzo Alexander, a Redskins backup linebacker and the special teams captain. "Here in the nation's capital—you know, Chocolate City—people see that. I think he brings hope to the city. He's probably the first franchise quarterback the Redskins have had in the last twenty years. And then, obviously, being a young African American male in the D.C. area, a lot of people can relate to him. He relates to people on so many different levels, outside of just being an elite quarterback. The way he carries himself, a role model—he's the full package."

When I spoke to African American Redskins fans about Griffin, that theme kept coming up: Griffin as a role model for the city's at-risk youth. It was one thing to have an African American quarterbacking the Redskins—that had happened plenty of times, from Williams to, more recently, Jason Campbell and Donovan McNabb. But it was yet another thing to have that quarterback possess Griffin's combination of dazzling talent, elite pedigree, sheer magnetism, and nationwide appeal. Griffin was someone who was viewed as an exceptional leader, someone who was actually praised for his character and "intangibles" (terms that usually were applied only to white quarterbacks) as often as he was for his athleticism.

"It's extra-special to have him here in Chocolate City," said Curtis Hughes, a season-ticket-holder from Capital Heights, Maryland (not far from FedEx Field), who wears a Griffin number 10 Redskins jersey to games. "I have two sons, and to show them that your franchise quarterback can be black, and hold himself with so much dignity, it's huge for me as a father."

Brian Mitchell, the former Redskins kick returner and running back, has been living in the D.C. area for the better part of twenty-three years and now cohosts a sports-talk radio show on the Redskins' flagship station, WTEM (ESPN 980). Searching for the proper way to characterize Griffin's potential impact, he brought up Michael Jordan's name.

"A lot of people in this day and age think there are no more role models, but he is one," Mitchell said. "He comes in with intelligence. He comes in without a lot of negativity—no negativity, basically. He's the ultimate gentleman. You hear a lot of people saying, 'Be like him.' Every once in a while someone comes along like that, someone who is the full package. Say what you want about Michael Jordan, but he knew how to handle himself both in an interview and on the basketball court. I'm not saying this kid will be Michael Jordan, but because of his ultimate intelligence, he can be at that level."

Once, not all that long ago, Robert Griffin III was just another kid who wanted to be like Mike. And now kids in Washington, D.C., and all over the country, wanted to be like RG3.

One person who would not want to be like RG3—who would not, in fact, want to have anything to do with him or any part in seeing him quarterbacking the Redskins—was George Preston Marshall. The team's original owner, having moved the franchise from Boston to Washington in 1937 in hopes of positioning it as "Dixie's Team," Marshall was an "arrogant, autocratic, meddlesome, bigoted and caustic" man, according to biographer Thomas G. Smith. While every other NFL team had integrated by 1952, Marshall would hold out another full decade—"I'll start signing Negroes when the Harlem Globetrotters start signing whites," he once proclaimed.

"Jim Brown, born ineligible to play for the Redskins," once wrote the *Washington Post*'s legendary columnist Shirley Povich, a longtime Marshall antagonist, "integrated their end zone three times yesterday."

Ultimately, it took pressure from the Kennedy administration, which threatened to withhold funds for the new stadium being proposed on the eastern side of town if the Redskins remained all-white, before Marshall finally and grudgingly traded for Bobby Mitchell, who in 1962 became the Redskins' first African American player.

Even still, Marshall went to his grave a stone-cold racist: when he died in 1969, his will called for the founding of a Redskins Foundation, with the stipulation that not a single dollar be directed toward "any purpose which supports or employs the principle of racial integration in any form." It is safe to say that this was not part of the official Redskins history that owner Daniel Snyder gave to Griffin after dinner that night in Waco following his Pro Day workout.

There are still old-timers in D.C., as well as children and grandchildren of those old-timers, for whom a lifelong love of the Redskins is qualified by a thin, not-quite-buried streak of resentment over the franchise's checkered racial history.

"There was a time not that long ago when a good thirty percent of black men in this city rooted for the Cowboys—just because of that history," said ESPN commentator Michael Wilbon, a former *Washington Post* columnist and longtime resident of the area. Wilbon gives Griffin something of a free pass, at least this early in his career, when it comes to absorbing all that complex history. "It's not possible for him to understand the angst, the pride, the whole nine yards. It's just not possible."

The Redskins have enjoyed a long history of great African American players, beginning with Bobby Mitchell himself, who was elected to the Hall of Fame in 1983, and continuing with Charley Taylor, Ken Houston, Doug Williams, Art Monk, Darrell Green, and others. But the distrust toward the franchise among the city's African American population never went completely away, and in fact it had been reignited in the last decade with the failed tenures of quarterbacks Campbell and McNabb. Campbell, a former first-round draft pick in 2005, was the Redskins' starter for three and a half seasons but never posted a winning record and never seemed to have the full backing of the team's management. McNabb, a six-time Pro Bowler in Philadelphia, came to the Redskins in the autumn of his career, in 2010, and departed after one forgettable season full of acrimony and sniping between the Shanahans and the McNabb camp.

"The black quarterback in this area," said Brian Mitchell, "hasn't had a long history and what seems like a fair shake."

That institutionalized distrust of the Redskins gave rise to one ancillary conspiracy theory regarding Griffin and the Redskins that was heard frequently in D.C.'s African American community. Neville Waters, a lifelong Redskins fan and a fifth-generation Washingtonian who is now a spokesman for the D.C. Taxicab Commission, told me that the drafting of Kirk Cousins in the fourth round in 2012 was seen as a red flag by many African Americans—who took it as a sign that the Shanahans intended to run Griffin into the ground.

"There was certainly some apprehension about the fact they drafted Cousins," Waters explained in October 2012—or three months before the knee injury to Griffin that lent the red-flag theorists some credence. "You mortgage the future to get your franchise quarterback, and then with a pick that could have been your starting cornerback or a lineman, you take a guy who under the best-case scenario will never play? It was like, what is [Mike] Shanahan doing? And then there was this option offense—kind of throwing [Griffin] out there. It's like, wait a minute, man. And you don't know. You want to give them the benefit of the doubt. But has Shanahan earned the benefit of the doubt with the black community? Not really. Hey, if they win, all is forgiven. But I would say there was certainly a suspicion. When you're sitting around with your buddies just talking shit, you look at that."

A nd then there is the name.

Outrage over the insensitivity of the Redskins' name (and its attendant logos, mascots, and other symbols) has ebbed and flowed over the years. If you step back from the rich franchise history and the team's insistence that the symbol is meant to "honor," not demean, Native Americans, there can be little doubt that the name is patently offensive. If you doubt that, simply replace "Red-" with "Black-" and see how it sounds. The Merriam-Webster online dictionary, under the entry "redskin," prefaces the definition by pointing out, in italics, that the word is "usually offensive."

The stance of Washington's African American community toward the name is best described as complicated, or fragmented. Given black America's own centuries-old struggle against prejudice and racism, it would make sense for there to be a heightened degree of sensitivity toward such outwardly racist symbolism—and in some corners, there is. "I hate that nickname," Neville Waters told me. But others in the black community are just as swept up in the tradition and glory of the Redskins and thus are as blind to the surface-level racism of the name as white fans are. For years, the team's unofficial mascot has been "Chief Zee," an African American man named Zema Williams who dresses in full Native American regalia, complete with a feathered headdress and—until

2008, when he dropped it from his act—a toy tomahawk. On any given Sunday, you'll see plenty of black folks, alongside whites, shouting out the final lines of "Hail to the Redskins": "Braves on the warpath / Fight for old D.C.!"

(The most unfortunate stance toward the Redskins' name on the part of an African American person was undoubtedly that of Clinton Portis, the great ex–Redskins running back, who once said to *Washington Post* columnist Mike Wise, "Hey, they used to call it the Negro Leagues back in the day. We didn't like it, but we had to take it. Now, the Indians have to take it.")

As 2012 flowed into 2013, the anti-Redskins'-name movement seemed to be gaining momentum—at least in the *Washington Post,* where anti-Redskins'-name columns appeared in the sports, local, and Sunday outlook sections over the span of one winter's month—and there was a growing consensus that the Redskins would eventually be forced to change their name, as most colleges featuring African American imagery already had. But how long it would take was anyone's guess.

There also seemed to be a consensus that one man had the power to hasten the change, if he saw fit to do so—Robert Griffin III.

In December, Wise, one of the most outspoken critics of the name, asked Griffin during one of the quarterback's weekly news conferences—unfortunately, the only access journalists had to him—what he thought about the team's name given the fact that many Native Americans deem it to be derogatory. This was right after the Rob Parker incident, and Griffin cast a get-me-out-of-here look at a Redskins media official before smiling sheepishly and saying, "I'm not qualified to speak on that. I didn't mean to stir up the other thing, so I'm not going to touch that one." It was undoubtedly the smart play. That was hardly the setting for such a difficult question—although given the Redskins' virtual quarantine of Griffin, it was the only opportunity Wise had available to him. And one could hardly fault Griffin for being gun-shy at that point.

"At just twenty-two years old, he has the owner's ear and the city's heart," Wise wrote in a subsequent column. "With his incredible QB skills and laid-back demeanor, this transcendent kid from Texas could be the Chosen One, all right—the one person who could make Redskins owner Daniel Snyder come to his senses and realize that it's time to stop demeaning Native Americans. . . . But I fear Griffin is not that guy. No young, dynamic leader of an NFL team is that guy. Pro players who take on controversial social debates are gone, replaced by athletes whose goal is to not offend—because that would mean fewer commercials, a loss of sponsors and, God forbid, a Q rating lower than Michael Jordan's."

There seemed to be a feeling that Griffin was shying away from any bold statements regarding race because of a desire to placate his corporate sponsors and remain consciously vanilla. After all, remember that Jordan—Griffin's onetime idol—upon being asked in 1990 why he wouldn't support a Democratic Senate candidate in his home state of North Carolina, famously replied, "Because Republicans buy shoes too." It very well could have been the case that Griffin's agents and sponsors and assorted other handlers were telling him to stay away from the name issue and generally to keep himself as race-neutral as possible. Maybe there was some sort of strategy to position him as a true postracial icon.

But there was at least one other plausible theory: that Griffin sincerely believed what he said about race—that he really did see the world in a color-blind way—and also that, at twenty-two years old and as a Washington-area resident for less than six months, he really wasn't qualified to weigh in on the appropriateness of the Redskins' name, or for that matter on the city's African American history and culture. What some might have seen as a cop-out, others could view as a young man who simply wanted to be liked and who was also smart enough to understand that the sort of nuance required of this subject simply wasn't possible in the sound bite–happy setting of a news conference.

"When people thought Michael Jordan [avoided social issues], it was a construct: 'I'm going to try to be this,'" Wilbon told me. "I don't think RG3 has to try. He might just be the guy."

"In reality, he's an easy person to stereotype, from his appearance—he's got the braids, he's dark-skinned," said former Redskins all-pro linebacker LaVar Arrington, who played six seasons for the team and now hosts a sports-talk show on Washington's WNEW-FM. "But you just see the kid, not his race. You don't say, 'I'm proud he's a black quarterback.' You're like, 'Man, that's RG3'. . . . I just see him as just a great person who doesn't need to conform.

"He transcends race—easily. He's postracial."

That's not a term—postracial—that you want to go tossing around, certainly not in Washington, D.C., where in many corners of the African American community it is considered a false premise, a white do-gooder's fantasyland, a red herring designed to distract folks from the prejudice that still pervades our culture.

"'Postracial' is the most dangerous concept in the English language," said my friend and former colleague Howard Bryant, a columnist and commentator at ESPN who often writes about sociopolitical issues in sports. "An African American man is only postracial until he gets stopped for the first time for driving while black."

Bryant, the author of three books, including *Shut Out: A Story of Race and Baseball in Boston,* said that superstar African American athletes have been forced into one template, one that requires them to "suppress race at all times"—with severe consequences if they don't.

"We've seen this all before—with Tiger Woods," Bryant said. "A guy who was going to revolutionize sports and unite people. But it's an impossible standard to meet. It's a setup." Where Griffin says he wants to unite people, Bryant would counter by saying, "You can't be a uniter and not talk about the source of the division. The division is race."

The problem for Griffin, at least in 2012 at the tender age of twenty-two, was that people recognized in him the potential to be The One—and at times tried to put that burden on him—before he even had the chance to figure out who he was and what he stood for. People seemed to want him to be another Arthur Ashe or Jim Brown, while conveniently forgetting that Ashe and Brown didn't become important advocates for social change until well into their professional careers. At twenty-two, they were still trying to figure out their new worlds. Perhaps in time, as Griffin gains maturity and perspective and comfort in his surroundings, he will be ready to step into such a role. Or he may never be comfortable doing so.

"Give him time," said Brian Mitchell. "He has to be responsible to himself first. Once he understands the whole aspect of being a professional, everything he needs to know to be the best football player he can be, he can do other things. I did the same thing. I had to learn to be a football player first, and after I did that, I got out in the community."

As for Parker, he apologized for his comments regarding Griffin soon after making them, saying via his Twitter account, "I completely understand how the issue of race in sports is a sensitive one and needs to be handled with great care. [On December 12], I failed to do that. I believe the intended topic is a worthy one. Robert's thoughts about being an African American quarterback and the impact of his phenomenal success have been discussed in other media outlets, as well as among sports fans, particularly those in the African American community. The failure was in how I chose to discuss it on First Take, and in doing so turned a productive conversation into a negative one."

In a subsequent column (titled "Allow Me to Reintroduce Myself") for TheShadowLeague.com, his new employer, Parker took a less apologetic tone: "We are black men," he wrote. "This is what we do. We challenge each other. It will never stop, nor should it. . . . Sorry to break it to all of those who thought I made it up or exposed something, but this isn't a new or outrageous conversation."

"Black people have those kinds of conversations all the time, every day," confirmed Michael Eric Dyson, a sociology professor at Georgetown University, a radio host, a cultural critic, and the author of books on Martin Luther King, Malcolm X, and Barack Obama, among others. "The reason Parker's comments caused controversy was because not many white people were used to hearing black people debate the inner-machinations of blackness in

America. Parker was merely making public a debate that happens among black people every day."

Dyson defended both Griffin's race-neutral outlook and Parker's questioning of it as legitimate stances toward race (though he also said Parker's approach was "clumsily stated and inelegantly conceived"). "I think Parker represented established blackness, and RG3 represented emergent blackness, and those views were in conflict," Dyson said. "Established blackness deals with the conventional ideas of how people live through racial identities and embrace them. Emergent blackness is about shattering the barriers and trying to overcome the boundaries of the traditional notion of blackness. [Griffin] is trying to challenge the narrow definition of what blackness is. There is no such thing as one right way to be black."

Dyson's nuanced views on race are of the sort that are mostly absent from the mainstream media's simplistic treatment of the issue—an absence that helps explain how Parker's comments became so incendiary. America may have come a long way from the days of segregationist owners and a black quarterback being a novelty, but there were still certain conversations that folks were not ready to have—not least of all Robert Griffin III.

THIRTEEN

THE QB REVOLUTION

As winter approached and the 2012 NFL regular season entered its fourth quarter, it was becoming clear that something was happening at the quarterback position in the league—something big, something fascinating, something perhaps even momentous. At the very least, it was a trend. At most, it was nothing short of a revolution. Begin with the fact that three rookie quarterbacks, piloting teams that had finished a combined 14-34 in 2011—Seattle's Russell Wilson, Indianapolis's Andrew Luck, and Washington's Robert Griffin III—had those same teams, a season later, pointed toward the playoffs. A fourth youngster at the helm of a playoff contender, San Francisco's Colin Kaepernick, might as well have been a rookie: though he was in his second season, he had barely played in 2011 and didn't make his first NFL start until Week 10 of 2012.

The rookie success was, in some ways, revolutionary on its own. Before 2012, only eight rookie quarterbacks in NFL history had led their teams to nine or more wins. In 2012, Luck, Wilson, and Griffin would all do so. Before 2012, only five rookie quarterbacks had thrown twenty or more touchdown passes in a single season. In 2012, Luck, Wilson, and Griffin would all reach that mark. By January, in fact, no fewer than half the twelve teams in the playoffs would be led by quarterbacks in their first or second season in the league, including an unprecedented three rookies.

For years, it had been accepted wisdom that most rookie quarterbacks, even some clearly great ones, would struggle, sometimes to extreme degrees. John Elway went 4-6 and posted a horrid 54.9 passer rating as a rookie. Peyton Manning went 3-13 and threw more interceptions than touchdowns. Troy Aikman went 0-11 and threw *twice as many* interceptions as touchdowns. Eli Manning went 1-6 and posted a 0.0 passer rating in one game.

"To have three rookie quarterbacks with winning records this year, it's really hard to explain," said Redskins coach Mike Shanahan, who had delved into statistical databases before the 2012 season, documenting and quantifying those rookie struggles in an effort to lower expectations on Griffin. "Obviously, [Griffin, Wilson, and Luck are] three excellent quarterbacks. I think now colleges are a little bit more sophisticated in the passing game. You have three quarterbacks who are excellent football players. I think you'll see more in the future."

But beyond the rookie success, something else was going on that fascinated observers and threatened to upend the way the NFL thought of the quarterback position. The Redskins, Seahawks, and 49ers, with Griffin, Wilson, and Kaepernick, respectively, were all running offenses featuring elements more typically associated with college football—zone-reads and options and pistol formations. (For that matter, even Luck, widely assumed to be a pure drop-back passer, ran some occasional zone-read plays for the Colts and proved to be a surprisingly adept and nimble runner, rushing for 255 yards in 2012.)

Though they were linked by the offenses they ran, each zone-read quarterback brought a different set of skills, as well as a different body type, to the equation. Kaepernick was a sinewy six-foot-five and 233 pounds, Wilson was a powerful five-eleven and 205, and Griffin, at six-two and 220, was in between. Griffin had nearly world-class speed (his 40-yard dash time at the NFL combine in March had been a sizzling 4.41 seconds), while Wilson (4.55) and Kaepernick (4.53) were not far behind. Wilson was perhaps the best pure passer in the group, having set an NCAA record for passing efficiency the year before at Wisconsin. What they shared was a combination of athleticism, pure passing ability, intelligence, and fearlessness.

Likewise, none of their teams ran the zone-read/pistol in precisely the same way, or in the same quantities—generally speaking, by the end of the season the zone-read package made up anywhere from 10 to 30 percent of their team's total offensive plays. But taken together—and adding in the success that second-year signal-caller Cam Newton was having in Carolina with some of the same concepts—they were changing the way the NFL viewed the position.

Of the new vanguard of read-option teams, the Redskins were the only ones who had been running the offense from Week 1—announcing its arrival on the second play of their season, in New Orleans, when Griffin ran the option to perfection on a twelve-yard run for a first down. It was well into the season before the Seahawks started using Wilson in a similar manner—unlike Griffin and Kaepernick, he did not have much experience with the offense in college—and head coach Pete Carroll made no attempt to hide the fact that he was persuaded to do so by what he saw out of Griffin and the Redskins. After a 19–13 loss at St. Louis in Week 4—the third time in four weeks the Seahawks had been held to fewer than 20 points—Carroll holed up in his office and watched all the tape he could find of the Redskins' new offense. After adopting the zone-read gradually, the Seahawks would go on to win seven of their final eight games—putting up 150 points in one remarkable three-game stretch in December—to earn a wild-card berth in the playoffs.

"I was impressed with how much [the Redskins] got out of it," Carroll told reporters in November. "They're way ahead of every-body else in terms of their commitment to a really college style of offense, and it's been very effective. . . . I was influenced a little bit more than I thought when I first looked at it."

Meantime, Kaepernick's success in San Francisco could be traced to the ballsiest decision made by an NFL coach in 2012—or perhaps ever—when 49ers head coach Jim Harbaugh chose to keep Kaepernick as his starter late in the regular season, even when deposed starter Alex Smith, who owned a record of 19-5-1 the past two seasons, came back from a concussion. The stunning decision was influenced at least in part by the success that Griffin (whom Harbaugh had tried to recruit to Stanford five years earlier) was having in Washington running an offense with elements of the zone-read and pistol formation. Kaepernick had run the pistol at the University of Nevada under the coach, Chris Ault, credited with inventing it.

"Quarterbacks that have a talent for running the ball can be very effective," Harbaugh told reporters in explaining his choice of Kaepernick over Smith. "A quarterback that can get out of the pocket, run, pick up first downs—that's a threat the defense has to account for."

You have to be careful when using the word "revolution." Clearly, three young quarterbacks (or four, counting Newton, whose Panthers finished the season 7-9) running the zone-read doesn't constitute a full-blown sea change, and it wasn't as if the league had never witnessed a handful of hotshot mobile quarterbacks who were supposedly about to revolutionize offensive football. Remember the mid-2000s heyday of Daunte Culpepper, Michael Vick, and Vince Young? It didn't stick then, and it may not stick now.

"I think the read-option is the flavor of the day," Pittsburgh Steelers head coach Mike Tomlin, who came up through the ranks on the defensive side of the ball, told reporters in March. "We'll see if it's the flavor of the year, see if [coaches] are committed to getting their [quarterbacks] hit. A few years ago, people were talking wildly about the Wildcat. It's less of a discussion now."

At the same time, just because Griffin, Wilson, and Kaepernick were having immediate success in 2012, by no means did these zone-read quarterbacks have a monopoly on winning. Far from it. Joe Flacco, who led the Baltimore Ravens to the Super Bowl title, was about as immobile a quarterback as the league had ever seen—he rushed for a grand total of twenty-two yards in all of 2012. (Griffin had six individual rushes at least that long in 2012.) Meantime, New England's Tom Brady, whom Flacco vanquished in the AFC Championship Game—and who owns three Super Bowl rings—had all of thirty-two yards rushing in 2012.

But who did Flacco beat to win the Super Bowl? That would be the 49ers and Kaepernick, who, in his tenth NFL start, put on a three-hour infomercial for the new generation of smart, mobile quarterbacks in the title game, throwing for 302 yards and rushing for another 62 and very nearly bringing the 49ers all the way back from a 22-point second-half deficit.

The vast majority of NFL teams were still running traditional offenses with drop-back quarterbacks, and that was unlikely to change anytime soon. But what had changed was the notion that you could not win with a young, athletic quarterback running the zone-read option out of the pistol formation.

H e's going to put some guys in this building in the Hall of Fame."
A Redskins official said that to me one day in early December, as Griffin's rookie trajectory was nearing its peak, following the *Monday Night Football* victory over the Giants that evened the Redskins' record at 6-6 and left them just one game out of first place. The conversation was about Griffin's transformative effect on every aspect of the franchise—not just wins and losses, but everything from ticket demand to the general mood of employees to, in this official's estimation, the legacies of individuals going forward.

"He'll have to win some Super Bowls, multiple ones," the Redskins official said. "But I don't see any way that doesn't happen."

The prediction of multiple Super Bowl titles aside, the official had a point in highlighting the legacy enhancement that an elite franchise quarterback—of the type that Griffin appeared to be—was capable of producing around a franchise. It was not so far-fetched to imagine, for example, that even one more Super Bowl title with the Redskins, combined with the two he won in Denver, would lock down Mike Shanahan's place in Canton. Likewise, talented offensive players such as receiver Pierre Garcon and left tackle Trent Williams can be made to look even better by the presence of someone such as Griffin—there could be Pro Bowls and, yes, maybe even Hall of Fame honors for them in the future, given another eight to ten years of this type of production. The Redskins went from 25th and 26th in the NFL in points scored in the first two years of the Shanahan regime—2010 (302) and 2011 (288)—to fourth in 2012 (436); while Griffin wasn't the only reason for the vast improvement, he was undoubtedly the biggest. And in the NFL that type of success tends to lift the entire boat: it turns offensive coordinators into head coaches, head coaches into Hall of Famers, and good players into Pro Bowlers.

Even amid all that young talent at quarterback around the league in 2012, Griffin stood out. As a runner, he simply had no equal at the position—by Week 13 he had already broken Newton's record for rushing yards in a season by a rookie quarterback. And as a passer, he was nearly as elite, hovering near the league leaders in passer rating, interception percentage, and completion percentage. By the end of the season, he would set NFL rookie records in the first two categories.

"I don't think anybody in the history of the league has played at his level," Shanahan said in December. "At least over the last forty years, when I take a look at the numbers and what he has done, I don't think anybody has played at his level. As we've talked about before, he's got a unique skill set—his ability to throw, drop back, play action, put a threat on a defense with his running ability—and he will just get better and better. He's just scratching the surface. And the reason I say that is because he works at it."

Of course, the two sides of Griffin's game, the passing and the running, went hand in hand. It was his running ability that to a large degree kept his completion percentage so high, since Griffin could tuck the ball away and scramble for a first down when other quarterbacks would have to throw the ball away or be forced into tight coverages. And likewise, his ability as a passer kept defenses honest and made it a gamble to stack the box—which, in turn, kept the running lanes open for him. (It also goes without saying that Griffin's supreme abilities contributed greatly to running back Alfred Morris's excellent season, although the effect is almost impossible to quantify. Morris may have sometimes waltzed through giant holes created by Griffin's mere presence, but just as important, he proved to be a punishing, hard-nosed runner who was almost never tackled by the first defender who hit him. Put it this way: any competent NFL running back would probably gain a thousand yards with Griffin as his quarterback. The other 613 yards Morris put up were all him.)

Of all the attributes Griffin displayed during his rookie season, it was his passing accuracy that was both the most surprising and the most auspicious for his future. Though his completion percentage in 2012 ranked fifth in the NFL, Griffin, according to advanced stats kept by the website ProFootballFocus.com, ranked second only to Green Bay's Aaron Rodgers in "accuracy percentage," which factors in drops, spikes, batted balls, etc., and he also led the league in accuracy percentage when under pressure. His ratio of four touchdown passes for every interception thrown in 2012 was bettered by only two quarterbacks, Brady and Rodgers.

Accuracy, though, is more than merely the avoidance of interceptions and incompletions; it is also about ball placement—being able to put the ball in the exact spot that will maximize the receiver's yards after catch. Many hard-core football stats gurus believe that accuracy is the single most dependable predictor of success, because it involves so many individual traits—not only ball placement but also timing, decision-making skills, patience, confidence. It is perhaps no coincidence that the top six active quarterbacks in completion percentage are Rodgers, Drew Brees, Peyton Manning, Tony Romo, Matt Schaub, and Tom Brady.

"I don't think enough credit was given to him as a quarterback because of all his athleticism, but he makes good decisions with where the ball goes," Cincinnati Bengals coach Marvin Lewis said of Griffin. "The ball gets out of his hand very quickly. He has an extremely strong arm and can throw the football a long ways. But he gets the ball in and out quickly, a very quick release, and gets the ball out and going. He seems to understand where the ball should go."

Kaepernick (62.4 percent) and Wilson (64.1) were right there with Griffin (65.6) in completion percentage—which only bolstered the case that the zone-read makes the passing game stronger. The number crunchers at ProFootballFocus.com found a way to quantify the advantage in the passing game offered by a mobile quarterback with a stat called "quarterback time in pocket"—the idea being that a quarterback with wheels can extend pass plays by avoiding sacks. And it was perhaps no surprise that the league leaders (among quarterbacks with at least 250 drop-backs) were, in order, Wilson, Kaepernick, Vick, Griffin, and Newton.

What was impossible to quantify, however, was how much Griffin's success could be credited to the creativity of the Shanahans in utilizing him and how much belonged to Griffin alone. In other words, would Griffin have been this good, this soon, no matter what offense he ran? Or did the Redskins' offense maximize his abilities and his production?

Chris Cooley, the veteran tight end, turned in his Redskins playbook on August 28, 2012, the day he was released by the team, a little less than two weeks before the season opener. He took possession of it again on October 21, when the team re-signed him following the season-ending Achilles injury suffered by Fred Davis. In the nearly two months that had passed, the Redskins' offense had changed dramatically—from the vanilla one on display during the preseason to the multifaceted, somewhat radical one that started to show up once the games began to count.

"When I got back here, the first thing [the coaches] said is, 'This kid is awesome,'" Cooley recalled, referring to Griffin. "He was above and beyond what they expected, especially what they expected this year. The game plan from Week Four of training camp to Week One of the season was a drastic change. When I came back in Week Seven, it was like, 'Okay, I'd better take some notes today, because this is another world.'"

All the way back in the summer, the Redskins coaches called their classroom and film sessions "Football 101." The zone-read package they were installing required an entirely new way of thinking about offensive football—not only different blocking schemes and receiver routes but different cues and different responsibilities. The running backs, for example, had to learn to read Griffin's movements to determine whether to squeeze the ball (a handoff) or let go (a quarterback keeper), while receivers often had to watch Griffin after the snap to determine whether they would be blockers or pass-catchers on a particular play.

"I remember when we first put it in, it was kind of like learning to walk again," tight end Logan Paulsen told *Sports Illustrated*'s Peter King. "All of a sudden, we're doing all this zone-read stuff and we're letting guys go and pushing the whole offensive line to different [defenders] than we normally do. The receivers, they have vastly different responsibilities now. I think this whole process has just been kind of a gigantic learning experience."

But the zone-read wasn't replacing the Redskins' 2011 offense—it was merely supplementing it. At its heart, the Redskins' offense remained the Shanahans' take on the West Coast offense, with its progressions, its bubble-screens, its zone-blocking schemes, and its three-, five-, and seven-step drops. But now they would be running it largely out of the pistol offense, with Griffin lined up about four yards behind center. Usually there would be a running back situated just behind him, and at various times other backs or tight ends or receivers might wind up in the backfield as well—added elements that Kyle Shanahan called "illusion" and "window dressing." Griffin became an active participant in formulating each week's game plan, his input sought out by the coaching staff.

"You have to credit Kyle and Coach Shanahan for being able to adapt to Robert's talents, but also being able to keep the integrity of the system that was here," backup quarterback Kirk Cousins said. "It's a tough balance to find, but clearly they found it. Credit goes both to Robert for communicating what he likes and what he's comfortable with, and the coaches for adapting to him."

(Because the Redskins built the zone-read/pistol elements on top of their standard, more conventional offense, as opposed to implementing a separate offense, it also made the transition from Griffin to Cousins somewhat seamless on the handful of occasions during 2012 when the backup was pressed into duty. In the three games in which Cousins saw action—including one start—he went a combined 33-of-48, with four touchdowns, three interceptions, and a 101.6 passer rating.)

The Redskins understood one thing when it came to Griffin and the zone-read/pistol offense: it wasn't something they had to use frequently in order to make it productive. Only a fraction of their total plays might feature the zone-read package, but the mere existence of it forced opponents to spend countless valuable hours during game week preparing for it, while on Sundays even the threat of it made everything else the Redskins ran that much more effective.

"It puts the defense in conflict," ESPN analyst and ex-quarterback Trent Dilfer said. "They may only run it a few times a game, but every time he takes a snap the defense has to be ready for it." Dilfer called the Redskins' offense the "perfect first- and second-down offense"—because the uncertainty in the minds of the defense was highest when the Redskins had many options for play-calls. (It was not, on the other hand, a great third-down offense, ranking 24th in the NFL in third-down efficiency in 2012, largely because the element of deception and uncertainty was min-imized when the Redskins were in obvious pass situations.)

The brilliant simplicity of the zone-read could turn a defensive player's aggression against himself. On a basic play, Griffin "read" the defensive end to determine whether to hand off or keep—if the end crashed down to stop the running back, he kept it, and if the end moved toward Griffin, he handed off. The Redskins could also run pass plays out of the offense, with Griffin pulling the ball back and throwing it, or they could send an additional "pitch man" (often receiver Josh Morgan) behind Griffin for a possible lateral after the faked handoff. And if a team chose to bring its safety up toward the line of scrimmage to help against the option—as the Cowboys did on Thanksgiving Day—Griffin was likely to throw a home-run ball over the top against the ensuing one-on-one coverage, as he did on the sixty-eight-yard bomb to Aldrick Robinson. Making all of this possible was Griffin's deadly combination of athleticism, passing acumen, and smarts.

Some teams dealt with Griffin by using a "spy" assigned to shadow his every move, but that made one defender unavailable to cover the Redskins' other skill-position players, altering the essential math of offense versus defense. Throw in the Redskins' heavy reliance on play-action (Griffin used it on 39.9 percent of his total plays in 2012, according to ProFootballFocus.com, by far the highest of any quarterback), and it all seemed like just a lot of sleight-of-hand—a shell game.

But all the way through the end of the season, NFL defenses couldn't stop falling for it.

"As far as shutting them down, I don't know if it's possible with a dynamic quarterback like him, who can kill you running and throwing," Giants defensive end Justin Tuck said of Griffin after the Redskins' *Monday Night Football* win on December 2. "Even when you're playing your best ball, he can run you all the way out to the edge. There were two plays in there where we should have had sacks and he outran us. . . . If he stays healthy, he's going to be havoc on defenses for a long time."

If he stays healthy . . ." was a common refrain from observers when it came to Griffin. The downside of the zone-read offense was obvious: the more the ball is in the hands of the quarterback, the greater the possibility that he'll get hit—and get hurt. There was room for debate, however, in regard to whether the danger was greater within the pocket, with defensive linemen and various blitzing linebackers and safeties bearing down on you, or outside the tackles on the sort of designed quarterback runs the zone-read called for. Put another way: Were the Redskins, by the nature of their offense, putting Griffin at greater risk for harm than would have happened with a more conventional offense? It was a question that would attract greater scrutiny in December 2012.

"I just don't think you can design your offense around a running quarterback, because in this league defenses will knock you out," ESPN analyst Ron Jaworski said on the *Mike and Mike* radio show, voicing the prevailing wisdom. "That's what the NFL is about—putting the quarterback on his back."

But Mike Shanahan would—and did—argue something else: that the zone-read, when run properly, actually protects the quarterback, because it both slows down the defense's initial attack and gets the quarterback out of the pocket, where all sorts of bad things can happen to him, from blind-side drillings to risky scrambles over the middle. The concussion Griffin suffered against Atlanta, Shanahan reminded everyone, had occurred on a scramble—not a designed run—and could have been avoided had Griffin slid or ducked out of bounds sooner.

There is no real evidence that mobile quarterbacks get hurt any more frequently than straight drop-back ones. Yes, it is true that Michael Vick has played a full 16-game season only once in his career. But it is also true that drop-back passers Tom Brady, Peyton Manning, and Carson Palmer have all suffered season-ending injuries when they were hit in the pocket as they were throwing, or just after—either way, the throwing motion had left them in a more vulnerable position than the position of a running quarterback with the ball on the outside, who can see the danger in front of him.

It really didn't seem to matter what style of quarterback you were—you would always be in danger. On one particularly gruesome weekend in November, no fewer than four starting quarterbacks, representing the entire spectrum of mobile-versus-drop-back styles—Michael Vick, Alex Smith, Jay Cutler, and Ben Roethlisberger—went down to injuries serious enough to cost them at least one additional game.

Still, the Seahawks, 49ers, and Redskins all were united in one sense—the way in which they limited their quarterbacks' exposure in the pocket. It wasn't mere coincidence that the three teams with the fewest pass attempts per game in 2012 were Seattle (25.9), San Francisco (27.1), and Washington (27.7). (Luck's Colts, by contrast, attempted an average of 40.1 passes per game, fifth-most in the NFL.)

"People notice when [Griffin] gets hit running the ball," Kyle

Shanahan told NFL.com. "But they don't realize how violent it is in the pocket. He doesn't get hit like [drop-back passers do]. With the threat of the zone-read, and the fact that he's not sitting there [in the pocket], defensive linemen aren't teeing off on him."

There was another reason the Redskins might not have wanted Griffin dropping back to pass more often: he wasn't always well protected in the passing game. The Redskins' offensive line ranked 17th in the NFL in "pass-blocking efficiency," a ProFootballFocus .com stat that measures how much pressure a quarterback is under. Individually, right tackle Tyler Polumbus was the main culprit: he ranked just 76th among all NFL tackles as a pass-blocker.

"The reason I don't think Shanahan should staple Griffin to the pocket is simple," *Sports Illustrated*'s Peter King wrote in October. "His line isn't good. And if Griffin tries to be a pocket quarterback . . . he's going to get blind-sided and ear-holed by the Jared Allens and Justin Tucks of the NFC, and he'll end up side-lined that way. So he's got to use his mobility, [but] for now he just has to be smarter."

The sudden prevalence of the zone-read option in 2012 caught the attention of the NFL headquarters, which in October—not long after Griffin expressed confusion over whether he could be hit after a zone-read handoff—sent around a video and a directive to all 32 teams that clarified the rules pertaining to when a quarterback has full protection and when he can be hit like any other offensive player. Essentially, the league said, when a quarterback hands off but fakes as if he has the ball, his only protection is the normal unnecessary-roughness penalty—and not even helmet-to-helmet contact is illegal.

In other words, when a quarterback runs the ball—or even fakes running it—he is the equivalent of a running back. And it probably would not surprise you to learn that running backs, on average, get injured the most often and have the shortest NFL careers of any position group. It simply isn't in your best interests to be the guy stuck holding the ball at the end of the play too often.

"Some of these [young quarterbacks] are great athletes—it's hard to get a really good shot at them," Giants coach Tom Coughlin told reporters two months after the Super Bowl, perhaps signaling the way defenses will approach the problem of mobile quarterbacks in 2013. "But [the hits] are cumulative in our business, and we play 16 games."

The dual-threat-quarterback revolution, if we're going to agree to call it that, came to the NFL about a decade after it took over collegiate football. Before 2001, no quarterback in NCAA history had passed for 2,000 yards and rushed for 1,000 in the same season—if you could run that well as a quarterback, you were typically in a wishbone, triple-option offense with few pass plays, and if you could throw that well, you were a drop-back passer, period. But then, between 2001 and 2011, the 2,000/1,000 double-milestone was reached 11 times (including three times by Kaepernick at Nevada), and in 2012 no fewer than five quarterbacks did it. (Griffin, in case you're wondering, isn't a member of the 2,000/1,000 club, having failed to gain 1,000 yards rushing in any of his seasons at Baylor.)

It seems safe to say the dual-threat quarterback is here to stay in college football. But what about the NFL? Do Griffin, Wilson, and Kaepernick represent the first wave of a new type of NFL signal-caller? The NFL, after all, is very much a copycat league. Or will this be just another fad that runs its course and disappears, leaving the league dominated, as always, by pocket passers? Opinion is more or less mixed.

"I've never seen a player like him," Hall of Fame wide receiver and current ESPN analyst Cris Carter said of Griffin on the *Mike and Mike* radio show. "I played with Randall Cunningham, and I've seen Michael Vick play a lot. But I've never seen a quarterback that has that type of athletic ability, that type of explosion—if he wants to. I mean, he [doesn't] have to use it. He is a pocket passer. . . . As far as revolutionizing the game and things like that, God doesn't make a lot of people like RG3. So I don't think [he's] going to be revolutionizing the game."

A dissenting voice comes from John Madden, the former coach and television analyst, who said on SiriusXM Radio, "I think it's going to be the pro quarterback style, I really do. If you go back and look at high school football, the way they play, and college football, the way they play, that's the type of quarterback that we're developing. And that's the type of quarterback that's going to come into the league, and I think eventually that's going to be the pro-type quarterback."

Griffin, in particular, may be more of an aberration than a revolutionary. Before him, no quarterback in NFL history had passed for more than 3,000 yards and rushed for more than 750 yards while completing more than 60 percent of his passes. (But if Griffin is an aberration, so too is Kaepernick—because if you ex-

trapolate the latter's 2012 numbers over a full season, he would
have joined Griffin in the ultra-exclusive 3,000/750/60 club.)

As much as we like to lean on historical comparisons, there
simply are no historical precedents for what Griffin—and to a
lesser extent Kaepernick and Wilson—did in 2012. Vick and
Cunningham, with career completion percentages of 56.3 and
56.6 percent, respectively, weren't nearly as accurate. Great scram-
blers such as Steve Young and Fran Tarkenton never came close to
Griffin's rushing totals. (Did you say "What about Tim Tebow?"
In 2011, when Tebow started 11 games for Denver and rushed for
an impressive 660 yards, he threw for just 1,729 yards and completed just 46.5 percent of his passes.)

But the extent to which offensive coaches continue to build on
what the Redskins, Seahawks, and 49ers did in 2012 is only half
of the equation as a new season beckons. The other half is what
defensive coaches do to combat the zone-read and this new wave
of super-mobile quarterbacks.

"Let's give it five years and then evaluate," Coughlin told reporters in March, staking out a reasonable middle ground for the
question of where it goes from here. "Let's not rush to judgment on
anything. Obviously, [the zone-read] is very effective. But some of
these defensive coaches, they're not sitting around looking out the
window and having coffee. They're into it. The energy level in the
defensive end of the hall in most buildings has been perked up by
what's happened."

Even among Redskins fans—and as you might expect, among
team officials as well—there were mixed feelings about how much
zone-read the offense should use with Griffin in 2013. On the one

hand, there was no better way to exploit and maximize the young man's abundant talents—and the goal here, of course, is simple: to win Super Bowls.

On the other hand, there was what happened to Griffin at the end of the 2012 season.

FOURTEEN

THE EMPIRE CRUMBLES

The vicious hit, applied by an opposing linebacker, came on an option play and caught the quarterback flush on his side, just under the rib cage. The pain was intense, nearly debilitating, each breath a struggle. But the quarterback picked himself up off the turf and stayed in the game—finished the game, in fact. That night, when the quarterback's roommate came home to find him in bed, writhing in pain—he had been urinating blood, the quarterback admitted—they went to the hospital, the quarterback now close to death. Unable to find the problem, the doctors finally cut him open to find his kidney had been both ruptured and relocated, shoved behind his spine. His heart stopped for half a minute. The kidney was removed. A priest was summoned for last rites. But the quarterback pulled through, and when he came to, he told his coach he wanted to play football again. When the coach said no, the quarterback petitioned the school, and when the school said no, the quarterback was devastated. "I was crushed," he recalled much later. "I should have been thankful I was alive, but all I could think about was never playing football again."

That anecdote comes from the football memoir *Think Like a Champion*, the author of which is the quarterback in question, a man named Mike Shanahan. He had been a junior at Eastern Illinois, in 1974, when football nearly cost him his life, but the injury also wound up giving him his life's work—because, no longer able to play football, he went immediately into coaching. He discovered he was very good at it.

Nearly forty years later, in the first week of 2013, Shanahan was standing at a lectern at Redskins Park in Ashburn, Virginia, addressing the Washington Redskins' media contingent a few days before the franchise's first home playoff game in thirteen years. Shanahan's quarterback, Robert Griffin III, had been dealing with a knee injury—diagnosed as a grade 1 sprain of the lateral collateral ligament—for nearly a month, ever since a hit to the leg in the fourth quarter against the Baltimore Ravens on December 9. It had forced Griffin to miss one game (the following week against Cleveland) and had limited his mobility in the two games since. But here, amid questions about Griffin's condition as the Redskins prepared to take on the Seattle Seahawks in the NFC wild-card playoff game, Shanahan was explaining the mentality of playing hurt.

"Guys play hurt," Shanahan said. "They're telling their teammates, 'You know what? I'm going to play. I'm not going to let you down.' I think that's one of the reasons why [Griffin] wanted to play [against Cleveland]. He understood that a number of football players on our football team are playing hurt. He did not want to let anybody down. When he sees London Fletcher, Trent Williams—guys who can hardly even walk—he wants to be in there. That's why he was mad at me. I said, 'You are injured, you are not hurt. You're injured, and you cannot play when you're injured. This is not the best for you and your future for me to put you in this situation.' I think his teammates appreciate that he wanted to be out there, and if I were to let him, he would have gone out there—or I should say, if the doctors would have let him. He's that type of guy. Once you have a guy that is going to put his body on the line when that might not be the best thing for himself or the future of him, they gain respect very quickly."

Griffin, in other words, was Shanahan's kind of man—a man's man, a football player's football player, the kind of guy who would sacrifice anything to get back on the field with his teammates. Shanahan, who once wanted to play with one kidney, and Griffin, who wanted to play on one good leg, were one and the same.

That mentality—which was hardly unique to Shanahan and Griffin and could be found in every NFL locker room—goes a long way toward explaining what happened to Griffin at the end of the Redskins' season. It explains how a brilliant young quarterback who was visibly hurt—whose knee was clearly getting worse over the course of the playoff game against Seattle and whose condition by the end was bad enough that fans both at FedEx Field and watching at home on TV were screaming, "Get him out of there!"—could be left to fend for himself until, ultimately, the knee simply gave out.

To understand how the Redskins and Mike Shanahan could let that happen to Robert Griffin III—his season ending with him crumpled on the chopped-up turf, his knee shredded and his future in doubt—you have to understand the culture of football, and you have to understand that the normal rules of decency and honor, and even medicine, do not necessarily apply in this strange and twisted world.

. . .

His first words, when someone finally got to his side, were these: "Just get me up, get me to the huddle—quick, we've got to hurry."

Griffin was on his back, in between the 4 and the 0 at the Redskins' 40-yard line at FedEx Field, and he couldn't get up on his own. It was December 9, 2012, and the Redskins trailed the visiting Baltimore Ravens by eight points with just under two minutes left in a game that was very much a must-win for Washington. On a second-and-19 from his own 27-yard line, Griffin had taken off on a scramble when the right side of the pocket collapsed. He was preparing to get down—more a side-roll than a slide—to avoid an onrushing Ravens defender when, from Griffin's right, Haloti Ngata, the Ravens' 340-pound nose tackle, crashed into his outstretched right leg. The impact buggy-whipped his leg, hyperextending the knee and stretching the lateral collateral ligament on the outside of the joint beyond its limits.

Griffin screamed out in pain—"Like a man, of course," he would joke later. The first person to get to Griffin's side was Logan Paulsen, the Redskins tight end, and he did as he was told.

"I got him up," Paulsen recalled. "And then I realized, man, he could barely walk."

Griffin didn't make it back to the huddle—at least not immediately. He limped slowly to the Redskins' sideline, but remained there for only one play. According to Shanahan's account the following day, Dr. James Andrews, the noted physician who serves as the Redskins' team orthopedist, cleared Griffin to go back into the game during a brief conversation. "He had a chance to look at [Griffin]," Shanahan said, "and he said he could go back in."

And so Griffin went back in. He would last only four more plays, hobbling badly but still completing two passes to get the Redskins into the Ravens' red zone, until finally, following a half-hearted incompletion that was flagged for intentional grounding, he crumpled to the ground, unable to take another step. Moments later, he was flat on his back on the training table behind the Redskins' sideline, being attended to by team doctors, unable to watch (but listening in on a headset) as Kirk Cousins, his backup, completed an improbable comeback. Cousins, pressed into duty by a Griffin injury for the second time that season, threw an eleven-yard touchdown pass to Pierre Garcon with thirty-six seconds remaining and picked up the two-point conversion himself with a quarterback draw to tie the game. In overtime, a long punt return by the Redskins' Richard Crawford set up a game-winning, thirty-four-yard field goal by Kai Forbath.

"I think the guys were proud of me for coming back in," Griffin said with satisfaction after the game.

And he was right.

"We knew the kind of guy [Griffin] was," veteran cornerback DeAngelo Hall told reporters. "To see him go out there on one leg and still be out there trying to throw the football . . . it just affirms who he is as a person, and it's the reason he has a [captain's] C on his chest.' "

"To will yourself back out there—that goes a long way," veteran linebacker London Fletcher echoed. "That resonates with your football team."

But the fact remained that, for the second time that season, Griffin had brought a sickening silence over the home crowd through his own actions. Just as with the concussion against Atlanta in October, the knee injury had occurred on a scramble, and just as then, he'd had the opportunity to avoid the debilitating hit—but didn't take it. Focused on getting the first down, he bailed out too late to avoid the hit.

"That play can happen to anybody," Griffin said a few days later, denying culpability. "It wasn't like I was waiting to get down until the last second, like I did against Atlanta. My leg came up, and [Ngata] hit my leg. [But] people need to realize football is a physical sport, and there are a lot of quarterbacks out there that aren't [mobile types] that aren't playing right now because of injury. It's not just because I'm a little bit athletic and can move around that I'm prone to injuries."

Not surprisingly, Shanahan also backed his quarterback, finding no fault with his intent. "It's like a playoff game to us, because we knew we had to win," he said, "and Robert was going to do anything he could to get the first down. I think in normal circumstances, he probably would've slid or took off to the outside, but in that situation he's trying to make a play. Most quarterbacks, at least quarterbacks we would want, would put themselves in that situation."

At least quarterbacks we would want. Shanahan probably wasn't referring to anyone in particular with that pointed phrase, but it was difficult not to read between the lines and think of Jay Cutler. On January 23, 2011, in the NFC Championship Game, Cutler, the Chicago Bears' cannon-armed quarterback, exited the game with a knee injury early in the third quarter and spent the rest of the game on the sideline, underneath a heavy coat, as a third-stringer completed the Bears' 21–14 loss to Green Bay.

The reaction was brutal. Bears fans burned Cutler jerseys in the parking lot. Former players crushed him on Twitter. (Sample tweet from former five-time All-Pro linebacker Derrick Brooks: "Hey, there is no medicine for a guy with no guts and no heart.") Meanwhile, an MRI on Cutler's knee the day after the game showed a grade 2 sprain of the medial collateral ligament, an injury that typically requires three to four weeks to heal.

The lesson from the Cutler example was clear to anyone paying attention: if you are an NFL player, especially a high-profile quarterback, never, ever—under any circumstances short of death, paralysis, or amputation—leave a game, or stay out of a game, willingly.

Griffin's own MRI after the Ravens game brought good news, under the circumstances. He had sprained his lateral collateral ligament, but it was a mild one (grade 1), and the anterior cruciate ligament—which had been surgically repaired in 2009 when he was at Baylor—was intact.

"Your positive vibes and prayers worked people!!!!" Griffin tweeted after getting the news. "To God be the Glory!"

With the best-case diagnosis out of the way, it was time to start speculating on the most pressing question facing the Redskins and their fans: Would Griffin be able to play the following Sunday at Cleveland? Nothing else in Washington—not even the approaching "fiscal cliff" that had Congress tied in a knot—was more debated. Griffin's was the most famous knee in Washington in at least fifteen years—since President Bill Clinton tumbled down Greg Norman's stairs in 1997 and tore a tendon.

Griffin himself treated the speculation as a game—when reporters were allowed to watch the first part of practice on the Wednesday before the Cleveland game, he waved and smiled at them, as if to say, "I see you." But once the media cleared away, it was later reported, all the first-team practice snaps were going to Cousins. Still, Griffin seemed to be genuinely disappointed and angry when Shanahan, at the Redskins' hotel in Cleveland the night before the game, informed him that he would be placed on the inactives list for the Browns game—benched.

"Players play, so I was not happy with the decision," Griffin said pointedly the next day after the game. "But at the end of the day, that's the decision they went with. I respect that, but it doesn't mean I necessarily have to like it. They said [they were] just protecting me from myself, not allowing me to go out there and put myself in harm's way."

(For his part, Shanahan pinned the decision on the doctors: Griffin "wanted to play," he said, "but when I hear [the] doctors saying, 'Don't play him,' I don't play him.")

Rather than taking his customary place four yards behind the center, Griffin watched the game from the Redskins' sideline, dressed in team-issued workout clothes and a winter hat and wearing a headset that allowed him to listen in to the offensive play-calls. In between offensive series, he filled the role usually performed by Cousins, conferring with Kyle Shanahan and the starting quarterback on the bench to go over what they had seen from the defense the series before.

Cousins's performance in place of Griffin was a revelation: in his first NFL start, he guided the Redskins to 430 total yards—nearly 50 yards more than their season average—and threw two touchdown passes in an authoritative 38–21 victory. Afterward, when Griffin embraced the now-undefeated-as-a-starter Cousins, television cameras picked up the latter, telling him, "Hey, take the reins back. Do this thing. Let's go to the playoffs!"

Meantime, while the Redskins were pounding the Browns, the New York Giants, who entered the day leading the Redskins by a game in the NFC East standings, were getting destroyed in Atlanta, losing 34–0. And so, by the end of the day, the Redskins—improbably—were in a three-way tie for first place with New York and Dallas.

The following week, at Philadelphia, Griffin reclaimed his starting-quarterback job and led the Redskins to a narrow 27–20 victory, a game that ended with the Eagles at the Redskins' 5-yard line, unable to punch it in for the game-tying touchdown. But from an individual standpoint, the game was a sobering reminder of what had been lost when Griffin hurt himself two weeks earlier. He simply wasn't the same player we had seen in the first three months of the season.

He kept tugging at the thick brace he wore on his right knee and adjusting it, as if it didn't fit properly. Between offensive series, he sat on the bench—rather than flitting around the sideline, encouraging his teammates—with an ice pack applied to his knee. In the game itself, the zone-read was all but abandoned, since without the threat of Griffin running the ball it was worthless, and he was under center, as opposed to in the pistol formation, for the majority of snaps. He was credited with only two rushes, but still completed 16 of 24 passes for 198 yards, with two touchdowns and an interception (his first in more than a month)—good enough for a 102.4 passer rating for the game.

"That's why they call me the quarterback," he said afterward, bristling at the suggestion he couldn't win without running. "I'm supposed to go out there and throw the ball."

It was the Redskins' sixth straight win, and coupled with losses by both New York and Dallas that day, it lifted the Redskins to a new, unlikely perch. They were alone in first place in the NFC East, and their 2012 season had come down to one simple equation:

If they beat the Dallas Cowboys at FedEx Field on December 30 in the regular-season finale, they would win the division and host a playoff game the following weekend—a staggering achievement for a team that only a month and a half earlier had been 3-6, with a coach who sounded ready to pack in the season.

There was a feeling at FedEx Field on the night of December 30 that hadn't been there in a long time. The frigid air, the prime-time kickoff, the enormous stakes, the Cowboys on the opposite sideline: it felt like playoff weather, playoff atmosphere, playoff football. For all practical purposes, that's what this Week 17, regular-season-finale matchup was. By kickoff, all the other play-off permutations had been exhausted, and Cowboys-versus-Redskins was a do-or-die game: Winner advances to the playoffs as the NFC East champ. Loser goes home.

The first chants of "R-G-3! R-G-3!" went up across the stadium even before kickoff as the captains, Griffin included, met at midfield for the coin toss. After the game, the same chant, now fortified with the twin fuels of alcohol and victory, echoed through the concourses and out into the parking lots. On the penultimate night of the year, everything that had transpired for the Redskins over the previous nine months—from the predraft trade with St. Louis to the installation of the Shanahans' new offense, from the sweat of summer to the aches of winter—had all been validated.

Thanks to the beauty that is NFL.com's "Sound FX" feature—in which a chosen player (you can probably guess who was chosen) is miked up for an entire game—we can tell the story of the Redskins' division-clinching 28–18 win over the Cowboys through sound bites:

- *Griffin to a group of offensive teammates before the game:* "All right, baby. Y'all already know what it is. Y'all, this is our house. It's our night. And it's our division. It's our job to go win it. This is it. Put it all on the line. We're gonna start fast and finish strong. Here ya go, 'Work' on three. One, two, three, work!"
- *Griffin, with a smile, to some teammates after limping through a ten-yard touchdown run around the left end:* "That was the worst-looking touchdown ever."
- *Griffin to Alfred Morris after the latter's thirty-two-yard touchdown run in the fourth quarter extended the Redskins' lead to 21–10:* "That's what I'm talking about, baby! Me and you, nobody can stop us." (*At another point, Griffin, channeling his inner Elway, tells Morris,* "You're my Terrell Davis, baby!")
- *Griffin to Morris in the huddle, late in the fourth quarter, as the Redskins faced a third-and-goal from the Dallas one-yard line, needing a touchdown to ice the game:* "Y'all know what

call is coming. They know what call is coming. Get in the end zone, all right?" (*Morris got in the end zone.*)

- *Veteran receiver Santana Moss to Griffin on the sideline in the final seconds:* "It's been a long time coming, bro. I appreciate you, man. Straight up, I really appreciate you. You played your ass off, man."

- *Griffin to Morris on the sideline, as the scoreboard congratulated the Redskins for their first division title since 1999:* "Look at that, man. Ain't been since '99. We came in here and did it in one year, you feel me? Sky's the limit for us, baby."

- *Griffin to embattled Cowboys quarterback Tony Romo as they shook hands after the game:* "Hey, Tony. I just wanted to say to you: Don't listen to what anybody is saying about you. You're a great quarterback, and this game doesn't mean anything. You feel me?"

It was the biggest game of Griffin's life, and almost certainly the coldest one he had ever played in—37 degrees at kickoff. At least statistically speaking, it also wound up being the worst game of his rookie year. He completed a season-low nine passes, none of them for touchdowns, and he posted a season-low passer rating of 66.9. But he also managed to pick up 63 yards on the ground—with the bulky brace on his right knee once again—and had the good fortune of handing off 33 times to Morris, which was the best thing he did all night. Morris, the unassuming sixth-round draft pick who drove a 1991 Mazda 626 that he called his "Bentley," turned those 33 carries into 200 rushing yards, the most by a Redskins running back in more than 23 years. He also set a new franchise single-season rushing mark, with 1,613 yards, breaking Clinton Portis's 2005 record.

"I'm not a star," Morris said when someone used that word to describe him after the game. "I'm just Alfred. I'm still the same. I'm not going to change. I couldn't change even if I tried."

In another week, Griffin would become the first rookie quarterback to start a playoff game for the Redskins since Sammy Baugh in 1937, but he and Morris, the rookies, were too young to fully grasp the enormity of what they had done, too young to understand all the angst that preceded them in this building or to know why there were tears being shed in the stands above them. In the context of the Redskins' tangled history, they were mere babies—many Redskins fans had emotional scars older than them.

"I was nine years old in 1999," Griffin said afterward, referring to the year of the Redskins' last division title. "I stand before you twenty-two, and the Redskins the champions of the NFC East. The Redskins haven't won the division since 1999, and we came in and we did it in one year."

The playoffs were coming to FedEx Field. The Redskins' first-round opponents: the Seattle Seahawks. Griffin and Russell Wilson would be meeting in what was only the second instance in NFL history of rookie quarterbacks going head-to-head in the playoffs. But Griffin wouldn't be facing Wilson, as he was fond of reminding people—he would be facing the Seahawks' defense, which was much scarier. It was arguably the best unit in the NFL, a defense that had already vanquished Aaron Rodgers and Tom Brady, knocked out Arizona's John Skelton, limited Christian

Ponder to 63 yards passing, gotten Mark Sanchez benched, and held Cam Newton to 183 total yards.

They were going to come after Griffin, and everyone knew it.

He tried to go on his bum leg, this stalwart of the Redskins' offense. He thought he could make it through with a shot of painkiller and some precautions. He was a tough guy, and he didn't have to prove that to anyone. But out there on that chopped-up dirt bowl of a playing field, in such a huge game as this—the franchise's first home playoff game in 4,751 days—he realized he was only hurting his team by continuing to play. The jig was up. And so, right there in the first series of the Redskins' playoff game against the Seahawks, with the Redskins inside Seattle's 5-yard line, left guard Kory Lichtensteiger took a knee and the trainers rushed out to help him off the field. He never returned.

"I felt I could give it a go, you know, with the proper medication and everything," Lichtensteiger recalled. He hadn't practiced the entire week of the Seattle game, in hopes his left ankle would heal enough to allow him to play. On game day, he told the coaches he could go, and the Redskins kept him on the active list. "I had it feeling right, or so I thought," he said. "At the goal line, I had to put pressure on my ankle. It just didn't hold up. I knew right away it was time. . . . If it were a normal regular-season game, I would've given it another week or two. [But] I wanted to be out there, and I probably didn't make the right decision."

By the end of the Redskins' 24–14 loss, after Griffin had made the opposite choice and suffered the consequences, nobody much remembered Lichtensteiger. But imagine if Griffin had done the same thing. What a different world this would be for the Redskins.

In the NFL, it tends to get left to the injured player himself to decide whether he can keep going or not. The coaches are too wrapped up in coaching to notice which of their injured players—and by that point in the season they are all pretty much injured to some extent—are too hurt to continue, so they rely largely on the doctors, who are paid by the team and thus are often in some degree of conflict between best medical practices and their obligation, real or imagined, to get the players back on the field as quickly as possible.

"You're waiting for someone to tell you [that] you can't play, because if it's up to us we'd gut out through anything, pretty much. It was hard for me to pull myself out, but I knew I wasn't helping the team," Lichtensteiger said. But he was careful not to indict Griffin for making the opposite choice. "Robert was still helping the team out there. . . . He did a good job not letting on to his teammates that he was injured. He looked [the same] the last two or three weeks and played through that as well. Him at 50 percent is still a pretty good option for us."

Griffin kept playing—and the Redskins kept running him all over the field—even after he appeared to reinjure his right knee late in the first quarter, when he planted awkwardly on a rollout pass play near the Redskins' sideline, immediately yanking off his helmet and rolling around with a grimace. Two plays later, he threw his second touchdown pass of the quarter, giving the Redskins an early 14–0 lead.

Back on the Redskins' sideline afterward, Griffin ducked into the small wooden shed behind the Redskins' bench that serves as an observation room, trailed by a figure in a burgundy-and-gold winter hat and a brown plaid overcoat: Dr. James Andrews. Moments later, Griffin walked back out—after having his knee retaped and the brace adjusted—and right there went the Redskins' last, best chance to avoid further injury to Griffin's knee.

The question of the doctors' responsibility for Griffin had come under greater scrutiny that very morning, when a *USA Today* story quoted Dr. Andrews as saying the conversation with Shanahan on December 9—in which Andrews, according to Shanahan's earlier account, had cleared Griffin to return to the Ravens game after missing just one play—never occurred. In fact, Griffin, according to Andrews, "didn't even let us look at him. He came off the field, walked through the sidelines, circled back through the players, and took off back to the field. It wasn't our opinion. We didn't even get to touch him or talk to him. Scared the hell out of me." The episode put Shanahan on the defensive, at least until Andrews pivoted slightly under follow-up questioning by a skeptical media, saying that while he had not actually examined Griffin, he had watched Griffin run around the sidelines and back on the field and had given the "high sign" signal to Shanahan that it was okay for Griffin to return to the game.

In any case, Andrews was on the sideline again as the Redskins battled the Seahawks—one of six physicians on duty that night, along with five trainers on the sideline and one in a suite above the field.

For the rest of the game, until the knee finally gave out in the fourth quarter, Griffin, by all accounts, had the green light from both the medical staff and the coaching staff. He played six more series, for a total of twenty-four more plays. But everything had changed after that tweak of his knee late in the first quarter: he was 6-of-9 passing for 68 yards and two touchdowns in the first quarter, but just 4-of-10 for 16 yards, no touchdowns, and one interception thereafter. With each series, his limp appeared more pronounced and his passes less crisp.

Those two first-quarter touchdowns would be the last points for the Redskins, the last celebratory, full-throated renditions of "Hail to the Redskins" all afternoon. With Griffin increasingly hobbled, the next six possessions for the Redskins went punt-interception-punt-punt-punt-fumble. This put enormous pressure on the Redskins' defense, which held as long as it could until, finally, Wilson and the Seahawks took control. By halftime, the Redskins' lead was down to one point, and midway through the fourth quarter Seahawks running back Marshawn Lynch—with Wilson himself throwing a key block downfield to take out Redskins cornerback Josh Wilson—scored on a 27-yard touchdown run to put Seattle ahead for good.

The odd thing, however, was the Redskins' play-calling. Despite the obviously compromised condition of their quarterback's knee—which got worse after the first quarter—the Redskins retained their commitment to the zone-read option, with the ball in Griffin's hands constantly. On the team's first offensive play of the fourth quarter, he ran another keeper around the left side, laboring as if he were dragging a fallen tree behind him, but still picking up nine yards.

"At some point," Fox-TV play-by-play man Joe Buck intoned ominously, "don't you have to think about Kirk Cousins coming into this ball game? [Griffin] is vulnerable. He's not able to do what makes him great."

There were discussions to that effect on the Redskins' sideline among the coaching staff, but Griffin never wavered in his insistence that he wanted to go on. "I think it's just a tough call because the communication from Robert is that he is fine," Cousins said later. "You don't want to sit the guy that has taken you this far when he is telling you he is fine."

"He said, 'Hey, trust me. I want to be in there, and I deserve to be in there,'" Shanahan said afterward, recalling one of several conversations he had with Griffin during the course of the game. "I couldn't disagree with him." When the end came for Griffin in the fourth quarter in that by-now-familiar sequence—the bad snap, the awkward lunge, the buckled knee, the deafening hush, the crumpled figured on the turf, the nervous "R-G-3!" chant, the trainers at his side, the halfhearted wave-slash-salute to the crowd—it was difficult for anyone present, or anyone watching at home, to know how to feel. Emotions ran high. There was anger, certainly. There was sadness for the kid himself. There was worry. There was something akin to regret that this brilliant star might have just been taken away from you. There was a feeling of sickness in the pit of your stomach that lasted for a good long while.

By the next morning, the reaction was immediate, sustained, and brutal. Everybody—fans, columnists, sports-talk hosts, your neighbors, your grandmother—wanted to blame someone, mostly Shanahan, but a sprinkling of others came in for criticism too: Dr. Andrews, Daniel Snyder, even Griffin himself.

"Many may question, criticize & think they have all the right answers," Griffin tweeted the morning after, suggesting he was aware of the firestorm. "But few have been in the line of fire in battle."

In a way, the sniping and criticism was all pointless, reflecting a fundamental misunderstanding of the nature of football. To assign blame for Griffin's injury is to make the mistake of thinking of football as normal, a realm where our regular societal mores and our notions of right and wrong apply—when in fact it is a singularly grotesque and twisted realm unlike any other, with the possible exception of the battlefield. This is a culture where pain is masked by shots, where injuries are hidden from coaches and doctors, where the code of honor says your teammates are brothers and you stay on the field for their sake, even at the expense of your own. This is a game where collisions don't occur by accident, as they do in other sports—they are the entire point of the game. Every single play holds the potential for disaster. Every single play, as football players like to say, is a car wreck. Violence and pain aren't just part of football—they are at the very heart of its ethos.

Shanahan, a guy who once wanted to play with one kidney, was not a monster, or a slave owner akin to Leonardo DiCaprio's character in the movie *Django Unchained* (a comparison made by one overheated radio host). He was simply the perfect, ultimate expression of football culture.

It calls to mind the old Chris Rock bit about the tiger that mauls a handler and everybody blames the tiger. "That tiger didn't go crazy," Rock said. "That tiger went tiger!" To bring the analogy home, Mike Shanahan didn't go crazy by leaving Griffin in the game—Shanahan went Shanahan. And for that matter, Griffin didn't go crazy either—he went Griffin.

"I did put myself at more risk by being out there," Griffin said in a moment of reflection after the game. "But every time you step on the football field, in between those lines, you're putting your life, your career, every single ligament in your body, in jeopardy. That's just the approach I had to take towards it. My teammates needed me out there, so I was out there for them."

In Super Bowl XXXII, Shanahan famously asked Terrell Davis to go back into a game in which he was suffering temporary blindness due to migraine headaches. "Don't worry about seeing on this play, because we're going to fake it to you—but if you're not in there, [the defense is] not going to believe that we're going to run," Shanahan can be heard telling Davis on a clip from that game featured on the NFL's website, under the heading "MVP Moment."

Those play-through-pain (or play-through-blindness) anecdotes tend to become essential parts of players' legacies. Most NFL fans, for example, could tell you that Ronnie Lott once played with a finger so mangled, it had to be cut off at the tip the next day. They know that Philip Rivers played an entire game on a torn ACL, or that Emmitt Smith played with a separated shoulder at the end of the 1993 season, or that Brett Favre played much of the 2002 season in a knee brace with a sprained LCL—the same injury Griffin was playing through. Or that Doug Williams himself, in the Redskins' victory in Super Bowl XXII, was forced out of the game for two plays in the first quarter by a "hyperextended" knee but came back in and played the rest of the game in pain, ultimately earning the game's MVP honors.

"It's a badge of honor," said former Redskins lineman Mark Schlereth, who also played under Shanahan in Denver and whose own badges of honor are his twenty knee surgeries and the fact that he once played in a game only a few hours after passing a kidney stone. "I checked out of the hospital on Monday afternoon and played that night against Oakland. That's just what you do."

"The quickest way to earn the respect of your teammates and coaches is to play through injuries," veteran quarterback Matt Hasselbeck told *Esquire* magazine. "The quickest way to lose respect is to say, 'Hey, I can't go.'"

Imagine for a moment that Griffin's knee had held up and that, though hobbled and hurting, he had led the Redskins to a dramatic victory over the Seahawks. The game would have gone down in sports lore—spoken of with the same reverence as the Willis Reed game and the Michael Jordan flu game, a pair of legendary performances that need no further description—and Griffin would have been lauded and praised, just as they were, for his valiant and gutsy performance.

Obviously, if Shanahan knew Griffin would wind up with his knee shredded—requiring surgery that could jeopardize his 2013 season—he would not have left him in. "I'll probably second-guess myself—should I have [pulled him] earlier? I think you always do that," Shanahan said, in a rare public instance of self-doubt, before quickly adding, "especially after you don't win." (That second-guessing apparently extended deep into the spring, as Shanahan, during a news conference a few days before the April 2013 NFL draft, spoke of trying to "learn from your mistakes" and vowed that as the Redskins head into the 2013 season, "one thing we're going to make sure of is that Robert never plays if he's not a hundred percent [healthy].")

But at the time of the Seattle game, nobody knew what would happen. Play out the scenario: if Shanahan takes Griffin out of the game against the quarterback's will, in such an important game, he loses the trust of Griffin and, by extension, the entire locker room. Griffin even said as much when he was asked after the game what he would have done if Shanahan had tried to take him out. "I probably would have been right back out there on the field," he said. "You respect authority, and I respect Coach Shanahan, but at the same time you have to step up and be a man sometimes. There was no way I was coming out of that game."

Many critics insisted that Shanahan should have overruled Griffin's choice to stay in—no matter what Griffin said or threatened to do—and in a normal sphere that would be a sensible, grown-up thing to do. But in the NFL that would be to invite mutiny. It's a twisted way of viewing things, but it's how the NFL works. There was a very good reason why few current football players, and none from the Redskins, took issue with what happened to Griffin.

"If he says he can play, he can play," Moss said later. "That's what players do. . . . When it comes down to what he was dealing with, [if] he was healthy enough to go out there and play, then he wasn't injured."

Shanahan "has to listen to the player in this situation," Fletcher said. "You're talking about the franchise quarterback, a guy who has made so many plays to even get you to this point. If he tells you that he can go, you have to . . . let him go. This is the playoffs, this is a do-or-die situation."

As for the doctors, even if we assume they are both competent and medically ethical—and there is no reason to think otherwise— their role on the sidelines is fraught with conflicting demands. For one thing, their commitment to the patient-player is often difficult to live up to when, as is often the case, players boldly try to evade the doctor and hide their injuries. As a result, amid the swirling chaos on the sidelines, the brand of medicine that gets practiced on an NFL sideline is often more like battlefield medicine—patch 'em up and get 'em back in there.

It's no wonder that survey results released by the NFL Players Association on January 31, three days before Super Bowl XLVII, showed that 78 percent of the players polled harbored a distrust of their team's medical staff. Meantime, according to the NFL's official tally, in 2011, the most recent year for which data was available, nearly 4,500 injuries were reported across the league, out of a pool of fewer than 2,000 total players.

"What we're asked to do as players—[the doctors] would never in a million years ask one of their patients to ever do what they allow us to do," Schlereth told my *Washington Post* colleagues Rick Maese and Sally Jenkins. "[Regular patients] would be on bed rest for something they tell us to practice with on Thursday."

The issue is made even thornier by the mind-set of the players, who are conditioned to want to go back into the game and will often do anything they can to make it happen. In that observation room behind the Redskins' bench, for example, where Griffin was examined during the first quarter of the Seahawks game, he suddenly popped up and told the medical personnel looking at his knee, "I'm fine. I'm ready to go." And that, essentially, was the end of that.

There is no defined threshold for when to order an injured player out of a game, no neon sign suspended above an injured player's head saying, "Done." You know there is risk in letting an injured player continue, but there are no calculators to tell you when the percentage of risk and the percentage of a player's health intersect in the danger zone. Maybe Griffin started the Seattle game at 75 percent health and was down to 50 percent by the fourth quarter, while the risk of further damage to his knee had risen from, say, 10 percent to 40. Does that mean he had to come out?

"This was a very special game for [Griffin]," Tom Yates, president of the NFL Physicians Society, told *USA Today,* in some very telling comments a few days after the game, "so the risk-reward ratio was changed. Everyone was willing to take the calculated risk, if you will."

In fact, the window for winning in the NFL is so small, the chances so few, the payoff so great, the pressure so mighty, that the risk-reward ratio is often so minuscule as to be nonexistent.

Within the NFL, the only criticism of Griffin's handling came from a handful of former players who probably would have done the same thing as he did back when they were playing, but who eventually made it out with all their faculties and who now have enough distance and perspective to understand the absurdity. "At some point you've got to protect a player from himself," former quarterback Rich Gannon, who had a seventeen-year NFL career and now serves as a radio and television analyst, said on SiriusXM Radio. "Griffin's the ultimate competitor. He wants to be out there. He's gonna tough it out. You could tell he was in excruciating pain, even with the knee brace. . . . I think at some point, somebody's got to step in. It's like stopping a fight in the 15th round or something, when the guy's been knocked around too much and he can't defend himself."

If the doctors weren't going to order Griffin out of the game, and the coaches weren't going to take him out, that left one person who could have altered history by doing what, by the conventions of normal society, would have been considered the right thing—and that, of course, was Griffin himself. And in football, however ridiculous it might have seemed outside of this sphere, the right thing to do was to keep playing.

"If you're healthy at that point in the season, it's because you're not playing," fullback Darrel Young said of Griffin. "He's a competitor. I respect him for what he did. I would've done the same thing in that situation."

Griffin never asked to come out of the game, and never let on that his injury was worsening—in fact, just the opposite. He insisted he wanted to play and insisted he was merely "hurt," not "injured" (a spurious distinction NFL players frequently use to justify playing through injuries).

But there was a disconnect between the Griffin camp and the Redskins over one issue: the play-calling. It had been the subject of some internal discussion both before and during the game, with the quarterback suggesting they abandon the zone-read, for the most part, and try to win the game with a more conventional drop-back passing offense, and the Shanahans sticking with the offense that had gotten them to this point, no matter what.

Why, in the same game, did Lichtensteiger stop and Griffin keep going? It certainly wasn't because one was more or less a man than the other—though some in the NFL would undoubtedly try to argue that. Maybe it was as simple as they said it was: Lichtensteiger knew he couldn't go on, and Griffin thought he could. Or maybe Griffin has the sort of ego—call it athletic arrogance—common in superstars but absent in grunt-worker linemen: a firm belief that, even when compromised, he represents the team's best chance to win.

After the Seattle game, when legendary former quarterback and current Redskins radio analyst Sonny Jurgensen suggested to Griffin that he should have taken himself out of the game as his condition worsened, Griffin shot back: "I don't feel that way. I'll say it time and time again: I'm their quarterback. [It] doesn't matter what percentage I am. If you can play, you play. [Teammates] know I'm going to play no matter what. I don't feel like me playing out there hurt the team in any way."

Don't kid yourself into thinking we don't prefer it this way—we want our football to be fast and violent and dangerous, and we want the players to be daredevils and warriors. This is our national obsession. We want a car wreck on every play, and so that's what we get—and we love it right up to the point where we have to see the brains splattered against the windshield. In scientific tests, sensors that measure the force of impacts have been placed in the helmets of NFL players and on some collisions have measured impacts akin to that of a severe car crash. It wouldn't take a great leap in technology to make those readings available and public for every play in every game—except we don't really want to know what those readings say.

We prefer football injuries to be invisible—concussions, painkiller-masked bruises and aches. We would greatly prefer not to have to be reminded of football's dark side—the toll the game takes on the players' bodies and brains—and when that dark side gets thrown in our faces and starts to color our enjoyment of the game, we get indignant, looking for someone to blame. As my colleague Mike Wise wrote after the Seahawks game, "We want our athletic heroes to leave it all out on the field, but the moment we get the face of the franchise face-down, unable to move . . . we want to know what barbarian did this to him."

One of the most electrifying rookie seasons in NFL history, and one of the most entertaining football campaigns in Washington Redskins history, had ended in the worst way imaginable, and there will never be another Redskins game where fans aren't holding their breath every time Griffin gets near a defender. And if the surgery is only a partial success, if we never see the same electrifying, transcendent player we saw in the first twelve games of 2012, well, at least we had those twelve games.

Could it have been avoided? Certainly. Somebody could have taken him out of the game. But in the context of football's twisted culture, letting it play out was the safe move. In the NFL, to have thrown in the towel would have been the risky move, the move that would have invited scorn. Most sane people outside the game probably thought just the opposite. In the end, Griffin was both a victim of the NFL culture and, along with his coach, its ultimate expression.

There was only one surefire way he could have avoided the serious knee injury in the Seattle game, and it had nothing to do with the play-calling or the culture of playing hurt or the ability to know when to slide or get out of bounds. If Griffin didn't want to end up flat on that turf, his next stop a hospital operating table, he might have considered never playing football in the first place.

EPILOGUE

THE RECKONING

E arly in the morning on January 9, 2013, three days after the playoff loss to the Seattle Seahawks that ended the Washington Redskins' season, Robert Griffin III sent a message to his Twitter followers: "Thank you for your prayers and support. I love God, my family, my team, the fans & I love this game. See you guys next season." At around 7:00 A.M., a team of surgeons at the Andrews Institute Ambulatory Surgery Center in Gulf Breeze, Florida, made incisions in both of Griffin's knees. From his left knee, the doctors cut away part of the patellar tendon, as well as a portion of the connected bone, which were then grafted to his right knee, where the tendon would become his new anterior cruciate ligament. The doctors had to take the tendon and bone from Griffin's otherwise healthy left knee because the same tissue in his right knee had already been used as a graft during his 2009 ACL reconstruction, which this surgery would be revising. The doctors also reattached Griffin's torn lateral collateral ligament and repaired a tear in the medial meniscus. From beginning to end, the entire surgery took nearly five hours.

Griffin had traveled to Florida from Virginia the day before on Redskins owner Daniel Snyder's private plane, along with some family members and team officials, including Snyder himself. Once the tests were taken, the options discussed, and the strategy plotted, the surgery was scheduled for as soon as possible. Every day that passed was precious if Griffin hoped to be ready for the 2013 season.

Griffin had a pretty good idea of what lay ahead of him over the coming weeks and months, having rehabbed the same knee three and a half years earlier while at Baylor, but this surgery was more complex and invasive, and estimates for the recovery time he would need before playing football again ranged from eight months to twelve. It didn't take a math degree to figure out that even the midpoint of that estimate would cost him a sizable portion of the 2013 NFL season. Nobody dared question Griffin's commitment to the rehab process. Just the opposite—those who recalled the way he threw himself headlong into his 2009 rehab, like a man possessed, predicted a speedy and complete return.

"Frankly, he was so much better on the mental side of things when he came back from his ACL [in 2009], I wouldn't be surprised if we saw an even better Robert Griffin," said Houston-based surgeon Mark Adickes, who happens to be a former Baylor and Redskins lineman and who performed Griffin's 2009 surgery. "I'm very confident that when he gets back on the field he'll be the same guy we saw [in 2012], and from a mental side we'll see an even more mature and accurate passing quarterback."

But here in the Florida Panhandle—where he would stay for another month, taking the first steps in his rehab—he was isolated, far away from his teammates, his fans, and the media, which gave him plenty of time and space to consider all that had transpired. It was a time of soul-searching and self-questioning. What could he have done differently to prevent this? What did he need to do in the future? What about the coaches and doctors? What were their responsibilities? These were not easy questions, and the answers, he knew, might be impossible to find without some similar soul-searching by the other involved parties and some honest conversations among them all.

The next time the public got a glimpse of Griffin, nearly a month after the surgery, it was the night before the Super Bowl, back in New Orleans, and he was walking—with a slight limp, but without the crutches he had required for the first couple of weeks post-op—down the red carpet prior to the NFL honors ceremony, where he would soon be announced as the winner of the league's Offensive Rookie of the Year Award. In several perfunctory interviews along the way, he said he was already ahead of schedule in his rehab and his goal was to be ready for Week 1 in 2013.

In 2013, he said, "You won't see the same Robert Griffin. You'll see a better Robert Griffin."

But the most revealing interview was carried on the Redskins' own video channel. There he said, "There's a few things in that [playoff] game that we wish we had done differently, and I'll talk to Coach [Shanahan] about that when I get back [to Virginia]. We'll have that conversation. It's a conversation that needs to be had. . . . I'll do my part to make sure that I stay healthy and keep myself out of harm's way, while at the same time making sure the coaches do the same."

Griffin's Offensive Rookie of the Year Award that night, which he won by a significant margin over runner-up Andrew Luck of the Indianapolis Colts, was an opportunity to ponder, one more time, everything he had accomplished in 2012. That there had been any debate at all over who deserved the award—Griffin,

Luck, and Seattle's Russell Wilson were the front-runners—was stunning. Really, when you lead the entire NFL in both yards per pass attempt and yards per rush attempt, becoming the first player in history to lead the league in both, *in your rookie year,* what more is there to say? In fact, the closest comparisons to Griffin's performance in 2012 weren't his contemporaries at all, but rather the short list of some of the best rookie seasons in NFL history.

Carolina's Cam Newton had set a standard of sorts the year before, throwing for a rookie-record 4,051 yards—but his passer rating of 84.5 was nearly 20 points lower than Griffin's. Miami's Dan Marino, in 1983, had a season that was statistically similar to Griffin's—he went 7-2, threw 20 touchdown passes against only six interceptions, and posted a passer rating of 96.0. And Pittsburgh's Ben Roethlisberger, in 2004, went 13-0 as a starter and posted a passer rating of 98.1—which stood as an NFL record until Griffin broke it in 2012.

But both Marino and Roethlisberger had taken over Super Bowl–ready teams. Much of Griffin's value was derived from how far he had lifted the Redskins franchise, more or less on his own. Remember, he was without his top receiver (Pierre Garcon) for most of the first half of the season and without his top tight end (Fred Davis) for most of the second half of the season, and he was saddled with a defense that ranked as the fifth-worst in the NFL.

When Griffin's name was called for the award, he climbed the steps to the stage, looked out at the crowd, and put the moment in the sort of context that only an NFL player/warrior could provide: "Sometimes," he said, "it's not what you get for your team, it's what you're willing to give for them."

Griffin had given plenty for the Redskins, as the scars beneath his suit-pants would attest, and now he would be justified in wondering—even if he was too loyal and discreet to say so publicly—what the Redskins were willing to give for him.

As the NFL off-season crept by, Griffin remained largely underground, at least in terms of media availability. His thoughts about his injury and his recovery remained mostly a mystery. But on every side of the question, the early part of spring in 2013 seemed to be a time for some subtle jostling for position on the issue, in advance of the media crush that was certain to greet the beginning of off-season workouts at Redskins Park in April and May.

In an ESPN.com interview in late March, Dr. Andrews, who had overseen Griffin's surgery, said that Griffin's recovery "has been unbelievable so far" and that Griffin "is one of those superhumans" for whom normal recovery timetables don't apply. He compared Griffin to Adrian Peterson, the Minnesota Vikings' great running back, whose ACL surgery Andrews had performed in December 2011 and who not only made it back for the 2012 season but wound up being the league's MVP. It would have been easy to accuse Andrews of unfairly raising expectations for Griffin's return, except that Griffin himself had been doing the same thing for some time, via an Adidas advertising campaign titled "All in for Week 1."

Redskins coach Mike Shanahan, too, appeared to be staking out his position when he told reporters at the NFL's annual owners' meetings in Phoenix in late March that Griffin would need to learn how to slide and get out of bounds better than he had in 2012 if he wanted to avoid injury.

"You go from the collegiate level to the professional level, [and] you don't realize the speed of these guys, and he took a lot of unnecessary hits," Shanahan told reporters. "But he'll look at film and protect himself, and I think it will be a drastic change from one year to the next." Shanahan also reaffirmed the Redskins' commitment to running the zone-read option with Griffin in 2013, arguing, as he had before, that it actually kept him safer by slowing down the pass rush.

That was the context for the statement Griffin released through the Redskins on March 27, reiterating his hope to be ready for Week 1, but vowing not to return until he was healthy. Within the same statement, however, he also made a cryptic reference to what happened in the Seattle game and what it would mean going forward.

"My first NFL season and my injury that ended it showed me a lot about the league, my team and myself," he said. "I know where my responsibility is within the dilemma that led to me having surgery to repair my knee and all parties involved know their responsibilities as well."

It was difficult to read Griffin's statement, in the context of the public comments from Andrews and especially Shanahan, and not see some sort of disconnect between the player and the team. But where was the disconnect? Griffin wasn't saying.

By early May, Griffin was sounding like someone who yearned to speak out but was muzzled by something or somebody—and could only hint at what he was feeling. In a cover-story interview with *ESPN The Magazine*, Griffin went right up to the edge of the canyon that separated his perspective from that of the Redskins, but didn't take the final step.

Asked by writer J. R. Moehringer about the Seahawks game, Griffin said, "I don't feel like playing against the Seahawks was a mistake. But I see the mistake *in it*." Asked by Moehringer to explain what he meant, Griffin replied, "With what happened and how everything was running—you take me out."

Parsing those words required a scalpel and a microscope, but the phrase "you take me out" certainly lent itself to one interpretation: that while it was impossible for Griffin to pull himself out of the game, because of how that would have been perceived by teammates and the media, someone in a position of authority ("you") needed to do it.

That was about as far as Griffin was willing to go, at least publicly, in discussing the events of January 2013. He and Shanahan had discussed the Seattle game several times in private by that point, and in the *ESPN The Magazine* piece, Griffin said his coach had impressed on him the importance of closing rank. "One thing [Shanahan] stressed to me," he said, "is we have to be a close group. We can't let people outside penetrate that and create a rift."

So, too, would it go with another source of potential discord: the offensive play-calling, which may have been the "dilemma" to which Griffin referred in his March statement. "Dilemma" was the right word: some of the very talents that made Griffin such a great NFL quarterback also made him more vulnerable to serious injury. But Griffin, who had been on a lifelong quest to rise above the stereotype of the run-first African American quarterback, may have figured there was an obvious solution.

Given the courtesy of having input on the Redskins' play-calling as the 2012 season wore on, Griffin occasionally tried to steer the offense away from the zone-read option—particularly after his original knee injury in December—while the Shanahans, who had spent months devising and installing their offensive blueprint, insisted it remain a significant element of that plan. And the facts suggested the offense had been wildly successful. Did it put Griffin in jeopardy? Perhaps, but the fact remained that it was a pair of scrambles out of the pocket—not designed runs—that had resulted in Griffin's two major injuries in 2012: the concussion against Atlanta and the knee sprain against Baltimore. Either could have been avoided by a well-timed slide or a quick duck out of bounds.

Still, how difficult could it be to reach some sort of middle ground on the direction of the Redskins' offense, perhaps with some sort of quota on how many zone-read plays they would run and a moratorium on flea-flicker passes that make Griffin a receiver? That would seem fair enough.

Shanahan would be wise not to alienate his quarterback. If some sort of Machiavellian power struggle arises at Redskins Park in 2013, there is every reason to think Griffin could win it. Not only does he have the longer contract—through 2015, as opposed to 2014 for Shanahan—and a far greater degree of public support, but he also seems to have an unusually close player-owner relationship with Snyder. (Snyder, as well as Shanahan, declined through a Redskins spokesman to be interviewed for this book.) When Shanahan was hired in January 2010, it gave Snyder and the Redskins a new face and an instant jolt of credibility. But by the spring of 2013, Shanahan was neither the face of the Redskins nor their biggest source of credibility.

Griffin, with his military upbringing and respect for authority, isn't the type to attempt a bold-faced power play, but people can sometimes surprise even themselves in the cause of their own self-preservation.

The biggest variable for 2013, of course, is the condition of Griffin's knee, and there is unlikely to be any definitive answer on that until deep into the summer, at the earliest. Griffin and his doctors can say all they want about how far ahead of schedule he has been in his rehab, but nobody will know anything until he is on the field. How many times have you ever heard of an athlete being *behind* schedule? They're always ahead of schedule—until all of a sudden it's game time and they can't go.

There is no reason to doubt Griffin—on the contrary, there is every reason to believe him—but in the spring of 2013, the Redskins had begun preparing backup Kirk Cousins to run the offense in the event Griffin had to miss part or all of training camp.

The truth is, as long as Griffin returns as a reasonable facsimile of his 2012 self, the Redskins' 2013 offense ought to be a colossal juggernaut. When the team re-signed top tight end Fred Davis in March, Griffin had his entire cadre of 2012 playmakers back for another year, and (at least for now) at full health. This is an offense, remember, that led the NFL in rushing yards and was second in overall yards per play in 2012—despite top talents Griffin, Davis, and Garcon missing parts of the season.

But there is also some question about what sort of quarterback Griffin will be when he returns. Most orthopedists believe that, while it is possible to get back on the field in six to eight months after a reconstructive knee surgery, it takes more like eighteen to twenty-four months before an athlete is back to 100 percent health. It seems fully possible that it will be 2014, and not 2013, when we get the full RG3 experience again.

It may seem counterintuitive, but there is an argument to be made that Griffin could actually stand to benefit from losing a step or two from his legendary speed and quickness when he comes back—because, presumably, such a reduction would limit his penchant for taking off on scrambles and also make the Redskins a little less inclined to run him around the corners so often. He would always retain enough speed and elusiveness to escape sacks and pick up an occasional first down with his legs, but it might not be such a bad thing if he doesn't feel compelled to do so at every opportunity.

"The silver lining is, this may ultimately be a good thing for RG3," said Dr. Neal ElAttrache, a Los Angeles–based orthopedist who performed Tom Brady's knee reconstruction in 2009. "I think this is going to change the way he plays when he gets back. He's going to evolve into the position, and their offense is going to evolve."

"Long-term, what I think eventually is going to have to happen is, he's going to have to play quarterback under center in an NFL system," ESPN analyst and former quarterback Ron Jaworski told my colleague Barry Svrluga in January. "He's going to have to do three-step drops, five-step drops. You can't last in the NFL running the offense off the spread-option. No one's perfected that yet. The quarterback's going to get killed. Eventually, you have to get to playing NFL-style quarterback."

The model could be someone like Green Bay's Aaron Rodgers,

who is one of the best passers in the game but who also rushes for three hundred or so yards each season. The transition into more of a drop-back passer was likely to happen anyway over time, as part of a quarterback's natural evolution. The Redskins always figured Griffin would be a different quarterback in 2022 than he was in 2012. At some point, he would expect to lose some speed, gain some passing acumen, and evolve.

And if the 2012 knee injury sped up the evolution process, so be it.

If the reckoning that followed the events of January 6 forced both the quarterback himself and the offense he ran to evolve, it stood to reason that the workplace that facilitated them should evolve as well.

NFLEvolution.com, the league's online campaign to promote the sport's safety measures, went live on February 3—Super Bowl Sunday. Early in the fourth quarter of the riveting Super Bowl XLVII between the Baltimore Ravens and San Francisco 49ers that evening, the 108 million or so viewers watching at home were treated to an accompanying commercial: a cinematic sixty-second spot, directed by former *Friday Night Lights* creator Peter Berg, that traced the evolution of the game of football, from its early days as a "bunch of guys running around in a pile of mud" to the modern spectacle it is today. As one generation of players morphed into another on-screen, the narrator (Baltimore Ravens linebacker Ray Lewis) highlighted the safety innovations along the way—from leather helmets to plastic helmets to face masks to rule changes that protect players.

"Here's to making the next century safer and more exciting than ever," it concludes. "Forever forward, forever football."

It shouldn't have been surprising that the league would use the platform of the biggest television event of the year to paint itself as being progressive on the issue of player safety. In many ways, the NFL is the greatest business model in the world. It operates as more or less a monopoly, with $9.5 billion in revenues in 2012, limited antitrust protection, and a built-in, completely free farm system in college football. Its television product is so good that it's almost *too* good, with innovations such as the RedZone Channel giving viewers at home a better experience than what the fans at the stadium are getting.

But in 2013 the sport was still under attack on many fronts for not doing enough to protect its players, as evidenced most vividly by the many lawsuits, representing more than 4,000 former players, that had been filed accusing the league of deliberately concealing information pertaining to the effect of repeated blows to the head on players' health.

As it turned out, three former players depicted in the "NFL Evolution" commercial were among those suing the league for damages, a connection first noted by *The Sporting News*. It was an embarrassing revelation for the league—but the NFL by that point had gotten used to the fact that it simply couldn't win on the violence issue.

Many of the safety measures the league has taken in recent years have been met with resistance from players and coaches alike. In 2011 it cracked down on blows to the neck and head, threatening to suspend repeat violators. There have been strict guidelines for handling concussions, a limit on the number of full-contact practices a team can have, and changes to the way kickoffs are executed. (After the 2012 season, the NFL would forbid ball-carriers from initiating contact with the crowns of their helmets—another rule change that drew heavy criticism around the game.)

Just a week before the Super Bowl, CBSSports.com senior NFL columnist Clark Judge quoted Ravens safety Bernard Pollard, one of the hard-hitting defenders in the game, as predicting that the game would no longer exist within thirty years—not because of the violence itself, but because of the league's overreaction to it.

"You've got guys who are 350 pounds running 4.5 and 4.4s, and these owners and coaches want scout-run blockers and linemen to move walls," Pollard was quoted as saying. "At the same time, they tell you, 'Don't hit here, and don't hit there, or we'll take your money.'" Later in the same interview, Pollard made a prediction that, far from being bold, had been made by others many times in the past: "I hope I'm wrong," he said, "but I just believe one day there's going to be a death that takes place on the field because of the direction we're going."

Super Bowl XLVII, of course, came and went—the Ravens triumphing with a 34–31 win—and the 2012 season went into the books without the dire death-on-the-field prediction coming to pass. Still, the bigger question persists: Is the violence so deeply ingrained in the nature of the game that removing too much of it will be fatal to the NFL itself?

During the course of reporting this book, I sometimes asked people close to Griffin what they thought he would be doing in twenty years. The answers were mostly predictable, given his interests and background: law, politics, broadcasting, even acting. It was only later that I realized I had the question wrong—it should have been: What will he be doing in *ten* years?

Griffin has dropped enough clues about his future to make you wonder if he will stick with football long enough to go down in its annals as one of the best to play the game—as his talent suggests he might someday be regarded. Back in April 2012, when I spent some time with him in Texas prior to the draft, he said this about the difficult time he had giving up other sports for football:

"It was tough having to close those doors—and I always say 'temporarily,' because I feel like it is temporary. [Playing] basketball may be a little more far-fetched than track right now, just because of everything that goes into it. But I know some basketball coaches that would take me right now, and I know some track coaches that would take me right now. But I'm trying to run through this door and kick it down in the NFL, and have fun with it and not look back. I don't look at it like, 'If this doesn't work out, I can do that.' I'm gonna make this work out."

In June 2012, when the U.S. Olympic Track and Field Trials were taking place—four years after his own near-miss in attempting to qualify for Beijing—Griffin watched the results closely and counted the number of hurdlers he had beaten over the years. It was a sizable number, and he made no attempt to hide how much he missed the sport at that moment.

"It does suck," he told the NFL Network. "I mean, that's the only way to say it. It sucks. But I'm definitely fortunate to be in the situation that I am, being in the NFL, being a franchise quarterback for a team, with the opportunity to go out and do an infinite amount of things. If I wake up one day and it's 2016 and I say I want to go run the hurdles again, I can do that."

Basketball, too, sometimes still tugged at his heartstrings. On the night he went to the Verizon Center in downtown D.C. to watch the Wizards play the Miami Heat, he called his father afterward, and the first thing he said had nothing to do with the fact that LeBron James had come over to hug him after the final buzzer. It was the fact that Griffin himself was as tall as Dwyane Wade (who is listed as six-four) and all the other guards on the floor.

"I had courtside seats—I was right next to some of them," he told his father excitedly. "I'm telling you—they're not any taller than me."

A second knee reconstruction in four years presumably puts at least a small dent in whatever aspirations he still has to run track or play basketball. But Griffin, it should be clear by now, is someone who doesn't want to be boxed in. You get the feeling that, in his perfect world, he would play in both the NFL and NBA, run the hurdles in the Olympics every four years—and practice law, run for public office, design augmented-reality worlds, make hit records, and star in movies on the side.

"The very word 'alternatives' bobs in and out of his speech with noticeable frequency," John McPhee wrote in 1965 of Bill Bradley, another young athlete with similarly varied interests. "Before his Rhodes Scholarship came along and eased things, he appeared to be worrying about dozens of alternatives for next year. And he still fills his days with alternatives. He apparently always needs to have eight ways to jump, not because he is excessively prudent but because that is what makes the game interesting."

To say that Griffin was disillusioned by his first year in the NFL would be to make the faulty assumption that he was naive about it going in, which didn't seem to be the case. In an interview with Grantland.com in 2011, he showed a preternatural grasp of what the league was all about: "With the NFL, if they come knocking at your door, you're not going to tell them no," he said. "But it's a tough business. The NFL doesn't like it when they have a smart guy who knows how much he's worth. The NFL now, it's about talent, and if you have talent, it doesn't matter what's going on . . . because as long as they can get people to watch them play, the NFL's making money. It's just about the spectacle. That's all it is."

People close to Griffin take it as a given that he will make good on his vow to go to law school and become a lawyer, and many of them also believe he will eventually run for office—something he doesn't exactly shoot down (other than to say it doesn't interest him right now). In March 2013, when Griffin was honored by the Texas State Legislature, Rep. Sarah Davis of Houston revealed that she had met privately with Griffin that morning and told reporters, "I think we will see RG3 run for office very soon—when he's ready to retire."

None of this speculation about Griffin's future is going to be of much comfort to Redskins fans, or to his fans across the country, who simply want to see him back on the field at 100 percent health as soon—and for as long—as possible. And it is hard to blame them. What a show it was.

To have seen Robert Griffin III turning the corner with the football and a head of steam in one of those first twelve games of the 2012 NFL season—before the knee injury changed everything—was to remember a young Michael Jordan with the ball in the open court, a young Rickey Henderson rounding second on a ball in the gap, a young Tiger Woods in the fairway with 285 to the pin, a lake to carry, and a 3-wood in his hands. At that moment, you were watching the only human on the planet capable of doing this very thing this well. It's the whole reason we watch. It's the force that moves us to the edge of our seats. It's the life-affirming thing—this possibility of transcendence signaling its arrival—that draws us toward any elite expression of human brilliance, whether in the arts or in sports.

But therein lay the central paradox within Griffin, within the game of football, and within those of us who watch. In none of those other sports does the athlete's brilliance itself correlate with danger; only in football could you say that it is because of Griffin's brilliance that his health is risked on every play; if he were a lesser athlete, or a lesser quarterback, or a lesser competitor, he would almost certainly be safer. When he returns to the field in 2013, we will be watching in hopes of glimpsing those same moments of transcendence we saw in 2012—but we will also implore him to be safer, more cautious this time. We want him to change, but we want him to stay the same.

And what does Griffin think? What does he want? Clearly, he has thought long and hard about what happened in the Seattle game—about his "responsibility within the dilemma," as he put it—but as of late April, he hadn't offered any firm answers. Perhaps there are none.

Here was a young man who had been reckoning for most of his life with the violence in his chosen sport—a man who, as a child, had made a Pinkie Promise with his mom that he wouldn't get hurt, a man who knew what it felt like to have his brain slammed into the inside of his skull, a man who understood the grueling monotony of a lengthy knee rehab. And still, with his ligaments giving out, he fought on. In some ways, Griffin was better than this. He knew better. He didn't need football to achieve great things. He understood better than most the difference between right and wrong; and between those white lines at FedEx Field, he was part of a team, part of a family, and he did what he thought was right at the time: He played on.

A man deserves to do what makes him happy, as long as that thing is achievable, and Robert Griffin III has every opportunity to find happiness, now and forever. He and fiancée Rebecca Liddicoat were making plans in the spring of 2013 for a summer wedding. Presumably, Griffin will be a father someday (hello, baby boy RG4). He might practice law, enter politics, and achieve great things as a statesman.

But the game of football, in my experience, rarely seems to make the ones who play it happy in the same way as, say, the game of baseball itself makes baseball players happy. Football players, either current or retired, might be satisfied, or content, or proud to have played, and they are often rich from having played—which might have the effect of making them happy. They might even genuinely love the game, in some warped and nostalgic way. But the game of football itself doesn't make them happy.

Only surviving it does.

ACKNOWLEDGMENTS

It was sometime in mid-March 2012 when Matt Vita, the sports editor of the *Washington Post*—and my boss—called to ask what I thought about the possibility of covering Robert Griffin III's rookie year with the Redskins. I remember exactly where I was at the time: standing outside the Seattle Mariners' spring training headquarters in Peoria, Arizona, on another perfect morning in the Cactus League. My response to Matt was, "Are you crazy?" No, come to think of it, I only *thought* that. What I said was, "Sure. Why not? Sounds like fun." And so, all these months later, Matt gets the first thank-you here, for putting me on this rich and fascinating (and challenging) story—as well as for doing things such as paying for me to fly across the country for what turned out to be a thirteen-minute interview with my subject. So it went on the RG3 beat.

The best part of the assignment, in hindsight, was being part of the *Post*'s Redskins coverage team, something I had somehow managed to avoid during my first thirteen years at the paper. To Mike Jones, Mark Maske, Jason Reid, and Mike Wise—thanks for the teamwork, the camaraderie, and all the great dinners on the road (never more than $35, of course). "The Ghost" will always have your backs. Rick Maese deserves a special thanks for

ACKNOWLEDGMENTS

letting me tag along on the first round of pre-draft interviews in Texas, for sharing all his notes, and for not telling the bosses that I nearly got our rental pickup truck stuck on one of those un-mapped back roads of Copperas Cove. Thanks also to Sally Jenkins for the generosity with her notes, her time, and her insight over a late-night Thanksgiving dinner of hot wings and cold beer in Fort Worth, and thanks to Dan Steinberg, whose *DC Sports Bog* was a godsend for chronicling all the RG3-related zaniness and transcribing all those radio interviews.

To the Redskins beat crew from across the D.C. media spectrum—Rich Campbell, John Keim, Grant Paulsen, Zac Boyer, Stephen Whyno, Nathan Fenno, Chick Hernandez, Sky Kerstein, Chris Russell, Tarik El-Bashir, Joseph White, David Elfin, Dan Hellie, Rob Carlin, Gary Carter, and the rest—thanks for the laughs in the workroom and the solid requests that night at the lobby piano in the Cleveland Key Center Marriott.

Plenty of people helped me by setting up interviews over the course of the year—Heath Nielsen at Baylor, Jack Welch of Copperas Cove High, Mark Heligman from CAA, Adam Woullard of Gatorade, and Tony Wyllie of the Redskins. Thanks to all of you. A handful of Baylor and Washington players were especially generous with their time and thoughts, so thank you to Chris Cooley, Jordan Black, Darrel Young, Kirk Cousins, and Lanear Sampson.

My good friends Rick Maese, Mike Jones, Barry Svrluga, Howard Bryant, Jason Reid, Dan Graziano, and Dan Connolly read various chapters during the process (or at least offered to) and provided some invaluable input—many thanks, fellas—and photog extraordinaire and good friend Jonathan Newton hooked me up with the headshot. Thanks also to Jeff Carroll, Cindy Plavier-Truitt,

ACKNOWLEDGMENTS

and the good people at Humanim, Inc., for allowing me to be a squatter for a couple of months in your beautiful office building.

A huge thanks to David Rosenthal and his staff at Blue Rider Press, and to my agent, Esther Newberg of ICM, for believing in the project (and in this first-time author), even after the story took its unforeseen turn in December and January—thus sparing me the ignominy, as plenty of friends have noted wryly, of being a two-time authorial jinx.

A special thanks to Jacqueline and Robert Griffin Jr. for their time and graciousness throughout this process, which included multiple interviews in their living room and countless calls, texts, e-mails, and sidle-up-tos on the sidelines at various games. I also like to think I learned something about parenting from you in the process. (I will let you know after my little girls grow up whether any of it took.) And to the rest of the Griffin/Ross family—especially Shane Griffin, Rodney Griffin Sr., and John Ross—thank you for sharing your family's story.

To Robert Griffin III—a special thank-you for your time before the season, and for the fun, fascinating ride during it. As many people quoted in this book have said to me, I can honestly say I've never encountered anyone quite like you in my career, and I wish you godspeed on whatever path(s) you follow.

Finally, to my wife, Amy, thank you for everything. None of this would have been possible without your love and support, as well as your knack for knowing when I needed a push or some words of encouragement, or when I simply needed the kids out of my hair for a while. And to Lucinda and Lyla—Daddy loves you to the moon and back. I'll give you anything you want if you Pinkie Promise me you won't grow up too fast.

337

INDEX

INDEX

INDEX

INDEX

INDEX

INDEX

INDEX

ABOUT THE AUTHOR

Dave Sheinin is an award-winning sports and features writer for the *Washington Post*, where he has worked since 1999. A graduate of Vanderbilt University, where he studied English and music and trained as an opera singer, he lives in Maryland with his wife and their two daughters.